PRAISE FOR THE SECRET OF CHANEL NO. 5

"[Mazzeo] explores interconnections between designer and perfume, teasing out the relationship with delicacy." —*New York Times Book Review*

"Engaging." —*Wall Street Journal*

"[In] the skilled hands of cultural historian Mazzeo, [the perfume] becomes a magnificent window through which to understand [Coco Chanel] and her milieu. . . . Impeccable research and crafting make a seemingly narrow topic feel infinitely important." —*Kirkus Reviews*

"This is one case where historical fact eclipses the legend and lore of the object itself—there's much, much more than meets the nose to discover in these pages." —*Booklist*

"Mazzeo's lush prose . . . never bogs down in the details—despite the extensive research showcased in the bibliography—and a smooth pacing keeps it moving along at a fast clip. This work is definitely recommended to lovers of twentieth-century cultural history, Coco Chanel, and, of course, the world's best-selling perfume." —*Library Journal*

"Mazzeo has written an account of the rarest of things—an international olfactory icon—that fairly rushes off the pages. Here is the life of one of the twentieth century's most interesting and deeply complicated women, a fascinating cultural history, and the story of an extraordinary perfume." —Chandler Burr, *New York Times* scent critic and author of *The Perfect Scent*

"The true brilliance of *The Secret of Chanel No. 5* is Tilar Mazzeo's ability to take a subject one would never have thought possible to think very deeply about and then cover it so captivatingly. Who knew that such a tiny bottle housed so many secrets?" —Michael Tonello, author of *Bringing Home the Birkin*

"Anyone who's ever dawdled in front of a perfume counter will love Tilar Mazzeo's fascinating history of the perfume known simply as No. 5; her rich and witty account is as compelling as the fragrance itself." —Karen Karbo, author of *The Gospel According to Coco Chanel*

THE SECRET OF CHANEL N° 5

THE SECRET OF

CHANEL Nº 5

THE INTIMATE HISTORY OF THE
WORLD'S MOST FAMOUS PERFUME

TILAR J. MAZZEO

HARPER PERENNIAL

NEW YORK ● LONDON ● TORONTO ● SYDNEY ● NEW DELHI ● AUCKLAND

HARPER ● PERENNIAL

First Harper Perennial edition published 2011.

Designed by Eric Butler

Frontispiece illustration of Marilyn Monroe with Chanel No. 5
© Michael Ochs Archives/Getty Images. Photograph on page 163 by Serge Lido.
Courtesy of Chanel.

The Library of Congress has catalogued the hardcover edition as follows:

Mazzeo, Tilar J.
    The secret of Chanel No. 5 : the intimate history of the world's most famous perfume / Tilar J. Mazzeo.
        p.   cm.
    Includes bibliographical references.
    Summary: "From Tilar Mazzeo, the author of the bestselling *The Widow Clicquot*, a captivating new book that shares her journey to discover the secret behind the creation, iconic status, and extraordinary success of Chanel No. 5, the world's most famous perfume"— Provided by publisher.
    ISBN 978-0-06-179101-7 (hardback)
    1. Chanel No. 5 perfume. 2. Parfums Chanel (Firm) 3. Perfumes industry—France—History—20th century. 4. Chanel, Coco, 1883–1971. I. Title.
HD9999.P3934C436   2010
338.7'6685540944—dc22

                                                        2010015284

ISBN 978-0-06-179103-1 (pbk.)

11 12 13 14 15   OV/RRD   10 9 8 7 6 5 4 3 2 1

FOR SUSANNE

Σαν έτοιμος από καιρό, σα θαρραλέος,
αποχαιρέτα την

Perfume, it's the most important thing. As Paul Valéry said it:
"A badly perfumed woman doesn't have a future."

—Coco Chanel, interview with Jacques Chazot, produced
as "Dim Dam Dom," director Guy Job, 1969

The most mysterious, the most human thing is smell.
That means that your physique corresponds to the other's.

—Coco Chanel, quoted in Claude Baillén, *Chanel Solitaire*
(New York: Quadrangle, 1974), 146

CONTENTS

Preface   xiii

PART I   COCO BEFORE CHANEL NO. 5

ONE   Aubazine and the Secret Code of Scent   3

TWO   The Pretty Perfumer   13

THREE   The Scent of Betrayal   23

FOUR   An Education in the Senses   37

FIVE   The Prince and the Perfumer   47

SIX   The Birth of a Modern Legend   59

PART II   LOVE AND WAR

SEVEN   Launching Chanel No. 5   75

EIGHT   The Scent with a Reputation   83

NINE   Marketing Minimalism   99

TEN   Chanel No. 5 and the Style Moderne   111

CONTENTS

ELEVEN   Hollywood and the Great Depression   119

TWELVE   A Broken Partnership   131

THIRTEEN   In the Shadow of the Ritz   139

FOURTEEN   Coco at War   151

FIFTEEN   Coco Plays the Numbers   165

PART III   THE LIFE OF AN ICON

SIXTEEN   An Icon of the 1950s   181

SEVENTEEN   The Art of Business   193

EIGHTEEN   The End of Modern Perfumery   205

Afterword   213

Acknowledgments   219

Notes   223

Bibliography   261

Index   269

PREFACE

eadlines around the world in the first days of December 2009 boldly announced something that came as a surprise to few: "Chanel No. 5 rated 'most seductive scent' in poll of women." Coco Chanel's iconic fragrance had once again been tapped as the world's sexiest perfume, handily beating out the designer perfumes of the contemporary fashion greats, including scents as ubiquitous and lovely as Calvin Klein's Eternity or Estée Lauder's Beautiful. Some of the world's bestselling fragrances didn't make the list at all. Among the fragrances ranked in the top twenty, there was something else remarkable, too: not one had a history that went back earlier than the 1980s—not one, that is, except for Chanel No. 5, now nearly ninety years old.

Chanel No. 5 is one of the few remaining "legacy" perfumes, and the idea that Chanel No. 5 makes a woman irresistibly alluring isn't a new one. When the story about the world's most seductive fragrance ran in the pages of the *London Daily Mail*, the reporter drily observed that "Marilyn Monroe never had trouble attracting men" either. Now, "it appear[ed] her colourful love life may have been down to a simple choice—her perfume." After all, who could forget that the starlet famously quipped that all she wore to bed at night were a few drops of Chanel No. 5? Certainly not the thousands of women who voted to name it the most alluring fragrance on the market and declared it the perfect scent not just for getting a date but also "for getting beyond it to boyfriend status." In fact, among these women, an astonishing one in ten claimed they met Mr. Right while wearing the iconic perfume.

If that's the case, Chanel No. 5 has to its credit a whole lot of love stories: according to the French government, a bottle of the world's most famous perfume sells somewhere around the globe on the average of every thirty seconds, to the tune of $100 million a year. The precise figure, like so much about this celebrated fragrance, is a closely guarded company secret. But those numbers—which translate into something upward of a million bottles sold annually—mean just one thing: a vast number of beautifully scented women for someone to adore. And this has been happening year after year, for decades.

Secrets, of course, give rise to legends, and both swirl around the story of Chanel No. 5. They have done so almost since Coco Chanel launched her signature perfume in the opening years of the 1920s— that pivotal moment after the first "Great War" when the world was determined to leave behind a painful past and to embrace all the promises of the new and the modern. Suddenly, once unimaginable things seemed possible. Albert Einstein won the Nobel Prize for reimagining the laws of physics, and once deadly diseases were tamed by the miracle of vaccinations. At the beginning of that decade, America had just a handful of millionaires. A few years later, the ranks of the super rich had swelled by more than 700 percent to a number approaching fifteen thousand, ushering in what promised to be a new gilded age. The bustling postwar economies created a new standard of wealth and luxury, and, for the first time, it all seemed within reach of the average person. There were wireless radios and talkie films, cars for the middle classes and chic ready-made fashions—and fine French perfumes—on the floors of glittering department stores, another phenomenon of this enticing new commercial era.

This was the decade of New York and Paris and of all the things that happened at a moment when the distance between those two great cities was beginning to seem just a little bit shorter. It was the decade of superstars and heroes. And, as the rise of rapid communication created the beginnings of an international cosmopolitan culture, it also became the era of celebrity icons. Babe Ruth led the New York Yankees to three World Series titles in that roaring decade, and Charles Lindbergh flew thirty-three hours from New York to Paris. Clara Bow became the world's first "It Girl"; Charlie Chaplin took Hollywood slapstick to dizzying heights; and on the nighttime stages in France's capital, the sultry Josephine Baker danced topless to breathless applause, night after night, during the interwar years. Among all the icons of the 1920s, however, none could touch Coco Chanel, already acknowledged as one of the most chic and influential women of an entire generation.

The line between legend and history, however, is wonderfully—and perplexingly—malleable. Much of what is told and retold as conventional wisdom about the spectacular rise of Chanel No. 5 and its transformation into an international byword for luxury is the stuff of half-truths, confusion, collective fantasy, and sheer invention. Sometimes, the truth that those legends obscure is more fantastic than any fiction.

Consider all the things you think you know about Chanel No. 5, which for most of its history has been the bestselling fragrance of all time and among the twentieth century's most coveted luxury objects. Perhaps you remember how this unique scent was invented in the summer of 1920 by the young fashion designer Gabrielle "Coco"

Chanel. Except it wasn't. In fact, it was already a scent with a long and tangled history—a history about nothing so much as the intimacy of loss and desire.

Perhaps you've read sources that tell how Chanel No. 5 stunned the world of traditional fragrance as a dazzling new technical innovation: history's first synthetic composition, its first abstract scent, with its novel use of the perfume materials known as "aldehydes." Indeed, it's likely that you have because this claim is a key part of the legend of how Chanel No. 5 became a phenomenon. The trouble is that none of this is true, either. Chanel No. 5 wasn't the first perfume to do any of those things. It wasn't even the second. Poised on the brink of what is still known as the "golden age" of perfumery, Chanel No. 5 *was* a genuine revolution that changed the history of fragrance forever and one of the great works of a new kind of art in a vibrant modern era. What makes it spectacular, however, is something different—something that makes it enduringly and genuinely sexy.

Among the widely held beliefs, there is one that is nearly universal: the idea that clever and persistent advertising created Chanel No. 5's international fame. Despite the beauty of a scent that perfume experts applaud as a milestone and masterpiece, who could doubt that its celebrity and staying power comes down to brilliant marketing and, especially, to the careful packaging of the scent in that wonderfully understated square-cut bottle? After all, the legend tells us how the bottle became revered, how it was recognized by Andy Warhol in his famous 1960s lithograph series as a twentieth-century icon. Then there is that spectacular photo shoot of Marilyn Monroe, the perfume's greatest spokeswoman, holding the Chanel No. 5 bottle provocatively close to her ample cleavage.

The trouble is that Chanel No. 5 was never one of the images in Warhol's famous pop art icon series in the 1960s. No one paid Marilyn Monroe for any endorsement, either. Even the well-known story about how the bottle became part of the permanent collections at the Museum of Modern Art in New York in the late 1950s is simply mistaken. Yet the idea that Chanel No. 5 is the creature of marketing is persistent because it seems so obvious. Look back through the archives, through the history of advertising and dusty copies of old newspapers and fashion magazines, however, and a simple and surprising fact emerges: Chanel No. 5's early success never came down to marketing at all.

Despite the widespread popular conviction that clever advertising made Chanel No. 5 a great name in the world of luxury, the truth is something stranger and a story far more compelling and complicated: for the first forty years of its fame, the marketing was run-of-the-mill and largely uninspired. It should have been nothing short of disastrous. The biggest competitors for Chanel No. 5 in the 1920s, '30s, and even '40s were a competition and confusion of the company's—and, later, Coco Chanel's—own making. Somehow, the marketing and promotion just didn't matter.

Consider again that one simple fact: a bottle every thirty seconds. The numbers are staggering, and they aren't part of a recent trend, either. Chanel No. 5 has been this kind of runaway success since the 1920s. As *New York Times* perfume critic Chandler Burr reminds us, in the fragrance industry today, the scent, which still dominates the global market, is spoken of in reverent tones simply as *le monstre*— the monster.

More than that, although it wasn't among Warhol's icons in the 1960s, Chanel No. 5 *is* one of those astonishingly rare products that has taken on a life of its own and breathes meaning as a symbol. It *is* an icon. As an exasperated competitor once anonymously confessed to Burr, "It's unbelievable! It's not a fragrance; it's a goddamn cultural monument, like Coke." The best metaphor, however, is still the one of the beautiful *monstre*, because this thing has a life of its own.

Few products around the world are more beloved than Chanel No. 5, and it inspires in its millions of fans—and there are millions—the kind of passion and loyalty that executives in slick advertising offices on Madison Avenue can only dream about man-ufacturing. The dilemma for any curious historian, savvy entrepre-neur, or fragrance aficionado is: what, precisely, is the connection? *How* did Chanel No. 5 become one of the most celebrated luxury products of all time? If it took decades for the marketing to catch up with the success of the world's most famous perfume, what *is* the secret of its fabulous destiny? More simply still, why is Chanel No. 5 the most sensual perfume in the world, and what exactly is it that makes this scent so sexy? This book—the unauthorized biography of a scent—separates the fact from the fiction, and teases out the truths from the jumble of half-truths and revealing silences, to tell the story of a familiar cultural monument whose history we've never really known.

In some ways, this is an unconventional book. After all, where, exactly, does one begin the story of a product, a consumable item? Does it start with the product's creation? Does it start with its first success? With the moment when the idea was planted in the mind of its creator? Despite being one of the twentieth century's iconic luxury products, sold around the world to millions of loyal enthusi-asts, throughout the history of Chanel No. 5 there is one thing that has remained unchanged: behind all the risks and struggles and tri-umphs that have created this product there are profoundly intimate stories. From the private losses that led Coco Chanel to imagine a signature fragrance to the heady days of its spectacular success; from the decades of tense courtroom dramas that ultimately led her to try to sabotage her creation to the bitter private war waged with partners under the laws of Nazi-occupied France and in the indus-trial factories of Hoboken, New Jersey; from a moment of glorious postwar fame to the present day, when the perfume maintains its extraordinary allure despite all the odds, *The Secret of Chanel No. 5* is the story of how a beloved product can have its own life.

This is the history of the world's most seductive scent, the pur-suit of the fragrance industry's glorious *monstre*—an intimate look into the secret life of a perfume that is about nothing so much as the production of desire. That story can only begin with the product's beautiful, but deeply flawed, creator—a woman whose fabled life becomes more complex and fascinating when viewed through the lens of one of her most famous creations.

THE SECRET OF CHANEL N° 5

PART I

COCO BEFORE CHANEL NO. 5

ONE
AUBAZINE AND THE
SECRET CODE OF SCENT

For the better part of a century, the scent of Chanel No. 5 has been a sultry whisper that says we are in the presence of something rich and sensuous. It's the quiet rustle of elegant self-indulgence, the scent of a world that is splendidly and beautifully opulent. And, at nearly four hundred dollars an ounce, it's no wonder that Chanel No. 5 suggests nothing in our minds so much as the idea of luxury.

It's a powerful association. Chanel No. 5 is sumptuous. In fact, the story of this famous scent is the tale of how a singular perfume captured precisely the fast-living and carefree spirit of the young and the rich in the Roaring Twenties—and of how it went on to capture the world's imagination and desires. Chanel No. 5, from the moment of its first great heyday, was the scent of beautiful extravagance.

The origins of the perfume and its creator, however, could not have been more different from all of this. Indeed, part of the complexity of telling Chanel No. 5's history is the great divide between how we think of this iconic perfume and the place where it began.

Chanel No. 5 calls to mind all that is rich and lovely. It's surprising to think that it started in a place that was the antithesis of what would later come to define it. The truth is that the fragrance that epitomizes all those worldly pleasures began with miserable impoverishment and amid the most staggering kinds of losses.

Gabrielle Chanel's peasant roots went deep into the earth of provincial southwestern France, and, in 1895, her mother, Jeanne Chanel—worn out by work and childbirth—succumbed to the tuberculosis that had slowly destroyed her. The disease spread quickly in the wet and cold conditions of the rural provinces, and in the nineteenth century it was called "consumption" for a reason. It ate away at the health of its victims from the inside, corrupting the lungs hopelessly and painfully. Gabrielle—named after the nun who delivered her—and her four surviving brothers and sisters had watched it all. She was just twelve years old at the time of her mother's death.

Her father, Albert, was an itinerant peddler, and perhaps he simply had no idea how to care for five young children. Perhaps he didn't particularly care. He had about him a rakish charm and a lifelong knack for dodging responsibility. Whatever the case, in the span of only a few weeks, the young Gabrielle would also lose her second parent. The boys were sent out to work and to make their way in the world as best they could. Albert loaded his three daughters into a wagon without explanation and abandoned them at an orphanage in a rural hillside town in the Corrèze, at a convent abbey known as Aubazine.

It was here that the girl who would become known around the world simply as Coco grew up as a charity-case orphan. It was a profound desertion, and the wounds of loss and abandonment were themes that would become as entwined in the story of Chanel No. 5 as they were in Coco's. They formed an emotional register that would shape the history of the world's most famous perfume and Coco Chanel's often complicated relationship to it.

Today, the abbey at Aubazine remains much as it was during her hard and lonely girlhood. Indeed, it remains much as it was during the twelfth century, when the saint Étienne d'Obazine—as his name was rendered in the original Latin—founded it. During their time at the orphanage, Coco Chanel and the other girls were assigned to read and reread the story of his exemplary life, and the unrelenting dullness of his good deeds is crushing.

The saintly Étienne, however, had a keen sense of aesthetics at a moment when Western culture's ideas about beauty and proportion were in radical transition. He and the monks who followed him to this wilderness in a remote corner of southwestern France were members of the new and rapidly growing Cistercian clerical order, which prized nothing so much as a life and an art of elemental simplicity. Étienne's isolated retreat from the world at Aubazine was—and remains—a space of echoing austere grandeur.

The road from the valley that winds up to Aubazine is steep and narrow, and the forests slant down sharply into long ravines. At the summit, there is nothing more than a small village, with a cluster of low stone buildings, a few shops, and quiet houses overshadowed by the looming presence of one of France's great medieval abbeys. By the middle of the nineteenth century, it had been transformed from a monastery into a convent orphanage for girls. For the children who lived there, it was a youth of hard work and strict discipline and, fortunately for the future prospects of the young Gabrielle, much of it focused on clothing. There was nothing luxurious about it, however. Days were spent washing laundry and mending, and it was here that she learned, of course, to sew.

Coco Chanel once later said that fashion was architecture, and the architecture she meant was based on this convent home, with its brutally clean lines and the stark beauty of simple contrasts. The connection has never been fully explored in any of the books that have been written on Coco Chanel's revolutionary fashions. Perhaps the first person to recognize Aubazine's profound importance was Coco Chanel's biographer, Edmonde Charles-Roux, who was one of the few people to know the story of this lonely childhood. She mentions it in passing. Thinking of Aubazine and Gabrielle's longing for a certain kind of starkness, Charles-Roux always believed that:

> Whenever [Coco] began yearning for austerity, for the ultimate in cleanliness, for faces scrubbed with yellow soap; or waxed nostalgic for all things white, simple and clear, for linen piled high in cupboards, whitewashed walls . . . one had to understand that she was speaking in a secret code, and that every word she uttered meant only one word. Aubazine.

It was at the heart of Coco Chanel's aesthetics—her obsession with purity and minimalism. It would shape the dresses she designed and the way she lived. It would shape Chanel No. 5, her great olfactory creation, no less profoundly.

Standing amid the scenes of Coco Chanel's childhood, the power of Aubazine is obvious. From the exterior, the abbey is an imposing structure of granite and sandy-hued limestone that towers over the village that grew up around it. Inside, it is a contrast of brilliant whiteness and lingering shadows. The keyhole doorways are dark wood against vast expanses of pale stone. There is the cool solidity of arching walls, adorned only with the play of light and the sun streaking in through colorless lead-paned windows. It possesses a striking and silent kind of beauty.

This building was also filled with meanings that would shape the course of Coco Chanel's life—and the life of Chanel No. 5. Everywhere in the world at Aubazine, there were scents and symbols—and reminders of the importance of perfume. St. Bernard of Clairvaux, who founded the Cistercian movement, made a point of encouraging his monks to give perfume and anointment a central role in prayer and in rituals of purification. In his famous sermons on the Bible's "Song of Songs," some of the most erotic verses anywhere in religious literature, he advised devout clerics to spend some spiritual time contemplating the perfumed breasts of the young bride described in the song's key passages. Soon, someone got the idea that this contemplation would be even more effective if it were combined with time spent simultaneously sniffing the aromas of the local jasmine, lavender, and roses.

For centuries, scent had been part of the life of devotion at Aubazine, and the traces lingered. Étienne had made a mission of planting richly scented flowers everywhere in the empty ravines and wastes around his abbeys. They were the same hills where the girls went for long walks with the nuns on Sundays. Just beyond, in the cloister courtyard, were the carefully tended remains of the original twelfth-century gardens, the source of all those scents. The echoing nave, where Gabrielle Chanel listened to endless sermons, had been the site of these perfumed rituals of meditation and prayer for hundreds of years. Even the worn, stone staircase at Aubazine that led to the children's bedchambers and the attics, where Gabrielle hid her secret romance novels, was the same one those medieval monks climbed every night on the way to their perfumed dreams. Scent had always been a part of her childhood.

It was a desperately unhappy childhood. Later, "Aubazine" was a word throughout her life that Coco Chanel would never speak. She surrounded it in silence and mystery, and it remained a guarded and shameful secret. In all the interviews that she gave in the years that followed, she would claim to have grown up with aunts and invented a fabulous and fictional story about her father making a fortune in America. In fact, she did everything in her power to jettison the past, going so far as to send money to members of her family on the condition that they never reveal those shared secrets.

What she lived with always, however, were Aubazine's smells.

They were the bracing scents of order and severity. Everywhere at Aubazine was the aroma of sheets boiled in copper pots sweetened with dried root of iris and the aromas of ironing. There was the scent from linen cupboards lined with pungent rosewood and verbena. There were clean hands and washed stone floors. Above all, there was the smell of raw tallow soap on children's skin and ruthlessly scoured little bodies. It was the scent of everything that was clean. Aubazine was a secret code of smell, and in the years to come it would be at the heart of everything she would find beautiful.

Aubazine was also filled with symbols and the mysterious power of numbers, and these numbers could be found—along with their meaning—literally in the walls and on the floors around her. It was an architecture rich in silent stories. The Cistercians who raised these abbey walls nearly a thousand years before believed profoundly in a kind of sacred geometry that ordered the universe. Their buildings reflected it everywhere. In the small chapel where the children were sent to pray, the entire scope of Romanesque numerology was carved into stone before them in the most mundane places, on the floors and walls and doorways. Before them was the singular unity of God's perfection in the simple shape of a circle. Double columns reflected the duality of body and spirit, earth and heaven, and three windows in a row were the threefold nature of the divinity. Nine represented the foundations of Jerusalem's walls and the number of the archangels, and six symbolized the days of creation.

The number five at Aubazine though was always considered special. It was the number of an essentially human kind of destiny. Or that, at least, was the idea of the monks who founded Coco Chanel's childhood abbey, and they built its entire structure on the power of this special number. Cistercian architecture flourished in Europe at the time of the Crusades, and these are the churches most closely associated with the occult mysteries of the Knights Templar. To those mysteries, the number five—the pentagon—was central. "Cistercian cathedrals, churches, and abbeys," writes one scholar, "are built on measures . . . which equal more or less [the] Golden Ratio of Pythagoras." It is the ratio of both the five-pointed star and the human form.

Coco Chanel understood the power of this number long before the nuns introduced the children to the esoteric symbolism of the abbey's architecture and its spiritual meaning in their lessons. In the long sunlit corridor that led into the dark solemnity of that cathedral, the path was laid with rough, uneven mosaics, ancient river stones arranged in geometric and symbolic patterns. Here, even the youngest girls waited in line to be summoned to their prayers, and Gabrielle walked this path daily. Laid out there in undulating circles, she found repeated incessantly the pattern of the number five, sometimes in the shape of stars. Sometimes, it was there in the shape of flowers.

The number five: she believed profoundly in its magic and its beauty. Those Cistercian nuns had raised their orphan charges to revere the power of symbols and spirit, and in this ancient branch of the Catholic faith it was a special number—the number of quintessence: the pure and perfect embodiment of a thing's essence. It was also, in a material universe of earth, water, wind, and fire, that other thing—ether, spirit—something mysteriously and untouchably beautiful.

There at Aubazine, the word she would never say, quintessence had been everywhere around her, and it hardly comes as a surprise, then, that the "No. 5 was her fetishistic number from childhood." It was part of her childhood games and her adolescent questioning: "she engraved it in the earth . . . with a branch she had picked up, [it was the number] she looked for, as a game, among the dates inscribed on the graves in the cemetery." When Gabrielle Chanel left the convent, she left behind its religion, but she never abandoned her belief in the occult mysticism of numbers.

She also already knew that the number five was about women in particular. From the beginning, the number five and its perfect proportions were tangled up with the secret sensuality of their allure—and with the symbolism of flowers. That connection was always, at Aubazine, elemental. Indeed, the very name "'Cistercian,' and that of [its] first monastery, Citeaux, both come from the word *cistus*, of the *Cistaceae* rockrose family, which we know today as the simple five-petalled 'wild rose'. . . . popular in medieval symbolism involving depictions of the . . . Virgin Mary, [whom] the Cistercians, Templars, Hospitallers, and the Teutonic knights all honored as the patroness of their respective Orders." Its image was carved into the stone tomb of St. Étienne, which the convent girls passed in the cloister daily, and the plant grew wild in the hills where they walked.

In the gardens of Aubazine, there was also another flower that looked remarkably similar: the white camellia blossom. It had a less ancient and less innocent history. Napoléon's empress Joséphine had made camellias popular throughout France in the nineteenth century, and Alexandre Dumas brought them to the popular vaudeville stage a generation later with the 1852 theatrical adaptation of his novel *La Dame aux Camélias* (1848)—"the lady with camellias"—the tragedy of a beautiful courtesan and her impossible love for a young gentleman. It was a novel that Gabrielle Chanel knew well, and as a young girl she once saw the legendary actress Sarah Bernhardt bring it to life on the stage in Paris. "*La Dame aux Camélias*," she once said, "was my life, all the trashy novels I'd fed on." Giuseppe Verdi would take the story as the basis for his opera *La Traviata* (1853). This long-lasting flower, the leaves of which are a source of tea, was already a symbol of a lover's devotion.

In the years after Aubazine, Coco Chanel would take the white camellia as a cherished personal symbol. It was the shape, she always said, of infinite possibility. It would also be for her a flower mixed up with the story of devotion, the glitter of the footlights, and the kind of love that had no good solution. Unsurprisingly, it was sometimes depicted having five petals. Soon, she would come to know something too about the heartbreak of rich young men and their mistresses.

Coco Chanel, after all, wasn't destined for the walls of a convent— far from it. When the orphaned girls at Aubazine turned eighteen, only those prepared to renounce the world and become nuns were allowed to stay at the abbey. No one ever imagined that the religious life was the vocation of this spirited and fun-loving young woman, and she certainly harbored no illusions. Instead, she dreamed of the big city. In this distant corner of southwestern France, the big city was a modest little place not far to the north called Moulins sur Allier.

When she left Aubazine to make her fortune, the girl who was not yet Coco Chanel had no idea that she wanted to create a perfume. She had no idea yet even of becoming a fashion designer. But she left this small village with a foundational catalog of scents and a powerful connection to the number that would later come to define her.

TWO
THE PRETTY PERFUMER

Moulins sur Allier felt a long way from Paris in the summer of 1905. Here in this rural province, life went on much as it had for centuries. The looming Gothic cathedral of Notre Dame de Moulins and a Renaissance palace dominated the village's medieval city center, and a large clock tower—its famous Jacquemart—tolled off the hours with a numbing persistence.

In the capital, however, change was coming furiously. At the end of a stately gilded age, Paris was already the refuge of those bohemians, innovators, and artists who would make it famous in the decades to come. In just another few months, the painter Henri Matisse and his compatriots would shock the art world with a new exhibit of wild work that would become instantly known as Fauvism. That summer, an infamously sensual young woman named Margaretha Geertruida Zelle would take to the stage under the name of Mata Hari and transform the cabaret striptease—invented in Paris only ten years earlier—into the quintessential French entertainment.

Moulins sur Allier, some two-hundred-odd miles from Paris, was another world entirely. But even Moulins had its cabaret dancers. At scrappy little dance halls like La Rotonde, sequined showgirls sang and strutted to entertain the local officers who were housed in the garrison nearby.

Had things worked out differently—had they worked out, in fact, as she planned—we never would have known Coco Chanel for her fashions or for her famous Chanel No. 5 perfume. We would have known her, along with Mata Hari and, later, Josephine Baker, as Coco Chanel, the sultry chanteuse.

It was a surprising turn of events, given that she had grown up in the ascetic surroundings of that remote Catholic abbey, surrounded by cloistered walls and, beyond them, farmland. When she had left the convent at the age of eighteen, a few years earlier, the lively Gabrielle Chanel—she wasn't yet "Coco"—put the sewing skills she had gained at Aubazine to use and found work as a shopgirl selling lingerie and hosiery at a boutique called À Sainte Marie in Moulins. On the weekends, to earn a bit of extra money, she worked for a local tailor, repairing men's breeches. At the end of 1904, the life of a shopgirl and seamstress looked very much like her future.

The work was dull, and it would never bring her great riches, but Moulins wasn't without diversions. Gabrielle was young and pretty, and soon thrilling flirtations began with the officers who came to have their breeches mended. They took her for coffees and ice cream and eventually to the local cabaret entertainments, where the girls on the stage belted out risqué tunes with catchy melodies while the audience sang along delightedly.

Gabrielle Chanel had no thought yet of creating a signature perfume—no thought yet even of creating her innovative fashions, let alone a couture fragrance. It was here in Moulins, though, that the kernel of an idea was first planted in her mind that one day would blossom so wonderfully. The favorite entertainment in Moulins that year was a familiar old comic opera from the last decades of the nineteenth century that continued to charm the audiences of rural

France. It was just the kind of thing that a fun-loving officer could take a spirited shopgirl to see on a summer evening. Called simply *La Jolie Parfumeuse*—"the pretty perfumer"—it was something for Gabrielle Chanel to remember.

In fact, the story of *La Jolie Parfumeuse* might have been prophetic. It was a popular piece in this small town for several seasons, and she is sure to have seen it. Its creator, Jacques Offenbach, was a celebrity in the world of café music—the kind of man who might "discover" a showgirl and launch her career spectacularly. Amid the lively tunes and ribald sexual comedy, *La Jolie Parfumeuse* was the story of Rose Michon—like Gabrielle Chanel, an orphan girl making her way in the world. The choice before Rose in the comedy was a familiar one: a choice between the pleasures of life on the vaudeville stage and the bustling and clever entrepreneurship of a perfume shop.

It was a sexy little drama, set in a cabaret, and the audience cheered on the adventures of the quick-witted and innocently sultry Rose, whose hopes of marrying the boy of her dreams are endangered by the rakish scheming of her would-be seducer and by her uncanny resemblance to a famously provocative showgirl from Toulouse. Rose naturally triumphs, and, in a comic final scene, her seducer's comeuppance arrives when he finds himself locked into a perfume storage room and gassed with the overpowering and lusty feminine scents of too much patchouli and tuberose.

Throughout it all, of course, the officers who came to be amused had plenty of scantily clad showgirls to ogle. Unsurprisingly, *La Jolie Parfumeuse* was an international hit for years, playing on stages in France, Germany, and the United States. In the world of early French boulevard music, it was well loved and emblematic.

It also might have been the young Gabrielle Chanel's story had she not made an entirely different choice. One day she, too, would open a shop and give the world its most famous fragrance. In her early twenties, however, that idea hadn't yet occurred to her. What had occurred to her was—as she put it herself years later—that she had "a hot little body," and, when she quit working as a shopgirl, it was to join the cabaret.

As a singer, Coco Chanel was not particularly talented. What she lacked in voice, however, she made up for in verve and youthful sensuality, and she was determined to make a career as a vaudeville actress and dancer. She dreamed of someday having a life in Paris, where women like Mata Hari were finding fame and fortune. She learned to wiggle her hips and danced in glittering, sequined gowns. She even earned her famous nickname, Coco, that year by making the tunes of "Qui qu'a vu Coco" and "Ko Ko Ri Ko"—a famous Offenbach tune—her signature numbers, to the delight of the officers who came to watch her.

It was fun, singing up there onstage and having so many gallant admirers. Before long, some of those gentlemen became more than just admirers, and it was from among these officers that Gabrielle Chanel—now simply Coco to everyone—soon chose her first lovers. Before long, she was pregnant, and the trouble was that Coco's officer knew well that marrying her was out of the question. She had strayed too far from the convent.

She was a showgirl actress, and it was a risqué line of work for a young woman, one that would make her, in the eyes of respectable men and their families, essentially unmarriageable. To put it bluntly, "For a large section of society, the similarities between the actress's life and the prostitute's or *demi-mondaine*'s were unforgettable and overruled all other evidence of respectability." Even talented singers and showgirls were forever condemned to the margins of polite society—that borderland known in French simply as the *demi-monde*, a shadowy "half-world" of those who would never be acceptable.

The *demi-monde* was a kind of social limbo, and Coco Chanel had entered it. No matter what came afterward—no matter what stunning celebrity she would achieve or vast riches she would accumulate, no matter how she would set the style for her entire generation or create the world's most famous perfume—she would never manage to escape this hard reality. She had consented to "be 'hired' for amusement," and this simple fact—and the consequences of what her biographers believe was a botched abortion that would leave her unable to bear children—would shape the course of her life in ways that were both profound and painful.

Coco Chanel's brief career as a showgirl would also lead, circuitously but inexorably, to the creation of Chanel No. 5 perfume. And not just to its creation but also to the very particular scent that it would capture. The aromas of the *demi-mondaines*—the women of the half-world—were something she would always remember.

With Coco pregnant and in trouble, one of her admirers—perhaps the responsible lover—helped her arrange the abortion. Étienne Balsan was a rich officer with the army's ninth infantry regiment who bred expensive horses and was heir to the vast industrial fortune his family had built by supplying textiles to the French army. He was handsome and enthusiastic in his admiration of women. He was also kind and generous. Remembering the patron saint of her stark convent childhood, Coco Chanel told him, "I've already had one protector named Étienne, and he performed miracles too." Soon, he offered the young Coco another kind of protection—the protection of becoming his mistress.

Actually, what he offered her was the position as his second live-in mistress. When Coco Chanel considered the options, her choice must have appeared quite simple. It had quickly become apparent to everyone that the young Coco, however lithe and charming, simply wasn't talented enough as a singer to make a brilliant career on the stage. She couldn't bear to go back to working as a salesgirl or seamstress, either; both meant a hard life with few pleasures. Choosing between becoming a kept woman on a rich man's grand country estate and a squinting life hunched over one pair of torn men's breeches after another wasn't difficult. Besides, she liked Étienne.

For better or worse, she chose life as a kept woman, and for the next six years lived as one of his lovers.

High society in France at the beginning of the new century was still a world of codes and rituals, and, during those years with Balsan, Coco Chanel—a girl with peasant roots— learned to navigate them superbly. Among those codes, she quickly understood that none was more revealing than scent. There was a fine line between respectability and the *demi-monde*, and there were even different kinds—and levels—of mistresses. Perfume was one of the essential ways of making a distinction between them.

Étienne's official lover, the celebrity courtesan Émilienne d'Alençon, was at the apex of this hierarchy. She had been mistress to the king of Belgium, and the French writer Marcel Proust immortalized her liaisons in his epic novel *À la recherche du temps perdu*, the famous scent-filled extravaganza known to English readers as *Remembrance of Things Past*. Émilienne was one of the so-called *grande horizontales*—the great horizontal women—of her era, and Coco Chanel admired her immensely.

What Coco Chanel liked about Émilienne most was that, unlike so many of the other mistresses who came and went on the weekends at Étienne's estate at Royallieu, where his male friends came to drink champagne and make love to women, she never smelled like a courtesan.

At the beginning of the twentieth century, there was a notable difference between the scent of a courtesan and the scent of a nice girl. Some aromas—like jasmine and musk, patchouli and tuberose—made a woman smell openly sexual, and only an actress or courtesan or *demi-mondaine* would dare to wear them. Respectable girls wore delicate floral scents of roses or violets. This was why the audience laughed so delightedly in *La Jolie Parfumeuse* when Rose, the pretty perfumer, punished her lusty would-be seducer in the back of her shop with more erotic perfume than he could handle.

A woman's fragrance told a silent story about her sexuality, and, for much of history, the connections between perfume and prostitution were nearly inseparable. According to archeologists, the world's oldest perfume was made on the Mediterranean island of Cyprus thousands of years before the common era, and this heady scent—a sweet and woody concoction with hints of citrus and vanilla—was dedicated to Aphrodite, the Greek goddess of sexual love. Long before anyone ever thought of the atomizer, this fragrant oil was burnt as an offering in her temples, and it's worth remembering that the very word *perfume*, after all, comes from the Latin *per fumum*: "through the smoke."

Also offered up in Aphrodite's temples on Cyprus, however, were beautiful young virgins. The island was at the heart of one of the ancient world's most famous cults dedicated to sacred prostitution. In veneration of the goddess, girls were required to offer up their bodies to strangers once in their lives. It was one half of a ritual sacrifice. Burning large quantities of expensive perfume was the other half.

Perhaps the reason the priestesses burned the fragrance in Aphrodite's perfumed temples with such abandon was that its fumes were believed to be powerfully intoxicating and sexually arousing. Some people still believe that the central ingredient of this ancient fragrance—a plant resin from the Cistercians' *cistus* or rockrose known as labdanum—is inherently sexy. It is used today in modern perfumery because it also smells uncannily like another of the world's most prized ingredients in the history of fragrance, the "floating gold" known as ambergris or "gray amber." Ambergris comes from whale excreta, and, perhaps surprisingly considering those origins, it is also considered irresistibly erotic. Jeanne Bécu, better known to history as the celebrated royal courtesan Madame du Barry, doused herself with ambergris in the eighteenth century and apparently both she and the king of France, Louis XV, were pleased with the amatory results. It all began in Aphrodite's temples, though, and aphrodisiacs are named after the goddess of lusty pleasures for a reason.

Since the beginning of its history, then, perfume has been associated with a woman's sensuality, and, during her time as Étienne's mistress, Coco Chanel learned just how important a woman's choice of fragrance could be in how she advertised her sensuality. While rich and languid perfumes based on scents like musk, jasmine, tuberose, and ambergris came and went as an aristocratic fashion in the nineteenth century—so much so that in the 1810s the empress Joséphine doused everything in the palace at Versailles in the intimate smells of animal musk to arouse Napoléon—the lines were clear and unambiguous at the dawn of the twentieth century. By then, these kinds of scents were associated with just one thing: the "*odor di femina* of prostitutes and other women of easy virtue." Everyone understood that "heavy animal-based . . . or jasmine fragrances," especially, "were marked as belonging to the marginal world of prostitutes and courtesans." Women "of good taste and standing" wore "only [the] simple floral scents" that captured the aroma of a single garden flower.

What Coco Chanel liked about Émilienne was that she broke the rules about a woman's sexuality—and about a courtesan's perfume. Émilienne didn't arrive for country weekends at Royallieu leaving the aromas of jasmine and musk in her wake. She eschewed the perfumes that the other women of pleasure used in those days when even country châteaux didn't have running bathwater to cover the scents of sex and bodies. To Coco Chanel, the scent of overpowering musk, with its hints of unwashed bodies, was simply dirty. She understood immediately that it was the odor of prostitution, and it was unbearable. So keen was her nose and so offensive did she find those perfumes that the way some of those other kept women smelled made her nauseous.

Émilienne didn't pretend that she was a dainty ingénue and douse herself in shy violet aromas, but she refused to smell like the boudoir either. Émilienne—the elegant and cultured Émilienne, who could pass effortlessly among the kings and princes of Europe—smelled to Coco Chanel of just one thing: the scent of clean. She was sexy and beautiful, but she carried her perfume lightly, and there was always somewhere around her the fragrance of warm skin and freshly washed hair.

The smell of something at once clean and sensual: that was the combination Coco Chanel admired. After all, there was also something distasteful in the idea that a woman could not be sensual or that sexuality itself was dirty. Although she had no idea in 1905 of creating a signature perfume—no idea, in fact, that she would become the celebrated Coco Chanel in the short space of a decade—she already knew that she was looking for ways to capture the essence of a new and different kind of modern sexuality. It was essential to how she thought about herself and her own decisions.

There was something fresh and modern about Coco Chanel's particular brand of frank sensuality, and it was part of what made her so attractive. She was far from being a convent prude, and she embodied a daring new kind of eroticism that the young men in the first years of the twentieth century found especially titillating. While the height of beauty then was still for voluptuous women with soft curves like Émilienne, there was a risqué fashion for women with the childish bodies known as *fruits verts*—green fruits. It was a fashion fueled by turn-of-the-century pornographic fiction, with tales of the secret lusts of orphaned Catholic schoolgirls, and Coco Chanel fit the image precisely.

In Coco Chanel's youth, this boyish look was charged with a very precise kind of naughty eroticism that no respectable woman would have dared to display. As one historian notes, what was titillating wasn't women who looked like men, "but rather like children." It was scandalous then, too, that these "green fruits" were often associated with a liberated lesbianism. Throughout her life, there were persistent stories that Coco took many different kinds of lovers. With the publication of Victor Margueritte's scandalously erotic novel *La Garçonne* (1922), it became a bohemian fashion. By the height of the

Roaring Twenties, it was the look to which every young flapper—as these *garçonnes* came to be known in English—would aspire. It lives on today on the runways of Paris and Milan thanks in no small part to the celebrity of Coco Chanel.

Someday, she would create the perfect scent for those flappers, too—a perfume that would refute all the conventional stereotypes about two kinds of women and the fragrances they could wear. It would be a scent that could define what it meant to be modern and elegant and sexy. Someday, but not yet.

THREE

THE SCENT OF BETRAYAL

The day when Coco Chanel first began to imagine this perfume came much earlier than we might expect, perhaps as early as 1911. By then, she was already another man's mistress.

In fact, by then Coco was in love. She was already on her way to becoming one of her century's great fashion designers as well. These developments were two small miracles for which she could thank Étienne Balsan in a roundabout way.

During the years at Royallieu, she was known among the men and their mistresses simply as Étienne's *petite amie*, his little friend, and she passed her early twenties lounging in bed until noon reading romance novels and learning to ride fast horses. Eventually, boredom struck. Besides, Coco Chanel had the sense to realize that she would not look young and boyish forever. Still dreaming of a glittering life on the Paris vaudeville stage, she considered returning to acting, but Étienne disapproved. With returning to the stage out of the question, she asked instead to take advantage of her knack for making pretty hats, and he couldn't see the harm in letting her pursue a more feminine hobby. In 1909, with Étienne's blessing, she set up a millinery shop, which she would run out of the ground floor of his Paris apartment. As the doors opened for business, Coco Chanel was launched in the fashion business.

While Étienne thought Coco's venture was a lark and a diversion, he was prepared to support her. But that next winter, when she asked for a loan to expand the business, which had been a success almost instantly, he turned her down flat. A former showgirl lover was one thing: it was scandalously and deliciously bohemian. A mistress who worked for a living in one of the trades was something quite different, at least in his aristocratic circles.

Anyhow, by that time, they both knew she was sharing her bed with someone else. One weekend at Royallieu, Coco met Étienne's rich English friend Arthur "Boy" Capel and was immediately infatuated. She liked that Boy smelled of "leather, horses, forest, and saddle soap," and, with the strange civility of two men swapping a mistress, Étienne and Boy agreed that Coco would become Capel's lover and that he would financially support her.

So, that next year Coco Chanel opened her millinery shop at the now famous address, number 21, rue Cambon in Paris, on a narrow street running along the back side of the Ritz Hotel. Only a decade or so later, the novelist Virginia Woolf would make the bold assertion that "On or about December 1910 human character changed," bringing along with it sweeping changes "in religion, conduct, politics, and literature." What Woolf forgot to mention was a change in the future of fashion, because Coco Chanel was part of that seismic shift in Western culture toward the modern.

She already had her eye on a larger and more ambitious vision. Coco Chanel was probably also already weighing the idea that perfume would be a part of it. Because one of the other tenants in the building made dresses, the initial lease on her boutique on rue Cambon had in it a clause that specifically forbade the enterprising young milliner from using it to sell fashions. If she wanted to expand her business, couture in 1910 was not the obvious direction.

In fact, there are hints that she had the idea of launching a signature fragrance perhaps a full two years before she ever sold her first fashions at new boutiques in the fashionable resort towns of Biarritz and Deauville. It's a curious if minor point. But, consider: had she begun with fragrance, the story of the house of Chanel might have been astonishingly different. There might have been no couture, and history might remember Coco Chanel first and foremost not as the inventor of modern classics like the little black dress but as a pretty perfumer.

Nor is it any wonder that in the summer of 1911 Coco Chanel's thoughts would have turned to fragrance. Perfume was the story of the moment. By June, all of Paris was buzzing with talk of scent. Fragrance had already made the young Corsican entrepreneur François Coty, whose family traced its lineage back to Napoléon, one of France's richest men. His Parisian home was considered the center of all that was extravagant and fashionable, and tidbits about his opulent lifestyle were forever in the papers. Even more important, though, the most celebrated fashion designer of the moment, Paul Poiret, had stunned the capital that summer with the launch of his new perfumes—making him the first couturier in history to have a signature scent.

The Poiret launch was a soirée at his Paris mansion, a costume ball provocatively called "*la mille et deuxième nuit*"—the thousand-and-second night. Inspired by the "heavily perfumed odalisques in *Scheherazade*," it was a sultan's fantasy. All of Parisian high society was invited.

That summer evening, on June, 24, 1911, the warm air was alive with the sound of low Persian music, and the lucky guests who arrived at the entrance to the opulent Poiret estate were greeted with the wafting scents of oriental perfumes long before they ever stepped foot into a world of fantasy. Servants dressed in silken robes ushered three hundred of the city's most glamorous socialites into a huge garden, brilliantly illuminated with glowing lanterns, and dotted with harem tents. Wildly colorful tropical birds perched overhead in trees; musicians played sultry beats somewhere out of sight; and, from her prison in a dazzling golden cage, the beautiful Madame Poiret played the role of a languishing odalisque entrapped in splendor. Everywhere there were the burning scents of rich myrrh and frankincense, the intoxicating smells of rare perfume, and glass after glass of sparkling champagne.

The guests reveled in this thousand-and-second night of sensual pleasures until the small hours of the morning, and at dawn there were fireworks that lit up the skies of Paris. As the ladies departed— ladies who included all the most fashionable names in aristocratic and artistic Paris—Poiret, their host and the evening's sultan, bestowed upon each a parting gift. It was a bottle of his first perfume, named Nuit Persane in homage to this night of Persian luxuries. The history of fragrance had never seen such a spectacularly imaginative launch for a new perfume, and all of Paris was enchanted.

It was hard not to admire Poiret's business acumen. Although he would deny such suggestions strenuously and always claim that he had thrown the party only for the enjoyment of his special friends, it was in fact a brilliant way of introducing the arbiters of fashion to his new line of fragrances, Parfums de Rosine, which he had finished preparing for launch only days earlier. The line was named after his daughter, Rosine, and the first scents took their names from the theme of oriental harems, with fragrances like Nuit Persane (1911) and Le Minaret (1912). The bottles of that first scent were decorated using motifs drawn from the window decorations that were the signature of his well-known boutique, in case any of the ladies was liable to forget the connection between his scents and his salon.

In launching perfumes from his fashion house, Poiret became the first couturier in history to link design and fragrance. He had delighted all of Paris with his dramatic flair for marketing this novel perfume, and the newspapers were filled with descriptions of his extravagant party—and of the new scents that could capture its spirit. Less than a decade later, in 1919, the obscure fashion designer Maurice Babani became the second couturier to launch a signature scent. Coco Chanel would be the third. And, when the time came, she would remember the flair for which Poiret was everywhere celebrated.

For the moment, however, Coco Chanel set any fleeting thoughts of perfume aside. She threw herself instead into her romance with Boy Capel and into the introduction in 1913 of a simple line of sportswear in her boutique on the coast at Deauville, where the rich and fashionable people of France spent their leisure time. The next year, the First World War began, and the uniforms of the volunteer nurses of the era inspired her to create, in inexpensive jersey fabric, a line of simple, chic, and liberating dresses for the upper-class women who had been part of her circle since her first days at Royallieu. Within a few short years, these new fashions had made her name and made her a small fortune. By the time the war ended, Coco Chanel was already a famous designer.

In fact, by 1914 she was even well enough known in high society to find her relationship with Boy Capel the target of gossip and public teasing. That year, the celebrity cartoonist and illustrator Georges Goursat—usually known simply by his signature "Sem"—published a sketch of her and Boy dancing at the fashionable resort town of Deauville sur Mer, titled simply "Tangoville sur Mer." In it, the polo-mad Boy Capel is satirized as a lusty centaur running off with the dazed milliner, who, in case anyone missed the identification, carries a huge hatbox distinctly labeled "Coco."

The caricature was a nod to the beginning of the tango craze that year in Europe, ignited by a bestselling book, *Modern Dancing*, written by the couple of the hour, Verne and Irene Castle. Irene Castle was a scrappy socialite, an aspiring fashion designer, and, with her bobbed hair in 1914, already—like Coco Chanel—an early flapper, at a moment when the *garçonne* look was still shocking. The cartoon was also a pointed and rather mean-spirited dig at Boy's decadent equestrian indulgences and a sly allusion to the lusts of the

Gabrielle Chanel and
Arthur Capel by the
cartoonist Sem in 1913.

mythological centaurs, known in Greek mythology for their habit of
brashly abducting women. After all, just because he and Coco were
in love didn't mean that Boy didn't have a stable of mistresses. And
everyone knew that Coco had been with Étienne before Boy Capel
had charmed her.

A caricature like this was not precisely the sort of coverage in the
fashionable press a conflicted young *demi-rep*—as women who were
only "half reputable" were called—would desire, but in a way it was
a sign that she had arrived. Sketches like this, however, would also
leave Coco Chanel wary of the press and determined to control her
public image in ways that would profoundly shape some of her most
critical decisions about business—and one day the business of her
Chanel No. 5 fragrance in particular.

During the next four years, the years of the First World War
in Europe, Coco Chanel flourished. By the end of them, she could
afford to treat herself to a seaside villa in the south of France and a

"little blue Rolls." She was a celebrity, and she was quickly becoming rich as well. "The war helped me," Chanel later remembered. "Catastrophes show what one really is. In 1919 I woke up famous." She had come a long way from the charity convent school of Aubazine and her days as a cabaret chanteuse.

She had done it by learning not to turn down lucky chances. When the war ended in November of 1918, though, there was one opportunity that Coco Chanel had missed completely: perfume. That winter in Paris, it would have been hard to miss. For months and months after the armistice, the city was still filled with many of the two million American soldiers whose return home it would take the United States government the better part of a year to coordinate. While they waited, French fragrances were the souvenirs they all wanted. It was because of those soldiers that French perfumers became some of the wealthiest entrepreneurs in the world during that decade. Perfume was Paris. Paris was chic and sexy. The returning soldiers wanted something to show they had been there, something to help to remember it.

The story of the fantastic rise of French perfume during the early twentieth century is in many respects also an essentially American story, because had it not been for the American market and the American passion for Parisian fragrances, the fortunes made would have been far, far smaller. That market would one day be at the heart of the century's great passion for Coco Chanel's No. 5 perfume especially—a fragrance that went all but unadvertised in France for decades after its invention.

The interest in French perfume had been growing in the United States steadily even before the First World War, and large fragrance companies like Bourjois and Coty had begun setting up offices in the United States by the 1910s. Now, these forward-thinking entrepreneurs were poised to become huge international successes with the frenzy for Parisian perfume that followed the armistice. No one had a story more amazing or more emblematic than the jaunty entrepreneur François Coty, who in 1919 became France's first billionaire. His wife Yvonne, who had also made her start as a fellow milliner in Paris, was a friend of the stylish and already celebrated Coco Chanel.

If Paul Poiret and the fabulous success of his Parfums de Rosine first gave Coco Chanel the idea of linking a perfume line with a fashion house, it was François Coty who was now her real inspiration. Later, they would become rivals. Coty had the gift of an incredibly keen sense of smell and had stumbled upon perfumery one afternoon in the back room of a friend's pharmacy, where rows of scented materials were lined up in simple, medicinal bottles. He sold his first cologne from the back of a pony cart to women in the provinces, and now, at the end of the First World War, he was one of the world's most celebrated industrial magnates and a man of high culture. His perfumes were worn by czarinas at the Russian imperial court and by thousands of middle-class women elsewhere. In the burgeoning American market, Coty was quickly becoming a household name, and he was raking in a vast fortune. His story was one of a self-made entrepreneur finding fabulous success, and the enterprising young Coco Chanel, keen to make her fortune too, understood it intuitively.

So, sometime in late 1918 or perhaps early 1919, Coco Chanel threw herself into seriously planning the creation of her signature perfume. Of the many possible explanations for how Chanel No. 5 came into existence, perhaps the most intriguing is the legend that a long-lost secret perfume formula was the basis for Chanel's decision to produce a new fragrance in 1919. It is a story shrouded in mystery, and, were it not for evidence in the Chanel archives in Paris that affirm the formula's existence, it would be hard to take such a romantic tale seriously.

It was probably during the winter of 1918 that Coco Chanel received an excited visit from a friend, the bohemian socialite Misia Sert, a woman whose great beauty was captured in paintings by

Pierre-Auguste Renoir and Henri Toulouse-Lautrec. Misia knew that Coco was researching the launch of a signature perfume. They had talked about it already, debated bottle designs, and even planned how Coco would market it to her couture clients—or so Misia always claimed afterward. Now, Misia had heard of an amazing discovery in an old library in a château in the Loire valley. There, during renovations, the owners had discovered a Renaissance manuscript, and among its pages was a recipe. It was a formula for the lost "miraculous perfume" of the Medici queens, an elixir said to preserve aging beauties from the ravages of time.

If authentic, both Misia and Coco Chanel knew that it would be an exciting discovery—and a fabulous way to promote her fragrance among her wealthy clients. After all, the history of perfume-making in France began at the court of the Medici queens, when the young Catherine de Medici was sent to France as the bride of King Henry II. Arriving from Italy, Catherine brought with her a certain Renato Bianco, better known simply as René the Florentine, as part of her entourage. René became the first official perfumer in French history, and, from his shop in sixteenth-century Paris, he supplied scented aphrodisiacal potions and fragrances for the art of seduction. When those went wrong and lovers strayed unaccountably, some said he also sold the occasional rare and deadly poison with which to dispatch the competition—or the offender.

This perfume recipe, however, was said to belong to Catherine de Medici's cousin, Marie, who had also married into the French royal family and who was an even more committed perfume aficionado. In fact, it is because of Marie de Medici that the French village of Grasse, which started out as an artisan center for the production of gloves and leather tanning, became the fragrance capital of the world in the seventeenth century. As perfume historian Nigel Groom tells the story, she "set up a laboratory in Grasse for the study of perfume-making in order to rival the fashionable Arab perfumes of the time, for which she is regarded by some as the founder of the

French perfume industry." The queen was obsessed with scents and aromatics—and especially with their beauty secrets. Because she remained strikingly beautiful well into her sixties, no one doubted that she had found something magical.

Now, an ancient manuscript with one of Marie de Medici's perfumes had been discovered. Misia Sert urged Coco Chanel to buy it, and she did. She paid six thousand francs—the equivalent of nearly $10,000 today—for the manuscript that revealed the secrets of this mysterious "cologne," as light citrus-based scents were still fashionably called. Surely, Misia told her, it would be the perfect foundation for her signature beauty products. Coco Chanel must have agreed, because that summer she was apparently planning actively for its production. On July 24, 1919, company records show that Coco Chanel registered a trademark for a product line that she planned to call Eau Chanel—Chanel water.

Misia Sert would later claim that this was the origin of Chanel No. 5. She also claimed that she and Coco Chanel spent hours together designing the packaging and hitting upon the elegantly simple idea of using a common pharmaceutical bottle for the flacon. Perhaps if the turmoil in Coco Chanel's personal life had not intervened in the autumn of 1919, Chanel No. 5 would have been invented earlier. But nowhere in the Chanel archives is there any evidence that Coco Chanel got as far as ordering bottles that summer. The only evidence that hints at the production of any perfume is the report of a mysterious undated receipt said to have been discovered in the Coty company archives as late as the 1960s, which shows that her friend François billed Coco Chanel for some perfume laboratory work. His wife, Yvonne, always claimed that when Coco first began considering the idea of launching a fragrance, François offered to let her use his laboratory for the development.

Perhaps that summer Coco Chanel had moved forward with some preliminary formulations and this is behind the story of the bill in the Coty archives. Today, there is no way of knowing for sure. Chanel, however, believes that the story of any connection between the Coty laboratory and Chanel No. 5 is simply apocryphal. François's granddaughter, Elizabeth Coty, who tells the story in the biography of her famous relative, seems less certain. What is certain is that a perfume called Eau Chanel never existed—and, for reasons almost equally as complicated and circuitous, its scent could not possibly have been the inspiration behind Chanel No. 5.

Even if the Medici manuscript didn't lead directly to the creation of Chanel No. 5 perfume, it was a crucial preliminary stage in Coco Chanel's thinking about the development of a signature scent. While she had set this ancient recipe and the idea of an Eau Chanel aside quickly, she was now convinced that the time had come to launch a couture perfume. She had missed the opportunity for fabulous fragrance sales at the end of the war, when American soldiers queued for hours outside boutiques in search of French perfumes, and she was about to make up for lost time.

Fragrance was an industry poised on the brink of a massive explosion. Indeed, the 1920s and 1930s are still known as the golden age of modern perfumery, and Coco Chanel had an inkling of it. If she had launched a perfume in 1919, however, it would not have been Chanel No. 5, or at least not Chanel No. 5 as we know it. Her relationship to the fragrance also would have been entirely different at that moment, with vastly different results for the history of this iconic perfume. Because what stopped her from moving forward with a perfume at that moment would soon become part of the reason that she became doubly obsessed with finding the perfect scent—the precise aroma of Chanel No. 5.

In 1919, Coco Chanel's private life was in tatters. In truth, it had been painful and tumultuous since at least the autumn of 1918, when Boy Capel, nearly a decade into an intense and powerful love affair with Coco, announced that he would never marry her. It was a heartbreaking reminder that there was no escaping her beginnings.

Being famous wasn't enough to make Coco respectable. In the circles in which she traveled, nothing ever would have been. She would always be the daughter of itinerant peasants who was abandoned by her father to the nuns of a rural orphanage. No one would forget that she began her career singing risqué cabaret tunes for officers in the dance halls, either. Nor would anyone overlook the fact that she gained a first foothold in the world of high society as a wealthy man's second mistress and as one of those shadowy and seductive *demi-mondaines*. Through talent and charm, she had made a brilliant career for herself. Now she wanted to make a life with Boy. "We were in love," she later remembered, "we could have gotten married." He refused. He wanted her only as his mistress. Respectable men at the beginning of the twentieth century didn't marry their illegitimate mistresses, even if one of those mistresses had become an international arbiter of high fashion and good taste.

Just as the first wave of those American soldiers were lining up outside boutiques in Paris in the autumn of 1918, looking for luxury scents to carry home to their girls and their mothers, Boy confessed what they both knew had been the truth all along. No matter where his heart might lie, he was now engaged to someone else, someone demure and respectable. The kind of girl who wore the simple floral scents of tea roses or violets and whose mores, at least on the face of things, were modestly old-fashioned. Coco, he hoped, would remain his lover and confidante—but she would be nothing more. For much of that year, they had lived together as always in his Paris apartment. Then he married the charming Diana Lister Wyndham. Coco Chanel was thirty-six.

It was a staggering betrayal, and Coco found herself facing an impossible dilemma. She knew what it meant to stay on as Boy's mistress. She had done it long enough to understand perfectly. She would live forever on the margins of the lives of others. It meant lonely birthdays and holidays among friends, and the apartment they shared would never be their home. Leaving, however, was almost equally unbearable.

By December, Coco still had not been able to make a final decision. She moved that fall into an apartment of her own in Paris, and the now-married Boy followed. Then, in the days before Christmas, he left for the south of France, to spend the holidays with his wife and her family. Coco Chanel stayed behind in Paris.

The French call the seacoast along the Mediterranean the Côte d'Azur—the "blue coast"—and the roads there are famously treacherous. South along the coast, they wind in hairpin turns along the cliffs that hang over the sea. Beyond are the *penetrantes*, roads twisting through the mountains and pine forests that are still among the most dangerous in France. Drive along them, and it is easy to understand how treacherous they really are. A car crash happened late one night: the result of a blown-out tire and perhaps too much champagne as well. It was December 22, 1919, on the road from St. Raphael to Cannes, and Boy did not survive.

"For a woman," Coco Chanel would later say, "betrayal has just one sense: that of the senses." Alone in the bed that they had shared, in the weeks that followed, she knew despair, and she doubtless knew as well how the lingering scent in the sheets of a man you had loved can bruise the spirit. That winter, Misia persuaded the distraught Coco to come to Italy for a long vacation. From Venice, Coco sent a telegram home, asking that everything be taken out of the apartment in Paris. In the end, she would live in rented rooms, sometimes at the Meurice Hotel, but mostly at the Ritz. It was all a reminder of the magnitude of her losses, all too much to bear. She turned, instead, to scent.

FOUR

AN EDUCATION IN THE SENSES

After the death of Boy Capel, Coco threw herself into the world of perfume. She wasn't simply immersing herself in work and a new project as a distraction during a personal crisis, however. The allure of scent was something more essential. The perfume that she would create in the aftermath had everything to do with the complicated story of her sensuality, with the heartbreaking loss of Boy in his car crash, and with everything that had come before. In crafting this scent, she would return to her emotional ground zero.

She sought something oddly contradictory. Her perfume had to be lush and opulent and sexy, but it also had to smell clean, like Aubazine and Émilienne. It would be the scent of scoured warm flesh and soap in a provincial convent, yet it would be unabashedly luxurious and sensual. In the world of fine fragrance today, a perfume begins with an idea—a "brief"—and if Coco Chanel had put into words what she was looking for in her signature scent, it would have been this tension.

She was fascinated by the art of perfume and the story that it could tell about a woman. She was also a sharp entrepreneur. With all those Americans eager for French perfume and with her celebrity on the rise, she was betting she could make a fortune. When it came to her perfume—the perfume that she was still only envisioning—there was always at the heart of it all a conflict between the scent as an intimate, personal story and as something public and commercial. This convergence of her entrepreneurial dreams and private losses would shape both the scent she set out to create and her deeply complicated, sometimes even antagonistic, relationship to it in the decades to come. She knew already that the perfume would be her calling card—the product most closely associated with her name and her story. She was going to do this right.

For Coco Chanel, precision was a religion, and she knew better than to commit time and resources to developing a signature perfume without first making an exhaustive study of the art and science and business of the fragrance industry. Those who worked in her fashion salon during the years of her great fame as a couturière would always remember how sometimes she would take a dress apart and reassemble it fifteen or twenty times before announcing it to be perfect and allowing it to leave her atelier.

She had the same approach to scent. For the next year, scent became her passion. She traveled to southern France with friends and toured small villages in the hills not far beyond Cannes, places like La Bocca and, especially, Grasse, which had long been established as the center of the French perfume industry. These were favorite summer retreats for artists, intellectuals, and impoverished foreign princes, who gathered here for the warm climate and the exquisitely scented breezes that blew in from the sprawling plantations of rose and jasmine and mimosa beyond the walls of these picturesque medieval villages.

It was here—and perhaps in conversations with her acquaintance François Coty—that Coco began studying perfume seriously. As her confidante Lady Abdy remembered, "When she decided on something, she followed her idea to the end. In order to bring it off and succeed she brought everything into play. Once she began to be interested in perfumery she wanted to learn everything about them—their formula, fabrication, and so forth. Naturally, she sought the best advice."

Coco Chanel was wise to have made a study of modern perfumery, because in 1920, when she was immersing herself thoroughly in the world of scent, the fragrance industry and the science behind scent were both changing in ways that would reshape the olfactory experience of the twentieth century.

For many of us, appreciating the finer points of a fragrance is something mysterious, and the same was true when Coco Chanel set out to learn about perfume-making. A perfumer—known in the industry simply as a "nose"—is charged with the delicate and complicated task of creating, out of all the hundreds of thousands of possible scents in the world, a composition that both captures a precise idea or feeling and is capable of evolving gracefully and beautifully in time as it slowly disappears from our perception.

As Coco Chanel quickly learned, the essentials of appreciating a fine fragrance begin with this art of blending aromas. Those who make perfumes talk about those scents in terms of "accords" and scent "families," and this language is key to gaining a connoisseur's appreciation for the art of perfume. Accords are a group of scents that blend naturally and provocatively together and, in blending, transform each other. They are fragrances within a fragrance, the building blocks of a complex perfume, and these accords are how experts define the different fragrance families.

Today, there are at least a half-dozen different rubrics for diagramming all the possible categories of perfume, and some of them are hopelessly, even occasionally comically, complex, with these families and subfamilies running into the dozens. In layman's terms, however, in the 1920s there were five traditional categories: scents designated as oriental, fougère, leather, chypre, and floral. Some had ancient origins and traditions; some were twentieth-century innovations.

When Cleopatra famously set sail to meet Mark Anthony, she perfumed herself with sandalwood and filled the air with an incense of cinnamon, myrrh, and frankincense. Today, we could classify Cleopatra's fragrances, based around the "amber" scents of plant barks and resins, simply as oriental perfumes. At the end of the nineteenth century, perfumers added to the warm, spicy aroma of those oriental ambers—materials like frankincense, sandalwood, and patchouli—another set of fragrance notes, another accord, based around animal musk and the orchid scents of vanilla.

At the time when Coco Chanel was learning about perfume and about the daring innovations taking place in the chemistry of fragrance, perfumer Aimé Guerlain's "ferociously modern" scent Jicky was considered the ultimate oriental. In fact, for many admirers it still is. Invented in 1889, Jicky was the first fragrance to use the then-exotic scent of patchouli, to which Guerlain added the aroma of vanilla. According to fragrance folklore, the classic oriental perfume Shalimar—Jicky's only rival as an oriental "reference" perfume—was invented in the 1920s when Jacques Guerlain, Aimé's nephew and the boy for whom Jicky was named, wondered what the perfume would smell like if he added an even larger dose of vanilla. The result was pure magic.

Contemporary perfumes in the oriental family are now recognized as having their scent based around vanilla—or, more precisely, vanilla along with the vanilla effects created by pinesap vanillin and the almond-and-vanilla-scented aromatic ingredient heliotropine, a synthetic molecule created in the mid-1880s—and blended in an accord with the scents of amber plant resins and animal musk. On the market today, familiar mass-market oriental perfumes include Calvin Klein's Obsession, Yves Saint Laurent's Opium, and even Old Spice cologne.

Oriental perfumes are meant to capture the scents of the East, but the perfumers with whom Coco Chanel talked that year also told her about a sea change in the approach to making fragrances. During the last decades of the nineteenth century and the first decades of the twentieth, dozens of new "synthetic" aromatic materials were being discovered in laboratories around the world, and this would change the direction of perfume-making to the present day.

For the first several millennia of its production, traditional perfumery relied on perhaps as few as a hundred natural scent materials, and now new scents and new aromas, capable of creating new accords and olfactory effects, were being created with the help of modern science. Modern abstraction and innovation were coming to perfumery, and it was a new and fresh aesthetic—just the kind of thing that had always fascinated and inspired Coco Chanel as a designer.

One of those new abstract fragrances was the family of scents known as a fougère. The word simply means "fern" in French, and these new scents were meant to evoke green leafy fronds and fresh woodlands—or at least the idea of them. As a rule, ferns don't have any smell at all, and the category is beautifully conceptual. The name *fougère* comes from a great early fragrance by the firm of Houbigant, marketed as Fougère Royale (1882), or "royal fern." It was a milestone in the history of modern fragrance: the first scent to use a synthetic aromatic, the compound coumarin, which smells of clean-cut hay. To this aroma, the perfumer Paul Parquet added the familiar cool scents of lavender and the dry-lichen aroma of oakmoss in a striking combination. The result was the refreshing coumarin-lavender-oakmoss accord still known today as a fougère. Fragrances that capture the essence of the fougère accord include such well-known scents as Geoffrey Beene's Grey Flannel, Davidoff's Cool Water, or the aromas of Brut Cologne.

The perfumes known as leathers were also a modern innovation in perfume-making when Coco Chanel was visiting perfumers and their laboratories. The scents in fact have no leather in them, and they depend on the late-nineteenth-century discovery of the scent materials known as quinolines. These molecules were first synthesized in the 1880s, and their smoky notes of tobacco and charcoal help these perfumes call forth the aromatic essence of soft, tanned leather. The most exclusive perfumes in this family—named after the premium birch-tar leathers of Europe's eastern empire—were scents known as *cuir de Russie*, or "Russian leather." It was the smell of the rare leathers used at the imperial courts to wrap precious jewels. Familiar staples today include perfumes such as Dior's Fahrenheit and Lancôme's Cuir.

Then, there is the scent of chypre—history's first international bestseller, the only real rival in the long history of perfume-making to compare with the celebrity of Chanel No. 5. Chanel No. 5 has been a phenomenon for the better part of a century. Only one perfume has ever been as famous and for even longer: chypre, that ancient fragrance with the warm wood-and-citrus notes of the rockrose plant resin labdanum and orange-scented bergamot, named after the Mediterranean island of Cyprus. The world's oldest perfume family and Aphrodite's scent sensation, it was popular until the mid-eighteenth century, when it mysteriously fell out of fashion. After 150 years in relative obscurity, however, perfumers in the first decades of the twentieth century were captivated by the idea of reimagining it for a new era. In 1895, the fragrance-industry giant Bourjois introduced a chypre to its catalog, and in 1909 Jacques Guerlain created Chypre de Paris. Parfums d'Orsay produced a chypre in 1912, and in 1913 came Bichara Malhame's Chypre de Limassol.

Coco Chanel knew perfectly well, though, that it was with the release of François Coty's Chypre in 1917 that history's most ancient and famously erotic perfume once again was sweeping the cultural imagination. It wasn't the same fragrance as that original chypre, which long ago sweetened the smoky air of Aphrodite's temples. That recipe had already been lost for centuries. In the process of creating a new version of the world's first perfume, however, François Coty also invented another of modern perfumery's central accords: a blend of citrusy bergamot and woody labdanum, to which he added as a delicate counterpoint the lichen scent of oakmoss.

These are still the essential notes of the family of fragrances known to perfumers as a chypre. Today, the family includes fragrances such as Estée Lauder's Knowing and Dior's Miss Dior. But those classic chypre perfumes were the scent phenomenon of the second decade of the twentieth century—the very moment when Coco Chanel was beginning to think seriously about scent and sensuality and what she intended to do with the connection.

The fragrance family that fascinated her, though, wasn't chypre. To follow in the footsteps of those recent innovations at Coty would have seemed too predictable and faddish for a designer intent on something that spoke to a new kind of feminine sexuality. It was the old, familiar category of floral perfumes that she wanted to reimagine—fragrances based on the heady scent of blooming flowers. Today, it is a vast family of perfumes that includes everything from Nina Ricci's L'Air du Temps and Jean Patou's Joy to that unlikely phenomenon of the 1970s, Charlie.

Fine fragrance begins with the quality of the materials, and this is especially true with floral perfumes, because the scents are so fleeting. In 1920, some of the finest natural materials in the world already came from Grasse. The roses and jasmine that bloom there are universally agreed to be nothing less than exquisite.

Roses and jasmine, however, were scents that told two very different olfactory stories about the women who wore them. The traditional scent for a woman's perfume, roses were discreetly and quietly lovely. Respectable women, women like Diana Lister Wyndham, could wear them without hesitation, and, until the second decade of the twentieth century, floral perfumes came in just one style, the style known today as soliflores.

These soliflores were perfumes that captured the aroma of a

single flower, and they were meant to be representational. Their formulas might blend several different floral essences, but one note—recognizably like the scent of some real flower—was meant to dominate the senses. At the turn of the century, the runaway bestseller was François Coty's La Rose Jacqueminot (1903), the scent that made him a millionaire almost instantly. It was based around the specific scent of an heirloom rose variety, the *rosa centifolia Jacqueminot*, which grew in the fields of Grasse.

A respectable woman who didn't like the scent of roses might easily choose a perfume with a different note. She might wear something scented with gardenia, lilac, or lilies. Violet fragrances—especially those made from the powdery and subtle scents of the Parma violet, cultivated in Grasse since 1868—were ladylike standards. A special formulation called Violetta di Parma (1870) was the signature fragrance of the empress Marie Louise Bonaparte, the second wife of Napoléon, and it became a nineteenth-century commercial powerhouse. When two chemists in 1893 perfected the technique of extracting from the Parma violet the precise compound that gave rise to its gentle aroma—molecules known as ionones—the scent became common even in ladies' soaps. It was the similar discovery earlier in the nineteenth century of geraniol and phenylethyl alcohol—the essential elements of the "rose" scent—that also made that fragrance so ubiquitous.

What a respectable woman would not do in the first years of the twentieth century was wear the scents of heavy "white flowers" like jasmine, tuberose, or ylang-ylang, known as "the poor man's jasmine." Their sweet and heavy scents were richly sensual, and, however gorgeous they might be, they were the smells of the licentious and illicit and arriviste.

Until the second decade of the twentieth century, no one wore the floral fragrances today known as multiflores—floral scents in a mixed bouquet—for the simple reason that they hadn't yet been invented. It wasn't until 1912 that the perfume house of Houbigant launched the first true multiflore fragrance, a scent known simply as Quelques Fleurs, or "some flowers." It was a perfume innovation: a scent that didn't smell recognizably like any particular flower. Instead, it was the *idea* of a new flower, one that had never existed. It was the scent of an invented and imagined and lovely floral creation. It became an instant sensation, and the idea behind it—the idea of the essential abstraction—was one that Coco Chanel found utterly fascinating.

After all, like the scent of fougère fragrances, Quelques Fleurs and these new multiflores that followed in the course of the next decade were wonderfully conceptual. As the scent historian Richard Stamelman puts it, the most experimental perfumers of the early twentieth century no longer "dreamed of imitating nature but of transforming the real," with a new "emotive perfumery." In order to create these effects, they turned to something else completely modern: the science of scent creation. The perfumer behind Quelques Fleurs, Robert Bienaimé, experimented boldly not only with the idea of blending floral notes but also with the pioneering advances in modern aromatic synthetics, materials able to give a perfumer just a single note within a flower. He used especially the revolutionary and largely unknown materials known as aldehydes. The combination allowed for the artistic creation of a scent that was powerfully original. The world was on the brink of a new and golden era in perfumery because this molecular precision freed perfumers from the bonds of representational art, as surely as Pablo Picasso and the other artists whom Coco Chanel called friends freed a generation of painters.

By the summer of 1920, although she still had a great deal to learn about the world of fragrance, Coco Chanel knew enough to understand her own vision clearly. She was already imagining a revolutionary integration of women's fashion—the founding of a couture house and a sense of style that would epitomize the freedom and verve of those young flappers. From her *maison* she would sell them everything from dresses and jewelry to fragrance. In fact, it is impossible to understand Chanel No. 5 except as part of this larger project of redefining twentieth-century femininity.

She also wanted that signature perfume to be a modern work of art and an abstraction. "[T]he perfume many women use," she complained, "is not mysterious. . . . Women are not flowers. Why should they want to smell like flowers? I like roses, and the smell of the rose is very beautiful, but I do not want a woman to smell like a rose." "I want," she had decided, "to give women an artificial perfume. Yes, I do mean artificial, like a dress, something that has been made. I don't want a rose or lily of the valley, I want a perfume that is a composition." A woman, she thought, "should smell like a woman and not like a flower."

She was imagining one more thing, too: a scent that would utterly confound those lines between the fragrance worn by a nice, respectable girl and one worn by a seductress. She wanted a perfume that would be sexy and provocative and utterly clean. That summer, she was finally ready to create it. "A badly perfumed woman," she once quipped, borrowing a line from the writer Paul Valéry, "is a woman without a future." She intended to have a dazzling one.

FIVE

THE PRINCE
AND THE PERFUMER

Coco Chanel was ready, but she needed still one thing: a perfumer.

She knew the outlines of the scent that she had in mind, and she had thrown herself into learning about the art and science of fragrance. That, however, wasn't the same thing as being able to craft a gorgeous perfume. It wasn't even close.

A wonderful fragrance—the kind of scent able to withstand the test of time, decade after decade—is always a feat of engineering and inspiration. A scent might easily have as many as five or six dozen different notes in it, and the old-fashioned racks on which perfumers in the early twentieth century arranged those materials in imaginary chords were called organs. The musical references in both cases are telling, because a perfume is a symphony of notes coming in and out, interacting, resonating, and, in time, disappearing. Coco Chanel had an excellent nose, and she knew the kind of scent that she wanted. But she didn't possess the training or mastery needed to create it.

So, instead, she set out to find the person who would be able to bring her vision into existence. She needed a talented perfumer, because she wanted something that would be daring and perfect. Once again, it was an affair of the heart that shaped the destiny of Coco Chanel and the story of the fragrance that would become Chanel No. 5.

The south of France that summer of 1920 epitomized the beginning of the debauched decade often known simply as *les années folles*—the crazy years. Women sunbathed on the beaches wearing ropes of pearls, and the bohemian rich staggered tipsy from extravagant party to extravagant party, from one bedroom to another. Coco Chanel, the rich and already famous designer, single-handedly made the suntan fashionable, and, as F. Scott Fitzgerald wrote of those times, "It was a whole race going hedonistic, deciding on pleasure."

After the death of Boy, Coco had certainly made the decision to pursue pleasure. She spent her summers on the French Riviera, where she entertained glamorous friends—among them some of her generation's most renowned artists. Everyone was there to celebrate, among other things, the end of the First World War just a few months earlier, and some people had more to celebrate than others. Among the luckiest but also the most impoverished were the aristocratic waiters who served the champagne cocktails in those seaside villas. These were the so-called White Russians, the princes and princesses, dukes and duchesses, who had somehow escaped execution in Soviet Russia after the revolution of 1917—an insurrection that had brought a brutal end to the rule of the imperial czars and swept the Communists to power. Throughout France in the years that followed, refugee princesses worked as seamstresses, and the handful of royal men lucky enough to have been at that moment in history somewhere far from St. Petersburg now took jobs as salesmen. Coco Chanel took one of the exiled princes as her new lover.

His name was Dmitri Pavlovich, and he was among the grand dukes of Russia and a cousin to the last czar, Nicholas II—who had been murdered, along with nearly all Dmitri's family, in the revolution. Like Coco, Dmitri had been raised an orphan. There, however, the similarities between their early lives ended, because this Russian beau's poverty was only a recent unhappy development.

Coco Chanel's new lover was a man with an astonishing history. Dmitri had grown up at the royal court in St. Petersburg during the twilight years of imperial splendor, but his childhood was anything but easy. While Boy Capel had balked at marrying Coco, his lowborn mistress, Dmitri's aristocratic father had made a different decision and had married his paramour. He would pay for it dearly. For the unforgivable transgression of falling in love with a woman beneath him socially, the grand duke Paul Alexandrovich was sent into forced exile and told that he would need to leave his two young children behind. Their royal uncle Sergei would raise them instead.

Uncle Sergei and their German-born aunt Elizabeth—the sister of the czarina and, through her mother, the granddaughter of Britain's Queen Victoria—embraced Dmitri and his sister, Marie, but even that story didn't have a happy ending. A few years later, Sergei Alexandrovich was assassinated on the street in front of them all during the first abortive efforts at revolution in Russia in 1905. Afterward, the orphans were sent to live at the royal court with their relations, the czar and czarina. There was even talk for a while that, if his sickly cousin Alexei died of his incapacitating hemophilia, Dmitri might someday inherit the imperial throne.

All that talk of inheriting an empire ended in 1916, when Dmitri was twenty-five. Horrified by the power of the "mad monk" Grigori Rasputin over the czarina and by the whispered talk of a palace revolt, Dmitri and his cousin Prince Felix Yusopov conspired to murder the mystic. An English aristocrat living at the Russian court later revealed why. "While in his cups," Rasputin it seems told the two young noblemen about the czarina's "fixed intention, early in January 1917, to launch a *coup d'état* to dethrone the [czar] . . . and herself to assume the reins of Government in the name and on behalf of her son." The prince and the duke were horrified, and they resolved to take action. First, they poisoned Rasputin with wine dosed with massive quantities of cyanide. When he failed to die, the prince shot him. According to the gruesome legend, Rasputin survived another three gunshots in the back, and, when bullets, too, seemed eerily ineffective, the young men finally drowned him beneath the ice of the city's frozen river.

When Dmitri's part in the murder was discovered, the enraged czarina shocked the royal family by having him illegally arrested. The result was scandal. A Russian grand duke stood apart from the law—part of what riled the revolutionary Bolsheviks. Even the czar didn't have the right to arrest a member of the royal family. Dmitri's imprisonment dragged on for days, and at first it seemed that the weak-willed czar would not be able to summon the resolve to counteract the czarina. Then, on the day before Christmas, the royal court was stunned again to learn that, instead of standing trial, Dmitri had been exiled from Russia. In the dead of night, he had been forcibly put, without food and under arrest, in the locked carriage of a train heading east to Kasvin, on "the confines of the Empire [at] the Persian border." He was being sent to serve in the disease-riddled battlefields of Persia, where it was expected he would die.

It was a bleak punishment. By contrast, Prince Yusopov got off lightly, simply being sent by train to comfortable exile at a family country estate near Moscow. The most scandalous part of that tale was that he was made to travel second class. Dmitri's destiny was far crueler.

In 1916, at the peak of the First World War, the Middle Eastern theater was the site of a bitter struggle over the oil needed to fuel this global conflict. It was a combination of cold trench warfare in the mountains and sweltering summer heats, and Dmitri was sent to Persia in order to be humiliated. He was attached to a supply chain in the army, and, as far away as America, there were reports in the *New York Times* that "Rumors spread he was traveling in fetters" and chains. No one misunderstood that it was intended as a death sentence.

Some of those closest to the czar wrote to him, begging that he change his mind about Dmitri. We "implore you," they wrote in their petition, "to reconsider your harsh decision concerning the fate of the Grand Duke Dmitri Pavlovich. Your Majesty must know the very harsh conditions under which our troops have to live in Persia, without shelter and in constant peril. . . . to live there would be for the Grand Duke almost certain death." The czar was resolute. Dmitri would never come home.

For the young duke, it was a terrifying and vicious retribution, made worse by the fact that he was singled out among the conspirators by the sentence. It was also a stroke of good fortune, for only this punishment would save his life. Just a year later, the revolution in Russia brought the Romanov dynasty to a bloody end. Scores of his friends—and nearly all of his family—were executed, including his cousin the czar, the czarina, the czarevitch, and all the royal princesses, as well as his noble aunt and even, in the end, his aristocratic father, who had finally been pardoned and had returned to Russia at just the wrong moment in history. If Dmitri had been in St. Petersburg, he would almost certainly have died with them.

Instead, in 1920 Dmitri was living on charity as a refugee between Paris and London, where he learned that his sister Marie, after a harrowing journey through Romania, somehow had also survived the revolution. In her memoirs she told how, at the time, "The past, our past, still held the most important part of our lives: we were like people roughly shaken out of a pleasant dream, waiting for the moment to go to sleep again and take up the threads where they had broken off." This princess soon found herself taking up threads of a different sort. She would go on to establish—with the support of Coco Chanel—one of Paris's most famous textile and embroidery houses, Kitmir, which supplied Chanel with many of her gloriously flamboyant fabrics during the 1920s and her famous "Russian period."

The past that Dmitri and Marie remembered was filled with every imaginable luxury and always with the richness of perfume. For both of these royals, perfume was a passion. The imperial palace at St. Petersburg was a famously perfumed court, and Dmitri's aunts and royal cousins had arrived amid the rustle of scented fur and velvet. There was one fragrance that both Dmitri and Marie remembered piercingly: an *eau de cologne* with the rich notes of rose and jasmine. Made in Moscow by the firm of A. Rallet and Company, it was known as Rallet O-De-Kolon No. 1 Vesovoi—or simply Rallet No. 1 perfume. It had been a royal family favorite, and the czarina—for whom it had been invented—cherished it especially. In fact, that scent may have been among the last beautiful things that Dmitri's murdered cousins ever experienced. Among the personal possessions looted from the Romanov royal family's prison chambers were vials of some unnamed perfumes.

For Dmitri, living in impoverished exile in the south of France, this was the scent of childhood: the smell of home and family and a life that had been shattered irrevocably. Scientists have long known that scent and memory are, in the neurological circuitry of our brains, inextricably connected. Dmitri knew it too, intuitively and without explanation. The scent of that perfume was among the familiar smells of a world that had disappeared. Some say his sister Marie still wore Rallet No. 1, and nothing could have been more natural than his effort to make it live on in other ways, too, by sharing it with his fashionable new lover—a woman whose passion at that moment was just this kind of a perfume. No one knows precisely what Dmitri's thoughts were about the fragrance that Coco invented that summer; he never wrote them down for posterity. But more than any other influence in Coco Chanel's life, at critical junctures Dmitri Pavlovich shaped the destiny of Chanel No. 5, and it's easy to understand why when we know the whole story.

· ·

When Coco Chanel met Dmitri, she was very much in pursuit of scent, and perhaps it was part of what drew them together. They may have met in Venice that first winter after Boy's death, in early 1920, when her grief was still at its keenest. More likely, though, they had met before in Biarritz or somewhere along the Riviera and were thrown together again later in the summer. By the summer of 1920, in any event, they were lovers.

Despite the vast differences in their backgrounds, they shared common ground: the same sense of longing in their emotional lives. The same sense of losing those they loved; the same sense of abandonment and betrayal. They both also understood what it meant to be alone and rootless. There is no documentary evidence to confirm what happened that summer, but there's a compelling emotional logic to the speculations and stories. Coco Chanel would have told Dmitri, of course, of her plans for a signature fragrance. Perhaps she told him of the ancient Medici formula, too, of this perfume made for their queens and how she had first planned to re-create it. She told him of the smells and all those sensations that she wanted a scent to capture.

In return, he told her of that scent he above all remembered, the favorite perfume of his lost imperial childhood, that fragrance that had been created especially in honor of his aunt and cousins to celebrate the women of the Romanov dynasty: Rallet No. 1. Some stories even say that he did the simplest thing imaginable: he bought her a bottle. It was produced, after all, in those foothills just beyond Cannes. Most importantly however, friends always thought afterward that he was the one who introduced her to a fellow Franco-Russian exile—the man who had created that imperial fragrance.

She had found her perfumer.

After all, it wasn't only the aristocrats who fled Russia in 1917. In the years after the Bolshevik revolution, those working in the luxury business quickly saw the wisdom of setting up shop somewhere else. Fabergé, the Russian-French jewelry firm famous for its jeweled Easter eggs, was nationalized, and its founders fled to exile in Switzerland. Russia's famed Imperial Porcelain Factory, known for its signature cobalt-blue patterns, was renamed the State Porcelain Factory, and its luxury craftsmen set to producing cheap works of pottery-turned-propaganda. A working-class communist revolution didn't hold many opportunities for families who had made their fortunes producing expensive perfumes, either—especially perfumes supplied to the late royal court.

This was the reason the Franco-German perfumer Ernest Beaux, when he was finally released from military service after the First World War, didn't go home to Moscow, where his family had emigrated to work in the Russian luxury trade, but came instead to the south of France. His family had strong French roots in particular and long ties to the firm of A. Rallet and Company, which had been purchased in 1898 by a prominent French family of perfume distributors who ran one of the largest fragrance businesses in the world in 1919. The Chiris family owned flower plantations around the world and sprawling factories in the village of Grasse, dedicated to the processing of jasmine and roses. They also owned research laboratories where aspiring young perfumers like François Coty had come for training and important offices in Moscow and St. Petersburg, where much of their business began.

Ernest Beaux had joined the firm of Rallet as a young man in Moscow in 1898, just after the Chiris takeover, and he was following in the footsteps of his older brother, who held an important position in the company. After beginning in the manufacture of luxury soap, he was soon shifted into a more prestigious line of work: creating innovative perfumes for the most famous and influential French fragrance house in czarist Russia.

He was keenly interested in all those new scientific developments that were reshaping the world of scent at the beginning of the twentieth century. He also possessed a dazzling talent. Ernest's first blockbuster fragrance, a men's cologne called Le Bouquet de Napoléon—"Napoléon's Bouquet"— hit the international market in 1912. He had created it to commemorate the hundredth anniversary of the Battle of Borodino, a decisive turning point in the final days of the Napoleonic Wars, and, as he later remembered, it "became an incredible success." Encouraged by the popularity of this fragrance, the company—already official perfumers to the royal family—urged him to create a new women's perfume in time for the celebration of the three-hundred-year anniversary of the Romanov dynasty in 1913.

Named Le Bouquet de Catherine after Catherine the Great, it was a lovely scent. Maddeningly, though, it was a commercial disaster; a perfume named after a German-born empress of Russia was doomed in 1914. It was a victim of its historical moment. In the early days of the First World War, Germany and Russia were already engaged in bloody conflict, and people increasingly resented the luxury-loving German-born czarina Alexandra and her strange, disturbing favorite, Rasputin. It was also staggeringly, even impossibly, expensive.

Ernest knew it was a brilliant perfume. Perhaps not yet perfect, but brilliant. It was daring and original in its use of new ingredients and new design concepts, and the only thing like it on the market was that beautiful—and extremely successful—multiflore perfume, Houbigant's Quelques Fleurs.

Le Bouquet de Catherine was a perfume destined for great things, and he was certain of it. Hoping that it was just a matter of marketing, the company tried changing the name: Le Bouquet de Catherine became simply Rallet No. 1. It was well loved by the imperial family, and a scent that, in the summer of 1920, Dmitri would remember. Somehow it never found an international audience under either of its names, however. It was a matter of the worst kind of unlucky timing. Had events in Russia unfolded differently, it might have been a bestseller. Based on Ernest's studies into Quelques Fleurs, which provided his initial inspiration, it was a scent that experimented boldly with pioneering fragrance materials. In the world of perfume, Rallet No. 1 was already a technical milestone and a scent innovation.

In time, perhaps it would have become famous. Instead came the First World War, the revolution, and the end of imperial Russia itself. Ernest spent those last years of the war, from 1917 to 1919, as a lieutenant stationed far to the north, in the last arctic outposts of the continent, surrounded by frozen tundra and the smells of snow and lichen. During the revolution, he threw in his lot with the Allies and the exiled aristocratic White Russians, and he served throughout the war interrogating Bolshevik prisoners in Arkangelsk, at the infamous Mudyug Island prison. It has since been called modern history's first concentration camp. These alliances—and the many wartime decorations that he earned for his service to France and Britain and in the cause of the White Russians—meant that he would never be able to return home to communist Moscow. He mourned for the life he had lost in Moscow and for the fate of an unsung fragrance masterpiece that had faded with the glory of the Romanovs.

When he received word in late 1919 that Rallet had moved its production to the village of La Bocca, just outside Grasse, the idea of the warm aromas of the south was a welcome reprieve. Mudyug Island was a cold and ugly place during the war.

By then the scent of the Arctic had captured his imagination, however. One of the Bolshevik prisoners at the camp in Arkangelsk later remembered a Lieutenant Beaux: how, unlike so many other officers who interrogated them, he was never a heavy drinker. Instead, he would go for long walks along the coast of the White Sea and spent his afternoons secluded in a small, towered lighthouse at the end of the surf. There, the arctic scents surrounded him. He was struck by the exquisite freshness of the seaweed and cold air, and he was already dreaming of ways to capture its aroma. He had already guessed that those aldehydes would be the key to unraveling its secret.

No one knows exactly when Coco Chanel met Ernest Beaux, and no one knows exactly how Dmitri might have framed that introduction. Coco's friends Misia Sert and Paul Morand both believed that Dmitri was the one who made it happen. There are no additional details to tell the story of that pivotal first meeting.

But the how and the when of that meeting make no difference. What matters is this: when these three people came together, their formative experiences—experiences that would shape how they thought of scent and fragrance and what was possible—had all been lived. Each knew precisely what it was that he or she imagined. Marvelously, there was sympathy of vision. The couturière had her perfumer.

All that remained for the future of Chanel No. 5 was for Coco Chanel to convince Ernest Beaux to work for her—and for him to invent it.

Precisely how that invention happened is one of the most fascinating, complex, and hotly contested parts of the entire Chanel No. 5 legend.

SIX

THE BIRTH OF
A MODERN LEGEND

All legends have their beginnings, and the story of the birth of Chanel No. 5 is more glamorous and complicated than many. In the summer of 1920, as the legend goes, the meeting of a prince, a perfumer, and a fashion designer changed the history of fragrance—and the history of luxury—in the century that followed. Nothing could have been more coincidental or more fortunate.

Coco Chanel had asked Ernest Beaux that summer to create for her the signature perfume she was imagining, and she wanted a sultry freshness. Ernest was hesitant. Creating a scent for a couturière, after all, was still largely unchartered territory. That summer, Coco Chanel would be only the third designer in history to venture into the field. All her time spent studying the perfume business now paid dividends—along with the keen sense of scent she had possessed from the outset. After several days exploring concepts together in the laboratory, Ernest was persuaded that the couturière was serious and that she knew what she was trying to accomplish. Still puzzling over how to unlock the clean scents of the polar north, he also thought that he knew precisely the note her fragrance needed. It was a vision shared by both creators.

Won over, Ernest accepted the commission. He would design for her the scent that they were both building in the imagination, and he worked for months crafting it. Finally the day came when he invited her to test the fragrances he had created. She would choose the perfect one from among ten different samples, each a variation on a theme that he already knew had fantastic potential.

There in front of them were ten small glass vials, labeled from one to five and twenty to twenty-four. The gap in the numbers reflected the fact that these were scents in two different—but complementary—series, different "takes" on a new fragrance. Each of these small glass vials contained a new fragrance innovation, based on the core scents of May rose, jasmine, and those daring new fragrance molecules known as aldehydes. According to the legend, in one of the vials a careless laboratory assistant had accidentally added a massive overdose of this last and still largely undiscovered ingredient, confusing a 10 percent dilution for the pure, full-strength material.

In the room that day, surrounded by rows of perfumer's scales, beakers, and pharmaceutical bottles, Coco Chanel sniffed and considered. She slowly drew each sample beneath her nose, and in the room there was the quiet sound of her slow inhalation and exhalation. Her face revealed nothing. It was something everyone who knew her always remembered, how impassive she could seem. In one of those perfumes, something in the catalog of her senses resonated, because she smiled and said, at last, with no indecision: "number five." "Yes," she said later, "that is what I was waiting for. A perfume like nothing else. A woman's perfume, with the scent of a woman."

What, Ernest asked her next, would she name her new fragrance? In Coco Chanel's mind, there was never any question. The number five had always been her special talisman. It was the

memory of all the childhood scents and the mystery of numbers surrounding her at Aubazine. It had been Boy Capel's magic number,
too, something else they shared. The number five was a special part
of theosophism—the fashionable religion of mystics and séances and
alternate dimensions that she and Boy Capel had enthusiastically
studied together. It was the number of quintessence. A fortune-
teller had told her that it was the number of her special destiny, and
she believed it. How lucky it was that the fifth sample—the one
with that overdose of aldehydes—had captured her imagination! "I
present my dress collections on the fifth of May, the fifth month of
the year," she told him, "and so we will let this sample number five
keep the name it has already, it will bring good luck."

Good luck, Coco Chanel, and the number five. There was a bit
of an inside joke that she was making with herself, too. Her other
little nickname was "Bonheur." In fact, despite its absence from her
birth certificate, it is often given as her middle name. In French,
the word for good luck is *bonheur*, and, although known around
the world as Coco, Gabrielle "Bonheur" Chanel seemed destined
for some good fortune. A perfume, she once sermonized, "should
resemble the person wearing it," and it seemed fitting that her signature perfume should carry her luck—and her number. In hindsight,
there is no doubting her intuition.

If that legend about the laboratory assistant's error is true, then
the creation of Chanel No. 5 was also a serendipitous turn of events
for Ernest Beaux. It was a perfume that would make him even more
celebrated than he already was in the fragrance industry. Much of
what had happened to create this scent—a scent recognized almost
instantly as something beautiful, something important—had nothing to do with luck, though. It was a matter of skill, insight, and
devotion.

A willingness to embrace modernity was part of his brilliance,
too. The floral heart of Chanel No. 5 mixed some of perfumery's
most luxurious and traditional aromas, scents like rose, jasmine,

ylang-ylang, and sandalwood. But the secret to Chanel No. 5 was in those aldehydes and what Ernest had done with them. They were ingredients that would change the smells of an entire century, and they would make Chanel No. 5 perhaps the greatest perfume of the golden era.

What is it about aldehydes that make the perfumes that include them so special? What, indeed, are they at all? This is where perfume meets chemistry. Today, aldehydes are in many of the scents around us. They are among the most familiar aromas of the world we inhabit, but they are especially recognizable in laundry detergents and room fresheners, in our shampoos and our antiperspirants. They are at the heart of the smell we think of simply as "clean."

In the first decades of the twentieth century, however, aldehydes were still a novel ingredient. While the earliest ones were discovered in the nineteenth century, most didn't exist in isolation until 1903, when the chemists Georges Darzens and E. E. Blaise, working independently, found ways to separate and synthesize a large group of fragrance molecules that would revolutionize the history of smell in the twentieth century. Chanel No. 5 played a seminal role in that scent story.

Understanding aldehydes is a long and complicated business, but at the most basic level they are molecules with a very particular kind of arrangement among their oxygen, hydrogen, and carbon atoms, and they are a stage in the natural process that happens when exposure to oxygen turns an alcohol to acid.

To put it simply, think of what happens when a bottle of wine remains open too long on the kitchen counter: it eventually turns to vinegar. Somewhere along the way, without anyone ever noticing it, the alcohol first turns to an aldehyde. A chemist would say that the hydrogen in the ethanol, the kind of alcohol in wine, combines with the oxygen in the air to create, through an organic reaction, first, acetaldehyde and, then, acetic acid—known simply as vinegar. Of course, what matters most about that bottle of wine is enjoying the fragrant notes of the bouquet long before then.

The problem for chemists at the beginning of the twentieth century was how to use science to stop that reaction artificially at the midpoint and to "create" aldehydes. Because the reaction that takes an alcohol to an acid doesn't stop naturally when there is oxygen present, scientists commonly talk of aldehydes as synthetic molecules—molecules created in a laboratory. It would be more accurate to say, however, that they are isolated and stabilized by chemists, thus making possible their revolutionary use as fragrance ingredients.

Aldehydes have the smell of many things. Some smell like warm wax and snuffed candles. Some have the scent of burnt matchsticks. Others smell like fatty soap or citrus pomade. Sometimes, there are hints reminiscent of rose and the rich oils of jasmine. Aldehydes are categorized in a general way by the number of carbon atoms they possess, and, smelled alone, one of the aldehydes in Chanel No. 5 (C–12) smells precisely of fresh laundry bleached in the sun. Other aldehydes, unfortunately, accost those unlucky enough to smell them with the dubious notes of rotting fruit or burnt rubber. They are often, however, beautiful scents, and perfumers have long noted that some among them have the scent of winter. The "unblemished whiteness of [these] aldehydes," writes one fragrance expert, is the smell of "powder snow."

Today, there is a certain wariness that comes with the idea of synthetics, but the art of modern fragrances could not exist without them. Chanel No. 5 might be perfume industry's modern *monstre*, but, if it comes down to it, aldehydes are actually perfectly organic: nothing more than carbon, oxygen, and hydrogen, the stuff of earth and air and our own bodies. They occur naturally all around us.

They are synthetic simply in the sense that the natural chemical reaction is arrested and the scent is isolated in a laboratory.

The trouble with aldehydes is that they are fleeting. They are part of what gives a fine wine its heady bouquet and smooth tannins, but every oenophile knows that these mellow and fade and finally disappear. One of the earliest aldehydes discovered, cinnamaldehyde, is the molecule that gives the scent to cinnamon. Aldehydes are also there in the peel of an orange, in those bright bursts of zesty aroma. They are in the needles of fir trees and the seeds of coriander in our kitchens and in stalks of lemongrass. In order to be used as independent ingredients in fragrances, however, they all have to be isolated by a chemist, who takes from the scent of fresh pine needles only that thing that is somehow waxy and greenly astringent and leaves behind the rest, which is the smell of fir trees.

The most surprising thing about aldehydes in the use of perfumery is that their effects aren't created simply through the unique smells that they lend to a fragrance. They have, of course, aromas of their own. As Jacques Polge, the chief perfumer at Chanel, likes to put it, adding aldehydes to the rich scents of florals is very much like what happens when a cook drizzles fresh lemon over strawberries. It isn't just a matter of a second aroma complementing the first. Instead, the lemon transforms and sweetens the experience of the fruit, lifts its flavors, and intensifies them. Aldehydes in a perfume have the same effect.

This aldehydic "lifting" of a perfume's rich aromas is, even to scientists, a perplexing business, but it probably has more to do with sensation than with scent. Certain aromas—but the aromas of aldehydes especially—set off complicated reactions in the nervous system. Chemists will also argue that aldehydes have the effect of stimulating what is known as the trigeminal nerve. It's the nose's way of experiencing feelings of hot and cold, pain and pleasure— the warp and woof of olfactory satisfaction.

As one expert explains, just as external temperature variations are registered with every inhalation, "most aromatic compounds can [also] stimulate trigeminal nerve fibers. Their stimulation induces sensations such as irritation, burning, stinging, tingling, and freshness." Aldehydes in a perfume give just those last feelings: the experience of tingling freshness, a little frisson of an electric sparkle. They make Chanel No. 5 feel like cool champagne bubbles bursting in the senses.

Rather than a bottle of bubbly, Ernest Beaux probably would have described the sensation more along the lines of taking an invigorating breath of cold fresh air, and he was right to connect aldehydes with the bracing scents of the Arctic. There at the northern reaches of the world, stationed along the Polar Circle, he guessed what modern science has confirmed and dissected: there exists a connection between the smell of clean snow on cold earth and the aromatic whiteness of these special fragrance materials. In the snows of the high alpine steppes and the blasted polar tundra, aldehydes appear today in concentrations sometimes ten times higher than in the snows of other places. The air and ice in the frozen hinterland is sharper and more fragrant than in other parts of the world, and Ernest could simply smell it.

Regarding that arctic note, Ernest remembered, "I finally captured it, but not without effort, because the first aldehydes that I was able to find were unstable and unreliably manufactured." It also made for a perfume with a kind of starkness. It was the scent of snow on cold earth, his student, perfumer Constantin Weriguine, later remembered: a "winter melting note." To balance that severity in Chanel No. 5, Ernest added even greater amounts of the exquisite jasmine from the perfume capital of Grasse, opulent and honeyed enough to leave the senses swimming. He warned Coco Chanel that a perfume with this much jasmine would be fabulously expensive. She simply told him that, in that case, he should add even more. She wanted the most extravagant perfume in the world.

Importantly, though, Coco was determined that the perfume not be completely defined by the jasmine; its scent was so heavy and languid that, alone, it was the smell of the *demi-mondaine*. Ernest also worried that the materials were literally so heavy that, without something to lift them, the scents would sink to the bottom of the bottle. In combination, these two elements of a perfume work together because the aldehydes give the effect of extraordinary lightness to these scandalously rich florals.

What this creates in Chanel No. 5 is nothing short of astonishing: the two bouquets—one natural and the other synthetic—working in an edgy balance with each other. The brighter and more expansive the aldehydes made the perfume, the more rich and luxurious the dosage of jasmine and rose could be. This essential contrast—between the luscious florals and the asceticism of the aldehydes—is part of the secret of Chanel No. 5 and its most famous achievement. In a simple stroke of innovation, Ernest rewrote those tired, old stories that a perfume could tell about a woman's sensuality. And that was just what Coco Chanel wanted.

Without the electric spark of whiteness, Chanel No. 5 would have been just another perfume—one of several beautiful multiflores newly created in the first decades of the twentieth century. It would have been a noteworthy departure from the generations of heavy single-note fragrances that had come before—the dozens of scents with names like Gardenia or White Rose—but it would never have become the most celebrated perfume in the world and the icon of a century. Even Coco Chanel's astonishing celebrity didn't have that kind of trendsetting power. More important, if it hadn't been both gorgeous and daring she never would have loved it—and she never would have made it her own.

Aldehydes are essential to Chanel No. 5, and Ernest used them in quantities and combinations that no one had imagined possible. They are part of what made the perfume famous. It's also easy to get carried away by the legend of their uniqueness. As recently as 2008, a journalist for a major newspaper claimed that Chanel No. 5

"was the first fragrance to make use of synthetically replicated molecules taken from products of natural origin called aldehydes." Among the many pervasive myths that swirl around the history of the world's most famous fragrance, the one that says that Chanel No. 5 was the world's *first* perfume to use aldehydes is one of the most persistent.

This is simply the stuff of legend. Yes, Chanel No. 5 does make amazing use of aldehydes—and Ernest Beaux used them at a moment when to do so was still an innovation. Yes, because it was the first popular perfume to use them in such large proportions, it created an entirely new fragrance family: the family known as the floral-aldehydic, the term for a perfume in which the scent of the aldehydes is just as important as the scent of the flowers.

Chanel No. 5, however, was never the first fragrance to use aldehydes. Even Robert Bienaimé's groundbreaking scent Quelques Fleurs—which used one of the so-called C–12 aldehydes to create its dazzling effects and which Ernest had carefully studied and even imitated—wasn't the earliest. Pierre Armingeant and Georges Darzens's Reve d'Or (1905) and Floramye (1905) claim the honors.

What has created this legend that Chanel No. 5 was the first is the wonderful synergy of a perfume launched at just the right moment and in just the right way, so that everything that came before was forgotten. The revolutionary—but not unheard of—use of aldehydes made Chanel No. 5 at the moment of its introduction a daring and unusual fragrance. Combined with the verve of Coco Chanel, it captured precisely the spirit of the Roaring Twenties. Its unimaginable commercial success also meant that, in the decades to come, no scent would be more widely copied or admired. As Ernest Beaux said years later, "it is the aldehyde note that, since the creation of Chanel No. 5, has more than anything else influenced new perfume compositions." In perfume laboratories around the world, it was the aldehydes that everyone seemed to think was its secret. Soon, it became impossible to think otherwise.

• •

Chanel No. 5 shifted the paradigm of fragrance, and the legend that it was the world's first aldehyde scent grew out of a sense of its cultural importance. Certainly, neither Ernest Beaux nor Coco Chanel ever made claims about its use of aldehydes being original. Ernest did claim, however, that the perfume was invented in 1920, saying, "When did I invent it? In 1920 precisely. After my return from the war."

Today, it is a statement capable of sharply raising eyebrows. One of the most shocking things about the legend of Chanel No. 5 is the fact that, in a fundamental sense, it wasn't invented in 1920 at all. There is simply no doubt about it: in 1920, the essential formula for Chanel No. 5 already existed. That fact, however, has given rise to endless rumor and speculation. With Chanel No. 5, nothing is ever as simple as it seems.

There are at least two distinct theories about the origins of the formula for Chanel No. 5. In the most titillating of those theories, people claim that Chanel No. 5 was an act of industrial espionage, its formula stolen from a competitor's laboratory in the south of France. This theory is part of that long, tangled history that connected Coco Chanel and her friend—and competitor—François Coty. As Edmonde Charles-Roux tells it:

the development of No. 5 . . . proceeded in a rather heavy atmosphere reminiscent of the whispered machinations that herald a palace revolution. . . . Plenty of intrigue, sudden reversals and secret alliances. Nothing was missing from the script, not even the spectacular disappearance of one of Coty's top chemists. The deserter fled, clutching to his bosom the fruit of long years of research: the formula for a perfume Coty could not make up its mind to put on the market because it cost so much to produce. That was one reason why this chemist went over to the enemy: he was afraid his invention would never be made available to the public. . . . Was his name Ernest Beaux? All queries being met by the impenetrable silence of those who know, we must be content to leave this point in darkness. But one thing is certain: about seven years later, Coty was producing a perfume that was almost exactly the same as No. 5. But although it sold tolerably well, Aimant never made a dent in the Chanel market.

A close look reveals a mixed-up, madcap story. On the one hand, Yvonne Coty always claimed that Chanel No. 5 was named not after the number of the fragrance vial but after the number of "a station in Coty's laboratory at either Suresnes or at the Rallet factory in the south of France." She seemed to believe there was some possible buried connection. On the other hand, Ernest Beaux never worked for Coty. He had spent his entire career at Rallet, so he couldn't have been the fleeing chemist. Perhaps another perfumer at Coty had absconded with the formula and passed it along to Ernest— who offered it to Coco Chanel. That is the logical chain of speculation. One thing, at least, is certain: in 1927, as Charles-Roux says, someone at Coty *did* have a copy of the Chanel No. 5 formula or something perilously near to it. Coty's fragrance L'Aimant, launched that year, was too close to have been any kind of an accident. The question was, had Coty really had it all along, and was Chanel No. 5 the copy?

As deliciously scandalous as this idea of a stolen formula and an errant chemist might be, the connection has never been confirmed conclusively, and it may simply be—as Chanel suspects—one of those whispered stories that have grown up around the Chanel No. 5 legend. There is a perfectly simple reason why Coty had a copy of the formula for a Chanel No. 5 perfume in 1927. The year before, François Coty's massive perfume company had swallowed up yet another of his smaller competitors, the perfume house of Chiris. In fact, Coty had been closely involved with the operations at Chiris already for several decades. He had trained in their laboratories at around the turn of the century, and he had become business partners with several of the owners of this family company. In some ways, he had acted as though Chiris was his business—and its perfumes "his" holdings—since the time of the First World War. It was a sense of proprietorship that would fuel an intense and not always friendly spirit of competition between Coty and Coco Chanel. Now, in 1926, Coty had formally purchased the business and all its holdings— holdings that already included that familiar little perfume outfit called A. Rallet and Co. All the information that François Coty needed to produce his own version of Chanel No. 5 was sitting right there in the archives.

But the name on top of that formula in the Rallet archives wasn't Chanel No. 5. What Coty acquired was the recipe for another perfume, a perfume invented in 1914. It smelled unmistakably like Chanel No. 5 for one very simple reason: it was the secret scent behind the world's most famous perfume. This time, the madcap story was perfectly true.

On that storied day in his laboratory, Ernest Beaux offered Coco Chanel ten samples of a fragrance that he had invented, variations on two slightly divergent but common themes. In each bottle was a fresh take on the kind of scent that they both wanted to bring to the world as a daring modern composition. But the scents in those vials had their own history. They were based on a previous formula. In fact, they were based on a previous perfume.

When Coco Chanel asked Ernest to produce a signature scent and described what she imagined during the summer of 1920, he knew that he already had the perfume she needed. He didn't need to invent it. Or at least he had the basic structure. He certainly didn't need to filch it from another perfumer's laboratory. What he proposed was simple: before the war, he had created a beautiful but unlucky perfume, inspired by his researches into Robert Bienaimé's revolutionary 1912 aldehydic multiflore fragrance Quelques Fleurs.

It had been a favorite scent of a certain unlucky czarina. Coco Chanel's aristocratic lover, Dmitri Pavlovich, knew it intimately and admired it. After all, that was why they were all there, wasn't it?

Ernest would give her Rallet No. 1—the perfume that began its life in 1914 as Le Bouquet de Catherine and that had been so evocative for Dmitri. Coco Chanel would make it her own. Perhaps she had explicitly asked him that summer for a scent like Rallet No. 1. It is hard to imagine that Dmitri would introduce Coco to Ernest without first introducing her to his creation. Or perhaps it was Ernest Beaux who first saw the link between the scent Coco Chanel wanted to give to the world and his unsung masterpiece and made the suggestion to her. On those subtle negotiations, history is silent.

What history is clear on is that the scent we know as Chanel No. 5 was perfected over several months in the late summer and autumn of 1920. That is what Ernest meant when he said "1920 precisely." But that was not when this scent was invented, not essentially. Coco Chanel, of course, knew it, but it wasn't until as recently as 2007 that molecular analysis was able to unravel unequivocally Chanel No. 5's secret lineage.

Working from the rose and jasmine heart of Rallet No. 1, the agreement was that Ernest would transform Rallet No. 1 to make it cleaner and more audacious. In the new formulas, he experimented even more boldly with ways to balance those rich natural essences with modern synthetics, adding to the blend, for example, his own rose-scent invention, "Rose E.B.," and the mixed notes of a jasmine field that came from a new commercial ingredient called Jasmophore. He added more of the powdery notes of orris—iris root—and contrasted natural musks with cutting-edge elaborations. The result was a scent, as heady with rose and jasmine as it was, that was actually less scandalously expensive than Ernest Beaux's original Russian creation—and Chanel No. 5 was still on target to be the world's most costly fragrance in 1920.

What he agreed to create that summer would be a new perfume, but it would also be a continuation of the past and its losses. It captured the scents of Moscow and St. Petersburg and Dmitri's gilded childhood. It was the exquisite freshness of the Arctic remembered during the last days of a fading empire. Above all, for Coco Chanel, here was an entire catalog of the senses—the scents of crisp linen and warm skin, the odors of Aubazine and Royallieu, and all those memories of Boy and Émilienne. It was truly her signature perfume. Like her, it even had a past that was obscure and complicated.

But for both Coco Chanel and the perfume she was about to launch to the world, the past was behind them. Now that it had been created, she was determined to make it a success. It would be a future that none of them could have ever imagined.

PART II

LOVE AND WAR

SEVEN

LAUNCHING CHANEL NO. 5

After Coco Chanel and Ernest Beaux had agreed on the scent, all that was left to do was prepare to bring it to the attention of the world of fashion. Coco originally planned to test the market by giving samples of her new signature fragrance to her best clients as holiday gifts at the end of 1920, but she realized immediately that this was a perfume destined for greater things. She planned to start, instead, by introducing it to some of her glamorous friends who set the trends in the world of high society.

What better way to introduce all these trendsetters to her perfume, Coco wondered, than to celebrate the invention of her signature fragrance at an exclusive restaurant in Cannes? She asked Ernest to join the party. She knew that, at the height of the season in this fashionable resort, some of the world's most stylish women were bound to pass right by her table. After all, the couturière Coco Chanel was already famous.

Coco Chanel desperately wanted to know whether everyone else would agree that the scent was as fabulous as she suspected, so she couldn't resist a private little showcasing of it that evening. There at her table, she stealthily perfumed the air with samples, and—as the world got its first intoxicating whiff of Chanel No. 5 that evening on the French Riviera—the result delighted her. Those lucky diners stopped dead in their tracks and wondered aloud, "What was that fragrance?" "The effect," she later said, "was amazing, all the women who passed by our table stopped and sniffed the air. We pretended we didn't notice." Just as Coco had predicted, it was unlike anything they had ever before experienced. It was spectacular, and, above all, it was very sexy.

What was it, precisely, that had these influential friends—the men and women who became the first to experience what would become the world's most famous perfume—so enthralled? Part of the answer, of course, is that Ernest's bouquet of aldehydes was quite literally unlike anything almost anyone had ever experienced. Only those in the most innovative laboratories of the 1920s had any idea how the smell of aldehydes would soon change the fragrance industry.

But aldehydes are just a part of what makes Chanel No. 5 special, despite the importance given to them in the legend. Long after they have faded—because aldehydes fade quickly—there is a rich depth of musks and florals in the perfume that is strikingly sensual. That was true, too, in the summer of 1920.

Musks and white flowers, especially, were the fragrance of something racy and a bit illicit in the 1920s. The idea that this was an erotic perfume didn't come down to cultural association alone, though. The sensual allure of some perfumes is far less a matter of personal preference than we might imagine. Those who passed Coco Chanel's table that evening were responding to something elemental. As those women who voted Chanel No. 5 the "world's most seductive perfume" in 2009 knew intuitively, some fragrances *are* simply more alluring than others. There are good reasons why scents like jasmine and tuberose, incenses like patchouli and sandalwood, and the powerful aromas of musks have been considered erotic for centuries, reasons why some fragrances have been called powerful aphrodisiacs.

Think of all the possible smells in the world. There are more than a hundred thousand. Even an average, untrained person can recognize upward of ten thousand. Then consider this basic fact: for several millennia, we have perfumed ourselves with a remarkably small and consistent number of scents, perhaps only a hundred. We are fascinated by a minute fraction of the vast olfactory extravaganza with which nature has presented us, and "we are as strongly attracted to roses and violets as any bee." When we begin investigating the chemical structures of the odors that have enticed us in the long history of perfume-making, it turns out that there are some clear connections between scent and the intimate smell of bodies.

Coco Chanel certainly understood—and felt—this relationship. Smell was always the keenest of her senses, and, to explain the intensity of how she lived with scent, she would claim, "In the lily of the valley they sell on the 1st of May, I can smell the hands of the kid who picked it." Or maybe she picked up on the notes of warm skin in the scents of flowers because her nose was exceptional. According to scientists, there is a simple reason why humans are so powerfully attracted to the scents of certain flowers: whether we know it or not, blossoms smell like bodies. And the bodies of others are enticing. When Coco Chanel caught hints of flesh in her flowers, there was nothing fanciful about her perception. There was nothing fanciful about the idea of Chanel No. 5 having the scent of a woman, either.

The idea that flowers smell like bodies, of course, seems like a strange proposition. But scent is an amazing thing, and the science is unequivocal. Take a close look at the hundred-odd ingredients that have formed the heart of traditional perfumery since the time of Aphrodite's first international bestseller, and the connection between scent and sex and skin is always there as soon as we look beyond the surface. From the chemist's perspective, many of the smells that humans like have something striking in common: they "share the same peculiar chemical architecture, carrying ten atoms of carbon and sixteen atoms of hydrogen in every molecule." Put more simply, it means that the smells that attract us fall into clearly delimited categories.

The fragrances that we have used to adorn ourselves for millennia tend to be divisible into four clear subgroups of compounds—alcohols, esters, ketones, and, famously for Chanel No. 5, aldehydes. They are aromatic molecules with shared elements in their structures. As Lyall Watson writes in her book *Jacobson's Organ*, however, "it does these magical fragrances no favour to reduce them to esthers and aldehydes." What matters is that they attract us, and they attract others.

When experts talk about the structure of a perfume, they speak of its apprehension in time, and they sometimes use the metaphor of the body—of head notes and heart notes and of what is euphemistically known as the bottom notes, or sometimes just the dry-down. The head notes are the most fleeting of all the aromatics, and they characterize the experience of a perfume during the first half-hour of its application. These are often the aromas of the most delicate floral and citrus fragrances. The heart notes are those scents that endure a little longer, during the next several hours, typically the stronger florals and hardy, sensual plant resins. The scents that linger longest—those at the bottom—almost always include a perfume's musks, which come, appropriately enough, from nether places. They have long been recognized as some of nature's most powerful fixatives.

Generally speaking, there are three kinds of materials that are used to make perfume—scents inspired by flowers; scents inspired by other parts of plants, such as their roots, barks, and resins; and scents inspired by the smells of animals. Chanel No. 5—one of history's most famously sexy perfumes—uses them all in generous doses. But Chanel No. 5 is especially about the florals—the ingredients of traditional perfumery that might seem to have the least in common with the smell of the body. Yet, reconsider. Flowers are, after all, the essential machinery of a plant's reproductive organs, and perfumes are often made from their sexual secretions. The difference between plant estrogens and animal estrogens is a slight one.

Roses and jasmine may not seem likely to smell like sweat and bodies, but to think otherwise would be wrong. As scientists who study the sexiness of perfumes explain, "many classical ingredients of natural origins [in perfume-making are] reminiscent of human body odors." It hasn't taken modern science to realize that, either. As early as the seventeenth century, the poet John Donne wrote about the "sweet sweat of roses." Among the most inherently sensual have always been the scents of jasmine, orange blossom, honeysuckle, tuberose, and ylang-ylang, flowers that, chemically speaking, have particularly high proportions of the scent molecule known as an indole. Those indoles are the smell of something sweet and fleshy and just a little bit dirty.

The same is true of those delicious plant resins: "several ingredients of incenses resembl[e] scents of the human body," one expert reminds us. When the perfumer Paul Jellinek was writing what is still the standard textbook on the science of fragrance chemistry, his testing on traditional incenses showed that myrrh and frankincense had identifiable notes of armpit odor; a common plant source known as storax was the scent of skin; and the coveted resinous gum known as labdanum had "the smell of head hair." When any of them were added to a simple, fruity *eau de cologne*, people consistently rated the perfume as more sexy. With its fragrant central notes of labdanum and storax, Aphrodite's perfume was an erotic bestseller for a reason.

The perfume materials that have the most direct connection to the smell of sex, however, are the traditional musks. Smelled on their own, the scent is often overpowering and even revolting. Yet used in small proportions and blended with other fragrances, these materials, with their strange and unsavory origins, have been among the most prized ingredients in perfume history. They come primarily from the private parts of some very unlucky fellow creatures, whose glands and sexual excretions have been harvested.

Natural musk—musk proper—comes from the male musk deer, an animal native to China and Southeast Asia, and the fluid stored in a small sac in his nether regions during the rutting season has been the object of a lucrative international trade for centuries. The word *musk* comes from the Sanskrit word *muṣka*, which translates simply as *testicle*.

Also classified in the scent family of musks is civet, which has an aroma that is unmistakably fecal and comes, not surprisingly, from the anal glands of wild cats. Castoreum, another common material, comes from the scent glands used by beavers to mark their territory. Because these ingredients—or the synthetic replicas of them that are used almost exclusively today—are capable of letting a perfume linger, they are used in nearly all fragrances, ancient and modern. That they smell like sex goes without saying.

If there are a hundred sexy scents in the history of perfume—aromas that appeal to us culturally and biologically—Chanel No. 5 uses many of them. This is, in fact, the structural principle of its composition: the bright freshness of aldehydes and the smells of skin and sweat, all of which means that there *is* something inherently sensual about Chanel No. 5. There was a reason why the smell of it evoked for Coco Chanel memories of clean sheets and warm bodies.

No wonder those diners passing by the table of Coco Chanel one evening at the beginning of a decadent era stopped dead in their tracks. They had just experienced something so alluring that, almost a century later, it remains mysterious and sensual and still modern. It was the aroma of confident sexuality, and within just a few short years it would be known around the world.

• •

Chanel No. 5 became a sensation in fashionable circles in just a matter of a few short months, and it was this night in a restaurant in Cannes that started its dizzying rise to fame. But using stealth tactics to introduce the perfume was an idea that Coco Chanel had borrowed. For years, she had been watching as some of the great businessmen of the era made spectacular fortunes in the perfume industry, and she had been taking note of how they managed it.

Coco Chanel got the idea for this guerrilla launch of Chanel No. 5 from a famous stunt that had set her old acquaintance François Coty on the road to his astonishing riches. When Coty was trying to convince a certain Henri de Villemessant, the man in charge of Paris's chic department store Les Grands Magasins, to sell his La Rose Jacqueminot on its shelves in the early 1900s, he made certain that the reluctant manager sampled his fragrance by clumsily breaking a bottle on the floor of the busy showroom. The customers were enchanted and began demanding bottles of the fragrance, and Coty had his first distributor. Coco Chanel was simply taking a page from the book of the world's most successful perfume magnate—a man who was because of it already among the world's richest people.

The enthusiastic response to Chanel No. 5 that night in the restaurant also convinced her that her intuition was right about the other idea she had for marketing it that autumn. Ernest Beaux had agreed to make her one hundred bottles. Having established No. 5's appeal, she returned to the idea of giving these samples of the scent to her most loyal clients as holiday gifts. It was generous—but not completely unmotivated. Rather, it was a clever move intended to ignite a whisper campaign and to test the market. Coco Chanel knew well that no one would mistake the exclusivity of her fragrance, not even the elite social trendsetters. She understood instinctively the powerful equation between envy and the height of luxury.

When these women of fashion came to her boutique and asked for more of that wonderful scent, she told them coyly that it had never occurred to her it was a fragrance that she might sell and hinted that it was just a little souvenir that she had discovered at some out-of-the-way perfumery in Grasse. She claimed that she couldn't remember even where she had found it and, feigning surprise at the eager response, fueled the fires of their interest by pretending to solicit advice: did they really think she should try to get some more? Perhaps it was possible.

All the while, she was creating buzz for its launch—and writing to Ernest, entreating him to increase the pace of production. She planned to sell it the following spring from her boutiques in Paris, Deauville, and Biarritz, as part of her collection. The legend that she officially released it on May 5, 1921, the fifth day of the fifth month, in homage to her magic number is, however, unfounded. In fact, Chanel No. 5 appeared quietly on the shelves of her boutiques in 1921, where it sold immediately—and fabulously—without any advertising. Advertising would not be part of the secret of its success for many decades to come.

EIGHT
THE SCENT WITH
A REPUTATION

Chanel No. 5 might not have been the only perfume named after Coco's favorite number to launch in 1921. This story has just as much to do with Coco's belief in her own good luck as it does with the pleasure she took in a bit of gambling. It was a friendly contest that she won handily. Later, however, there were moments of regret and loss that came with it. Her wager should have made Coco Chanel realize just how intimate her connection with this new signature perfume really was.

One of her friends in the fashion business was a couturier and former military officer named Edward Molyneux, who had just opened his atelier in Paris, first at number 14 and, later, at number 5, rue Royale. Coco Chanel had long been at ease with men of his experience—they had been, after all, her first admirers and lovers in the dance halls of provincial France. She and Molyneux also shared a certain sense of chaste minimalism that would make him one of the most famous fashion designers of the 1920s and 1930s.

That winter they hit upon a bit of friendly competition. Each would launch on precisely the same day a perfume with the same name, and the contest would be to see who would be more successful. She was being sly and more than a bit superstitious when she suggested number five—her lucky number. There was no harm in stacking the decks in favor of good fortune.

Edward Molyneux did, in fact, launch a perfume called Numéro Cinq—"number five." Rare bottles of it still survive, and, depending on the date of its first production, it may be the first modern oriental in perfume history. As Luca Turin writes:

> [Edward Molyneux's] Numéro Cinq is surpassingly beautiful and strange, the only example I know of an iris oriental. Assuming the fragrance wasn't changed, the uncertainty about its age then becomes as exciting as the discovery of an Egyptian mummy clutching an iPod. 1921 is when the first oriental, Coty's Emeraude, came out. 1925 is the birth date of its famous successor Shalimar. If Molyneux' [Number] 5 dates from 1921, perfume history needs to be rewritten.

In fact, archives reveal that Shalimar was invented and briefly launched in 1921 as well, only deepening the enigma. About Numéro Cinq, nothing is certain. Some believe that it was launched, as planned, at the same time as Coco Chanel's No. 5 in 1921. Others believe that Molyneux didn't release his fragrance—along with perfumes Number 3 and Number 14—until a few years later. The whole thing is shrouded in more than a bit of mystery, and those who knew the facts never put them on the record.

Two things are certain. First, there's no debating just who won this little entrepreneurial contest. Second, Coco Chanel's changing attitude toward Molyneux's Numéro Cinq perfume speaks volumes about the instant fame of Chanel No. 5—and about her passionate identification with it. In the beginning, a wager over two number-five perfumes seemed like an amusing bit of innocent competition. It didn't take long, though, for Coco to lose her sense of humor.

What happened, of course, was that in the space of a few short years Chanel No. 5 became successful beyond all imagining. Suddenly, she didn't want anyone else riding on her coattails. Coco Chanel now insisted that Molyneux change the name of his perfume. Everyone in the world of fashion knew that Chanel's signature scent already had a cult following, especially among the trendsetting beautiful young things who already called themselves flappers, and these fashionable trendsetters weren't exactly rushing out to buy Molyneux's Numéro Cinq perfume. It was Chanel's No. 5 that everyone coveted, and she hardly needed to bother. However, Coco's possessiveness was also legendary. In the end, this change of heart would be the beginning of a pattern of having second thoughts about business deals and entrepreneurial gambles—a pattern that would cause her, especially with Chanel No. 5, no end of trouble.

Molyneux found her ire amusing. In fact, he couldn't resist the opportunity to needle his quick-tempered competitor. Mademoiselle Chanel was upset at his calling his perfume Numéro Cinq, he told his customers. With a bit of sly irony, he began simply advertising it instead to anyone who would listen as Le Parfum Connu: the known perfume, the perfume with a reputation. What he meant, of course, was the perfume with that familiar number. Then again, Coco also had a bit of a reputation herself.

When Coco Chanel began selling her signature fragrance from her busy fashion-house headquarters in Paris, the result was, as Misia Sert put it, "success beyond anything we could have imagined. . . . like a winning lottery ticket." "Eau Chanel," as Misia still stubbornly—but mistakenly—insisted on calling it, was "the hen laying the golden eggs." For the first four years of its existence, from its commercial launch in 1921 until 1924, Chanel No. 5 was sold only from her shops through word of mouth. Coco Chanel's boutique strategy had been a stunning success, and among the fashionable elite of Europe it was almost immediately—as Molyneux's joke testifies—the perfume everyone knew.

One of the most amazing things is the simple fact that advertising had nothing to do with it. Chanel always proudly insisted that, during those first years, she never paid for any kind of promotion—despite the fact that what is lauded as the first advertisement for Chanel No. 5 appeared in 1921. Astonishingly, it came from a man who had made a habit out of mocking her in public for years and making her and the rest of French high society the butt of some of his deliciously funny satires.

The artist of this first Chanel No. 5 tribute was none other than Georges Goursat, who had skewered her and Boy Capel in his 1914 caricature "Tangoville sur Mer." Coco Chanel never paid him for any of his promotion, and, for that matter, he was the last person she would have hired if she were going to hire anyone. Sem—as Goursat was more familiarly known—had kept Coco Chanel in his sights ever since that first satire depicting her and Boy in a randy embrace. He had roasted her again in 1919, with an even nastier cartoon called "Mam'selle Coco," published in his album *Le Grand Monde à l'Envers*. That title translates roughly to something like "high society upside-down," and in it Coco Chanel is a droopy-breasted woman with a distinct slouch, shown selling her summer hats in one of her resort boutiques. It is not a flattering portrait.

He did always think of her, at least, as a genuine arbiter of fashion, though, and in 1921 even Sem couldn't help but be impressed by what this upstart young milliner-turned-designer had accomplished. The result was one of the earliest and most lasting images of Chanel No. 5 in this perfume's long history, a graceful flapper gazing up longingly and wordlessly at a floating bottle of Coco Chanel's signature scent. It was lovely and elegant, and it captured perfectly the kind of reverence this perfume immediately inspired.

That first 1921 sketch has been mistakenly lauded and reproduced as the first Chanel No. 5 advertisement, and it is conventional

Tribute to the perfume Chanel No. 5 by the cartoonist Sem in 1921.

wisdom that the lovely young flapper in the image is Coco Chanel. This is wishful thinking, too; Sem was applauding the success of Chanel No. 5, not endorsing it. He acknowledged the phenomenon that Coco's perfume had instantly become and nothing more. In fact, he was even impressed enough to go out of his way to visit Ernest Beaux in January of 1922 at his laboratory. Chanel No. 5, Beaux remembered, "was already a remarkable success . . . and it was the time of the Conférence de Cannes and the factory at La Bocca was the kind of thing that attracted distinguished visitors." One day, Sem was among them. The caricaturist was quite taken with the beauty of the perfume, declaring in a witty punch line that Ernest Beaux was the new "Ministre de la Narine"—the "nostril minister" of France. He was willing to give Coco Chanel some credit, too. But he drew the line at flattering her personally.

The reason that the flapper couldn't possibly be Coco is simple. The caricature doesn't look like her, and, without a doubt, Sem knew perfectly well how to make Coco Chanel immediately recognizable to anyone who saw his satires. He had been doing it already for years. In fact, just two years later, in 1923, when it was clear that Chanel No. 5 was on its way to becoming a cultural institution, he published a wickedly clever cartoon that was devastatingly direct in its message. It was his second "tribute" to Chanel No. 5. This time, no one confused it with paid promotion.

This next Sem image was a message about Chanel No. 5 and Coco Chanel's illegitimate sexuality—and about the kind of "reputation" both had in the 1920s. It is only the second time in history that the perfume appeared in the world of print. For that reason, at least, it is a milestone in the history of this fragrance. It was also an image that would inevitably have consequences for how Coco Chanel would think about her signature scent.

The picture in this caricature is a scene in Coco Chanel's atelier, and it was a stark reminder to the French public of facts that Coco was keen to forget: that she started her career as a cabaret singer and was clearly *nouveau riche*. In it, the designer—this time clearly recognizable—is lounging on a divan, while a fashionable client is having an evening gown fitted by a kneeling seamstress. It is a seamstress who was likely, in this strange, new world, to have once been a princess. Everyone knew that, by the 1920s, Coco Chanel—who began life as a peasant—was employing those unlucky exiled Russian aristocrats to sew in her workshops. It all takes place inside the silhouette of that square-cut modernist bottle.

If the image wasn't enough of a jab, the words written below the caricature are an even more barbed little bit of humor. They are the lyrics of a song, written in imitation of the flirtatious old dance-hall tune "Ko Ko Ri Ko" that earned the young Coco Chanel her nickname. They read:

> *I declare quite shamelessly,*
> *There is nothing less coco,*

The atelier of Coco Chanel by the cartoonist Sem in 1923.

Than a design by Coco
Perfumed with eau de Coco
De Coco, de Cocologne.

Her low-class social origins and history as a showgirl were no longer something Coco Chanel wanted to advertise. The entire thrust of the caricature, however, was at the expense of her peasant upbringing.

In fact, the last line—a reference to Coco's famous *Cocologne*—has another joke buried in it: a reference to the legendary land of Cockaigne (in French, the *pays de Cocagne*), the mythical land of luxury and ease, the workingman or workingwoman's dream, where everything in the real world is turned topsy-turvy. Here, peasants are kings and nuns take lovers. In this astonishing "New World"—the title of the collection in which this caricature was published—poor convent schoolgirls turned *demi-mondaine* mistresses luxuriate in riches and splendor, while a princess labors on her knees.

For Coco Chanel, this image can only have been painful. While being caricatured was a mark that she had arrived in high society and had achieved a kind of chic celebrity, the point of the satire was still to poke fun at her—and she was a proud woman. Most difficult of all was the way that Sem had unerringly chosen her perfume as the way to ridicule her past—a perfume that privately captured something essential about her sensuality. It cut close to the bone.

She had identified with Chanel No. 5 intimately from the beginning. Bringing together the scrubbed asceticism of Aubazine and opulent invitation of musk and jasmine, it was the scent of her past. The trouble was that Sem recognized it, and now those complicated affairs of the heart were being publicly satirized. Because the connections between Coco Chanel and her signature scent seemed so obviously intimate, the cartoon's appearance had become a public occasion to tease her personally in a way that had never happened with her daringly understated dresses. This kind of mockery and the pain it caused must have been considerable.

Part of what makes any scent potentially painful is the way in which it can serve for any of us as an intimate emotional repository. As Coco Chanel once put it, thinking of the loss of Boy Capel and her scent memories, "Suffering makes people better, not pleasure. The most mysterious, the most human thing is smell. That means that your physique corresponds to the other's."

Whatever we think about the value of suffering, Coco Chanel was right about scent. It does mean that our bodies somehow correspond. In the circuitry of the human brain, scent and our feelings for each other are also hopelessly entangled because there is a specific part of the human brain—"ancient," if we think about it in evolutionary terms—known as the *rhinencephalon*. This part of the brain processes two things: smells and emotions. In fact, *rhinencephalon* in Latin simply means "nose brain." As neuroscientist Rachel Herz writes in her book *The Scent of Desire*, "the areas of the brain that process smell and emotion are as intertwined and codependent as any . . . could possibly be." This is why the scent of a missing lover's shirt or a mother's favorite perfume can move us so deeply.

The basic structure of the human brain means that scent and sensuality are hopelessly—and wonderfully—caught up together in a network of desire. This was at the heart of Coco Chanel's relationship to her No. 5 perfume. When a journalist just a few years later suggested that she invented the little black dress in order to put the whole world into mourning for Boy Capel, Chanel was furious. The idea was tasteless. She was equally defensive about her identification with No. 5; it had always been a scent about her most private emotional terrain.

Those satires by Sem—the first public images of Chanel No. 5 in its history—had a powerful impact. They are an eloquent and silent testimony to the astonishing desire that this fragrance instantly inspired, but they are also probably part of the reason Coco Chanel set out to create some public distance between herself and her perfume. It was the beginning of an ambivalent relationship to her creation that would wreak professional and emotional havoc for decades to come. Chanel wouldn't willingly appear in an advertisement for the fragrance for almost twenty years—not until 1937—and, even then, she probably didn't know that she was posing for one.

So it is easy to understand why, if this was the early "advertising" she was getting for Chanel No. 5, Coco decided to place the product in the hands of talented marketing professionals whose job would be to manage not just its distribution but its image. Soon afterward, she would do precisely that. She would always regret it.

What she did next was an astonishing thing. Just at the moment Chanel No. 5 was becoming a stunning success, Coco Chanel signed away her rights to it.

The decision would shape the direction of her life, and it would be at the heart of her increasingly tangled relationship with this legendary product. But Chanel was also a shrewd businesswoman, and the decision was a pragmatic one.

Ernest Beaux had a research laboratory in Grasse, but he was not, after all, a manufacturer. Rallet was a relatively small perfume house, with its own line of fragrances to sell and bring to market. Creating perfumes for a fashion designer was still a pioneering enterprise. That first autumn of 1920, after their invention of Chanel No. 5, Ernest Beaux had produced for Coco Chanel just one hundred bottles, and Sem's tribute of 1921 is testimony to just how popular her signature scent became and how quickly. Now, keeping pace with demand was a huge challenge.

In the south of France, the laboratory at A. Rallet scaled up production, but there were limits. Coco Chanel was never good at accepting limits, though, and she had her sights set on something more ambitious. Once again her model was her friend François Coty, whom she had already known for the better part of a decade.

While Coty had launched his fragrance business at Les Grands Magasins, Chanel had been doing business in the millinery side of her couture house for years with Théophile Bader, the man who owned the flagship Parisian department store Les Galeries Lafayette. Convinced that Chanel No. 5 was destined for the world stage, she asked if he would sell her fragrance there. Bader knew a blockbuster-in-the-making when he saw it. The only problem, they agreed, was supply: they would need enough perfume to meet the insatiable demand they both imagined.

She needed, he told her quite bluntly, a partner capable of managing the large-scale manufacture and distribution of her perfume. Already she could see the obvious advantage, too, of someone to manage promotion and advertising. So, in the spring of 1923, at the fashionable Deauville racetrack, Théophile Bader made one of the great entrepreneurial introductions in the history of the twentieth century. There, Coco Chanel met the industrialists Pierre and Paul

Wertheimer, brothers who owned one of the world's largest perfume manufacturing and distribution companies.

The Wertheimers' firm, Bourjois, had originally been founded by an actor and was bought by an earlier generation of Wertheimers in 1898, when it had already established a reputation for producing perfumes, theatrical makeup, and a bestselling face powder. Coco Chanel had begun her career as a showgirl, singing in the dance halls of provincial France. The Wertheimers had made their fortunes at Bourjois selling perfumes and cosmetics manufactured for the theater and vaudeville stage. There was a kind of delicious irony about it, and they were willing to cut a deal with her. She piqued their interest.

When Paul and Pierre Wertheimer took over the direction of Bourjois in 1917, the new focus was on a more contemporary style of perfumes, a move away from the traditional floral fragrances that had first established Bourjois as a major player in the market and toward the new, more modern scents that would carry it into the future. Their fragrance Mon Parfum was marketed from 1919 onward with the idea that "my perfume reflects my personality," and it was the beginning of a trend that would transform both the fragrance industry and the world of fashion. Within just a few years, magazines would begin encouraging women to "analyz[e] one's own personality to discover 'its' style," and soon the idea followed that every woman needed a signature scent. When Coco Chanel offered her fragrance, backed by all her considerable celebrity, it was again a perfect match. Or so it seemed to them all at the outset.

In the beginning, someone later remembered, there was only one lawyer.

When they entered into negotiations, everything was agreed to very simply. Coco Chanel needed someone to manufacture and market her fragrance to the world, and she was ready to give up control over its distribution. This was a break from the past and from the emotional complex that the scent of Chanel No. 5 had represented. One had to be sensible and entrepreneurial. She was adamant, however, that control of the fashion house, which represented her future, would remain entirely in her hands. A partnership that infringed on her autonomy as a couturière was her greatest fear, and it shaped the plan that she suggested. In was an anxiety heightened by what she had seen happen to the people who did business with François Coty. His reputation as an unrelenting competitor who took pleasure in swallowing up the smaller companies with whom he partnered was already well known.

Chanel wasn't willing to risk her fashion business for anything. So, when it came to the perfume, she effectively washed her hands of it. She wanted to keep "her association with the Wertheimers . . . at arm's length," a friend later suggested. Others who knew the terms of the agreement believed that "her fear of losing control over her fashion house made her sign away the perfume for ten percent of the corporation." The Wertheimer brothers, Paul and Pierre, who were to front the costs of producing, marketing, and distributing Chanel No. 5, suggested that she could retain complete control of the couture house by simply agreeing to create a second company, Les Parfums Chanel. Each of the partners would take a share. Coco Chanel told them, "Form a company if you like, but I am not interested in getting involved in your business. I'll give you my calling card and will be content with 10% of the stock. For the rest, I expect to be the absolute boss of everything." That was the bargain, and she had brokered it.

Perfume was *their* business, and from now on the business side of Chanel No. 5 was their concern, their product. She would give them the right to use her name on it, and in exchange she would get a share of the profits. It was perfectly simple. The contract read:

Mademoiselle Chanel, dress designer . . . founder of the company, brings to the company the ownership of all the perfume brands sold at the time under the name of Chanel, as well as the formulas and processes of the perfumery products sold under this name, the manufacturing processes, and designs registered by her, as well as the exclusive right of said Company to manufacture and put on sale, under the name of Chanel, all perfumery products, makeups, soaps, etc.

They agreed that, to protect the status of her name as a designer, they would sell as Chanel "only first-class products" that she deemed sufficiently luxurious. She kept the right to sell perfumes—which she could have manufactured elsewhere if she wanted—from her fashion houses in Paris, Deauville, Cannes, and Biarritz, but she was otherwise out of the perfume business. Coco Chanel would receive 10 percent of the profits of the company and would put up none of the capital; Théophile Bader was given a 20 percent share in Les Parfums Chanel as a finder's fee and distribution partner; and the Wertheimers would control the rest of the company. In exchange for developing the brand, they would get 70 percent of the profits—and take all of the risks. That spring of 1924, Coco Chanel had owned Chanel No. 5 for just four years.

It was an extraordinary decision from an emotional perspective. She had been driven to create not just a signature scent but also a fragrance that encapsulated both her sense of loss and the story of her life and loves. She had named it after her lucky number, and she thought of luck as her middle name. She had wanted it to be a success, and she had identified with it deeply. In fact, she would consider it "her" fragrance for decades. With it, she scented her house as well as her body. Despite these intense personal connections to this perfume, however, she licensed it to the partners at Les Parfums Chanel just as it was poised to become a blockbuster.

If the decision was emotionally complicated, as a business move it was clearly brilliant. Here was a product with amazing potential, and anyone who had tracked its meteoric rise in those first few years knew it. For Chanel No. 5 to reach an ever-broader market, however, she would need the help of experts in the fragrance industry, and that was precisely what she now had negotiated. Having worked to develop the fragrance, she naturally had always planned to have it succeed brilliantly.

However, she never imagined what it would become or how hard it would be for her to disentangle herself from it emotionally. After all, her initial fear—that the scent that captured something essential about her style wouldn't reach a wide enough audience—had proved unfounded. Indeed, it was immediately successful. She should have been thrilled. Instead, there were painful jabs in the society papers like that 1923 caricature to rattle her.

At that moment, it was the public face of her fashion house that she associated with her persona, and her greatest anxiety was that anyone or anything would be able to co-opt it. But she was above all in her own mind a hardheaded businesswoman. In 1924, Chanel No. 5 still seemed like something that could be—with a bit of distance and some expert marketing—turned to account and managed.

In the years to come, the difficulty was that the product would go on to have a life and a legend of its own, one that she couldn't control. It was also a perfume that would make them all wealthy almost beyond imagining. The money rolling in wouldn't satisfy Coco Chanel forever, though. Increasingly she would also sense that she was no longer at the center of the Chanel No. 5 story.

Les Parfums Chanel was established on April 4, 1924, and—despite the conclusive evidence that Chanel No. 5 was based on a Rallet perfume—there are no records of any formal arrangement with the perfume house of A. Rallet, still at that time a subsidiary of Chiris. People in the perfume industry in Grasse remembered later how the firm had offered Coco Chanel the formula for Rallet No. 1 when she had first approached Ernest Beaux, and perhaps they had all negotiated the rights free and clear from the outset. Perhaps they had not, and the company now balked. Certainly, in 1920, Ernest Beaux had been looking for new career opportunities, knowing that the legendary perfumer Joseph Robert already occupied the position of chief "nose" at Chiris, and there is a chance that Ernest took it on as a private commission. In any event, by 1922 he had broken ties with the company and moved to Charabot, a company specializing in perfume materials. When he left, he quite understandably took his work with him.

Even if Coco Chanel and the partners at Les Parfums Chanel didn't make a formal arrangement with Chiris to use the formula for Chanel No. 5, it would hardly have mattered. Ernest Beaux had invented the perfume, and he knew the formula. Perfume formulas even today, like other recipes, aren't protected as intellectual property. That has always been part of the reason for the urgent secrecy of the fragrance industry. The loss of the formula would have been the occasion for considerable consternation and teeth gnashing in the Rallet division, where the perfume had been invented, but there was nothing anyone could do.

Ernest Beaux had created Chanel No. 5 and unlocked the secret of its innovations, and he was well paid for it. Alone among the key players, however, he had no share in the business or in the vast riches that were on the horizon. Poised to take on a greater role in the perfume's success, in 1924 Ernest was hired as the technical director and perfumer for fragrances at Bourjois and Les Parfums Chanel.

Chanel No. 5, created at the height of Coco Chanel's first celebrity, was poised for great things, and this was clear almost from the first moment. For the first four years of its existence, the scent had been available only to clientele in her fashion boutiques, and it had been wildly successful even then. Soon there would be international distribution. All that was left was to make customers aware of the perfume and to generate desire in them. The job fell not to Coco Chanel but to the partners at Les Parfums Chanel, who had—Coco put it best—made the perfume *their* business now.

NINE

MARKETING MINIMALISM

With the creation of Les Parfums Chanel in 1924, the Wertheimer brothers, with Théophile Bader and Coco Chanel as minority partners, set out to make Chanel No. 5 a perfume with a global distribution and, by doing so, to gain worldwide fame for the product. These efforts were the first serious attempts to market the fragrance traditionally—a fragrance that had become a favorite among the fashionable women who shopped in Paris, despite Coco Chanel's strategic refusal to pay for any advertising. Indeed, it had become a sensation among these social elite—women who could afford to have their clothing made for them by the famous Coco Chanel—based on word of mouth alone. Those who bought their clothing off the rack at the world's great department stores couldn't yet pick up a bottle of Chanel No. 5 at the beauty counter, unless they happened to be shopping at the Galeries Lafayette after 1923.

This would all quickly change. The transformation of Chanel No. 5 into the world's most famous perfume would happen with the opening of the vast American market. By the 1920s, American women had, in the words of one historian, "the greatest value of surplus [money] ever given to women to spend in all of history." The postwar years saw the rise of a new kind of luxury market that included the middle-class consumer. The goal at Les Parfums Chanel, where Ernest Beaux had now been hired as the head of fragrance, was to bring Chanel No. 5 to the cultural mainstream, where it could reach the women who read fashion magazines like *Vogue* and patterned their hemlines after news from Paris.

Ironically, Coco Chanel imagined her minimalist perfume in opposition to the world of salesmanship, and, even after the partners at Les Parfums Chanel took over the marketing and distribution of Chanel No. 5, the advertising was determinedly understated—not just for the first few years but for most of the next two decades. The persistent idea, then, that Chanel No. 5's original success was the result of heavy advertising and cunning marketing campaigns could not be further from the truth. In fact, the real surprise is that the early marketing didn't manage to undermine it completely. Those first advertisements are baffling.

The partners at Les Parfums Chanel outlined their strategy succinctly in the first sales catalog, sent to retailers in France immediately after the creation of the partnership in 1924. It was a remarkably simple affair in black and white, with a plain brown paper cover, black edging, and a white ribbon: the signature Chanel colors. It tells us everything we need to know about how Coco Chanel imagined her signature scent—or how the partners at Les Parfums Chanel, more precisely, imagined it for her—and it cuts to the heart of why there was, in the beginning, so little marketing. "Luxury perfume," the brochure reads,

> this term has lost much of its value because of how it is abused. Modern advertising touches everything, but that is only a matter of an attractive bottle or fine packaging. The Chanel perfumes, created exclusively for connoisseurs, occupy

a unique and unparalleled place in the kingdom of perfume. Committed to the creation of an original perfume, different from anything else obtainable, Mademoiselle Chanel succeeded in finding some extracts of an exceptional quality and so evocative of the Chanel style that they take their place among her earlier creations . . . the perfection of the product forbids dressing it in the customary artifices. Why rely on the art of the glassmaker or the manufacturer of cartons! This so often brings an air of prestige to a dubious product and brings mercenary cheers from the press to sway a naïve public. Mademoiselle Chanel is proud to present simple bottles adorned only by their whiteness, precious teardrops of perfume of incomparable quality, unique in composition, revealing the artistic personality of their creator. Sold at the beginning only by Mademoiselle Chanel in her stores in Paris, Deauville, Cannes and Biarritz, these perfumes became highly prized in elegant circles in France and abroad. The great demand convinced Mademoiselle Chanel to consent to sell her products in different countries around the world, at a few renowned and chosen houses.

In rejecting the idea of fussy advertising, it was the quality of her fragrance that they wanted to showcase, and the clear message to the consumer was that, in the world of luxury, flashy marketing was part of the problem. Unlike the ornate and florid perfume bottles being famously created by the luxury glass firm of Cristal Baccarat in the 1920s, Les Parfums Chanel would make a simple, pharmaceutical bottle its signature.

Immediately after that meeting with Ernest Beaux in 1920, in which she selected his famous fifth sample, Coco Chanel had started planning for the Paris launch of her new fragrance. She had picked out the bottle, however, much earlier. The decision about the bottle had been a long and fascinating one. "Elegance," she once said, "is refusal," and the bottle for Chanel No. 5 was an act of both memory and defiance.

What the bottle would *not* look like was one important consideration. Most perfume bottles before Coco Chanel were as ornate and as flowery as the fragrances within them, decorated with swirling, gaudy flourishes of color and design. She wanted something with cleaner lines, something that would be distinct and simple. It would have lines as clean as those notes of the aldehydes in the fragrance.

Like the perfume, it would also have to be sensual. Selecting her signature perfume had always been wrapped up intimately with Boy Capel, and the bottle—this simple glass shape—was nothing if not an intimate memory. The story usually told about her inspiration, however, isn't accurate. Boy had carried with him in his traveling case a set of matching toiletry bottles, and leather cases with flacons and brushes were common. Boy's set came, some say, from the shop of his shirtmaker, Sulka; others say it came from the tailors at Charvet, already in the 1920s the most exclusive couture house for men's fashion, where nearly all the men of Coco Chanel's acquaintance bought their shirts hand-tailored. Coco Chanel shopped there herself on occasion: the company also produced the gorgeously patterned silks that even she couldn't find anywhere else.

Both toiletry bottles shared the same economy of lines that she admired in the Romanesque architecture of Aubazine and in the fall of a dress, and, when asked years later where the design had come from, Chanel's artistic director, the late Jacques Helleu, remembered hearing from his father, Jean, that the Charvet bottle was behind it. But that wasn't where Coco found her inspiration at all. Her real model was one of Boy Capel's whisky decanters.

Her friend Misia Sert described the original design for the Eau Chanel bottle—as she insisted on calling Chanel No. 5—as "solemn, ultra-simple, quasi-pharmaceutical," and Coco ordered copies of just such a bottle—adapted in "the Chanel taste"—made in delicate and expensive glass and sometimes, for special clients, in crystal from the elite manufacturers at the firm of Brosse. Everything about it was pure transparency. What Coco Chanel wanted was an invisible bottle—an invisible bottle that, ironically, would one day become one of the world's most recognizable icons.

Ernest Beaux had created an abstract floral perfume in the scent of Chanel No. 5, a fragrance that Coco Chanel would celebrate as a composition not unlike a dress. The bottle would be its complement: the abstraction of a bottle, from which everything was erased except the essentials of line.

It was a surprising decision, maybe even a daring one. In some ways, though, the bottle wasn't nearly as radical as it appears. The history of early twentieth-century perfume bottles reveals something entirely unexpected: this style of bottle was already being used in the fragrance industry. The mainstream might have preferred those overwrought crystal creations, but by the early 1920s there was a fledgling movement in design toward a new kind of artistry in perfume bottles. It's the elaborate designs of René Lalique that everyone remembers—and collects today—of course. Already "the art of the bottle tend[ing] . . . to simplicity of line and decoration" was gaining momentum, however. Even Lalique was producing elegant, streamlined modernist flacons.

Some of them strongly resemble that first Chanel No. 5 design. The 1907 Lalique bottle for François Coty's La Rose Jacqueminot (1903)—a perfume that was a huge commercial success—is strikingly similar. It's the same delicate pharmaceutical style, with a discreet label and a square stopper. The only notable differences are some extraneous art nouveau flourishes. Coty himself had been introduced to the world of perfume-making in a friend's pharmacy, where he had seen dozens of understated, elegant glass bottles—bottles, it's worth noting, not entirely unlike the one Coco Chanel designed for her signature scent.

Throughout most of the first part of the century, Coty was the world's largest fragrance house, but one of the other international powerhouses was Bourjois, the parent perfume company that had first made the Wertheimer brothers' fortunes. At least as early as 1920, Bourjois's bottle for its Ashes of Roses (1909) also used a flask whose lines are a close echo of the Chanel No. 5 bottle: simple, clear, square, with just a small maroon paper label.

Coco was a careful businesswoman, and she made her name by paying attention to details. When she began her study of fragrance in 1919, she assessed her would-be competitors, and, with her gift for timing, she selected a bottle that reflected a new, chic direction in the industry. From the marketing perspective, the achievement of Chanel No. 5 has not been that its packaging has been entirely revolutionary but that it has always pushed what some have called the soft edge of the avant garde. This is precisely the case with the famous bottle.

Or, rather, with the bottle that would *become* famous as it evolved over the years. Because the first bottle used for Chanel No. 5 isn't quite the same as the one that today is among the world of luxury's most recognized icons. In the beginning, the flask wasn't sold in the now-ubiquitous square-cut bottle, with its sharp and beveled shoulders. The original bottle—the one shown in that 1921 tribute to Chanel No. 5 by Sem—was gently curved at the edges. Its shape was sleek, the tiniest bit masculine, and spectacularly understated.

The innovations that directly led to the bottle we know today happened in 1924, when the original rounded and ethereally thin glassware was proving too delicate for distribution and the partners at Les Parfums Chanel ordered a new design, produced at the celebrated Cristalleries de Saint Louis, in glass and only rarely in crystal. Later, in the course of nearly a century now, there has been only one substantial modification to the shape of the bottle. In 1924, the corners of the bottle were first faceted and squared.

Over the years, the stopper, however, has changed more dramatically. In fact, it's the variations in the stoppers that experts use to date bottles of vintage Chanel No. 5 perfume. In 1921, when Coco Chanel first launched Chanel No. 5 from her boutiques to her admiring clients, the top was nothing more than a small, utilitarian square glass plug. Although the Charvet boutique was just a stone's throw from Paris's ritzy Place Vendôme, the original flask didn't yet have that familiar faceted large stopper that some people insist was inspired by the monument in the center of that famously chic square. The signature octagonal stopper was also added in 1924, when Les Parfums Chanel redesigned the bottle. Since then, there have been only three other alterations. In the 1950s, the bevel-cut stopper was made thicker and larger. In the 1970s, it was made even bigger. The last change was in 1986, when the size of the stopper was scaled back to balance the proportions.

There is another small controversy about the origins of the famous Chanel No. 5 bottle, however, and it's a story that suggests that the updated flacon in 1924 might have come with some hard feelings. The original flask for Chanel No. 5 hadn't ever been entirely original. But some fragrance historians suspect that the changes to the bottle in 1924 also had their inspiration in the bottle for another perfume—a perfume that was already intimately entangled with the story of Chanel No. 5.

At Chiris, Ernest Beaux had a former colleague by the name of Jean Helleu. Helleu was an accomplished painter who, because of his keen sense of aesthetics, was highly sought after as a designer of fragrance packaging. Some of his earliest designs were for Coty. But he had also worked for Chiris designing bottles in 1923, when—after the success of Chanel No. 5 and Ernest Beaux's departure—Rallet No. 1 was being relaunched in the French market. This is where the controversy comes in: experts have uncovered at least one rare example of Rallet No. 1 packaged in a bottle that is immediately recognizable. In fact, it is iconic. It is the same bottle as the 1924 Chanel No. 5 flacon. Precisely.

Who designed that Rallet No. 1 bottle? And what was the

direction of the influence? It's all a mystery of chronology. Jean Helleu—and his son Jacques after him—went on to spend distinguished careers working for Chanel, but according to the company archives there is no evidence of Jean Helleu having worked for the house before 1930. Meanwhile, the surviving Rallet No. 1 bottle, produced for export to the American market, is impossible to date precisely. Either way, though, the undercurrent was electric. If the 1924 updates to the Chanel No. 5 bottle were borrowed from the design for the 1923 Rallet No. 1 relaunch, then it's difficult to imagine that the businessmen at Chiris—François Coty already among them—were anything but furious. Using a formula developed at Rallet was one thing. Packaging the new perfume in the same bottle as the predecessor must have seemed outrageous.

More likely, it happened the other way and Rallet No. 1 was packaged in the "Chanel No. 5" bottle after 1924 in order to capitalize on its obvious success. But designing the Rallet No. 1 packaging to imitate deliberately the Chanel No. 5 bottle was still a pointed kind of irony. Only a small group of people knew or suspected the connections between those two scents until the 1990s, and, if that's the case, then someone had a sharp sense of humor—someone who also knew the entangled history of those two fragrances and didn't mind advertising it.

Either way, the 1924 Chanel No. 5 bottle, of course, went on to become iconic. So did the distinctive small, white label that the company still uses, with its famous typeface. For the relaunch of the Chanel No. 5 flacon, the tag read simply "N°5—Chanel—Paris," and, when not in the standard *parfum* concentration, it included the strength in *eau de toilette* or *eau de cologne*—two other early versions of the fragrance. The sans-serif font was drawn from contemporary avant-garde design. From the very beginning, however, even as early as 1921, on the top of each stopper Coco Chanel placed her symbol, also formally trademarked in 1924: those instantly recognizable double Cs. That has been there always, and it was Coco Chanel's original contribution.

There are conflicting tales about where those double Cs came from, too. One is a romantic story about the glittering world of the Roaring Twenties along the Riviera. In the south of France, Coco Chanel's friends were wealthy socialites and some of the twentieth century's great artists, including Igor Stravinsky, who was famously besotted with her. Since she only met Stravinsky for the first time in the summer of 1921, any notion that he directly inspired the scent of Chanel No. 5 is mere romantic fantasy. One of her other friends, however, was the American heiress Irène Bretz—known during the 1920s as simply *la belle Irène*—who owned a soaring, white-stuccoed wedding-cake villa in the hills above Nice called Château Crémat. According to the legend, one summer night Coco Chanel looked up at a vaulted arch at one of Irène's famous parties and found her inspiration in a Renaissance medallion: two interlocking letter Cs. Those double Cs became from that moment her signature.

There are, however, other stories of where the symbol came from, and according to the officials at Chanel this tale about the medallion at Château Crémat is also nothing more than a persistently fanciful legend. After all, Coco Chanel also knew well the Château Chaumont, where one could find the very same motif, a famous symbol that dated back to the sixteenth century and the days of the Medici queens. At the royal château in Blois, the symbol was carved in white in the private apartments of France's Queen Claude, who found in the initial "C" an inspiring personal motto: *candidior candidis*—the fairest of the fair. Everywhere at the royal court and on the jousting fields, Cs blazoned forth, in homage to her. A generation later, Catherine de Medici became the next queen to live in those chambers, and she sensibly—and more famously—adopted the symbol and the motto as her signature as well.

For Coco Chanel, nothing could have been more fitting. An

ancient Renaissance perfume recipe used by the scent-obsessed Medici queens set her on the path that led to Chanel No. 5. The coincidence seemed almost destined. Because the initials for "Coco Chanel" weren't the only inspiration she found in the iconography of two Cs, eternally embracing. It was also the symbol of those two last names that were never united: Chanel and Capel.

When we think of Chanel No. 5 today, what comes to mind above all is the bottle. It's the part of the product for most of us that is immediately iconic. In fact, it's one of the curiosities of its history that far fewer people are able to identify the perfume by its scent alone—a strange state of things for a legendary fragrance. Our familiarity with the bottle of Chanel No. 5 certainly can't hurt those staggering sales figures, but it was never the reason this perfume became world famous. If we are looking for the answer to Chanel No. 5's mythical success in marketing, we will have to look deeper.

What is boggling, considering the marketing of the perfume in the 1920s and the selection of its original bottle, is that Chanel No. 5 ever became iconic at all. That first sales catalog in 1924 laid out the marketing strategy at Les Parfums Chanel precisely, and, while the simplicity of the bottle was always part of the conception, the focus was on the luxurious singularity of the perfumes.

Perfumes plural.

Because there is one bewildering thing about the first sales catalog: nowhere does it single out Chanel No. 5 for any particular attention. In fact, the scent that Coco Chanel had turned into a boutique bestseller was jumbled together with a whole new line of Chanel-labeled perfumes, all sold in precisely the same bottle—and nearly all of them had numbers.

In 1924, with the creation of Les Parfums Chanel, Chanel No. 5 went from being *the* Chanel perfume to one among many. In the first sales catalog, there were almost a dozen perfumes for sale. Some of those new fragrances, oddly, were very traditional, old-fashioned scents like Rose. They were precisely the kind of girlish soliflores that Coco Chanel had been renouncing. This mixture of old and new wasn't the most surprising thing, though. It was that suddenly Chanel No. 5 had plenty of competition—and it was of the partners' own making.

If Les Parfums Chanel were looking to create an international brand identity for Chanel No. 5, it is difficult to imagine a more curious marketing strategy. They advertised for sale that year a host of fragrances, including extracts Chanel No. 1, Chanel No. 2, Chanel No. 5, Chanel No. 7, Chanel No. 11, Chanel No. 14, Chanel No. 20, Chanel No. 21, Chanel No. 22, and Chanel No. 27, along with Rose, Chypre, and Ambre. All were packaged in identical fashion. In decades to come, they would add to the litany of perfumes Chanel No. 9, Chanel No. 18, Chanel No. 19, Chanel No. 46, and Chanel No. 55.

There were so many numbered Chanel perfumes that, by the 1930s, the American chronicler of the Jazz Age, novelist F. Scott Fitzgerald, could write of the character of Nicole, in his masterpiece *Tender Is the Night* (1934), that

> She bathed and anointed herself and covered her body with a layer of powder, while her toes crunched another pile on a bath towel. She looked microscopically at the lines of her flanks, wondering how soon the fine, slim edifice would begin to sink squat and earthward. . . . She put on the first ankle-length day dress that she had owned for many years, and crossed herself reverently with Chanel Sixteen.

He could rely on his readers to get the joke. Chanel No. 16 was almost the only one that never really existed.

Part of the great puzzle of Chanel No. 5 is why, among all these numbers, it became the only perfume we all remember. Some of those early numbered perfumes were lovely fragrances in their own right—one or two even rivaled for a short time the success of Coco Chanel's original. Yet most of the early ones have since disappeared completely, and no one even knows any longer what some of the first scents—especially the mysterious and very popular Chanel No. 55—might have smelled like. Yet, even in the 1920s, it already seemed that Chanel No. 5 was marked for some special sort of future. Consumers were poised to make Chanel No. 5 the world's most famous perfume. It happened despite a decade of what should have been a modern marketing disaster.

TEN
CHANEL NO. 5 AND THE STYLE MODERNE

When Coco Chanel licensed her signature perfume in 1924, Chanel No. 5 was already a coveted luxury object. In the fashionable circles of Paris, it was the scent everyone wanted—and only the lucky few could manage to get it. That had been the whole point of the partnership at Les Parfums Chanel: to bring Chanel No. 5 out of the boutique and to introduce it to larger markets on both sides of the Atlantic.

For the partners at Les Parfums Chanel, the United States was always a target market, and New York City—already with nearly six million inhabitants—was the commercial and cultural epicenter of that market in this famously fast-paced decade. Luxury ocean liners carried thousands of wealthy tourists each week between New York and the French port of Le Havre, and perfume was still the ultimate souvenir of Paris. In the grand department stores of Manhattan, sales of luxury goods were skyrocketing in the booming postwar era, because the economy of the United States was growing at a stupendous rate, while much of Europe, on the other hand, languished in a recession. Sales of French perfumes in America increased more than 700 percent in the decade from 1919 to 1929, and by the early 1920s nearly all the major fragrance houses—Bourjois a leader among them—were opening or expanding offices in New York to capitalize on the growing sales. The extent to which the American market and American cultural contexts created the legend of Chanel No. 5 is also part of this perfume's untold story. In fact, the history of Chanel No. 5's success cannot be disentangled from the scope of the American century—or the consumers who helped to create it.

The advertising for the Chanel fragrances, however, was remarkably modest, and it was confined exclusively to the American market. The first known advertisement for Les Parfums Chanel ran in the *New York Times* on December 16, 1924. It was a small corner advertisement on page five, taken out by the high-end department store Bonwit Teller, which was located on Fifth Avenue at 38th Street back in the Roaring Twenties.

Bonwit Teller specialized in bringing to the women of New York City the latest Parisian fashions, and the advertisement alerted readers to "Chanel's New Perfumes," encouraging city gentlemen to "choose one of these exquisite fragrances that will be a subtle compliment to her taste." Again, the emphasis was on many perfumes, and among them was Chanel No. 5. But it was only one among several. Also offered for sale were the perfumes Chanel No. 7, Chanel No. 9, Chanel No. 11, and Chanel No. 22. The prices ranged by size from a modestly expensive $4.50 to an astonishing $175 for an impressively large bottle, the modern-day equivalent of from fifty dollars to nearly two thousand. All that the reader saw in the advertisement was a row of bottles. In it, every single bottle was precisely the same.

There was simply nothing singular about its presentation. The surprise wasn't so much the uniformity of the bottle alone—other perfume companies sometimes used standard flacons. But the identical bottles, combined with the proliferation of numbered perfumes, were an odd way to capitalize on the growing international fame of Coco Chanel's signature scent.

New advertisements appeared only sporadically for a decade.

If Les Parfums Chanel intended to launch Chanel No. 5 in the American market, they chose a strange way to do it. Their strategy in Europe, when viewed in hindsight, would be no less perplexing.

Back in Paris, the partners at Les Parfums Chanel missed a spectacular marketing opportunity just a few months later. In fact, they arguably missed one of the greatest advertising spectacles of the century. It wasn't because the partners didn't know about it, either.

In 1925, Paris hosted an international commercial exhibition dedicated to showcasing the world's great luxury products—and French luxury products in particular. First planned for 1915 but postponed due to the First World War, it was a massive effort to stimulate the flagging French economy and to remind the world that Paris was the world's fashion capital. The event spread out across the city and drew sixteen million visitors that year, and it changed the history of art and design. Officially titled L'Exposition Internationale des Arts Décoratifs et Industriels Modernes—the International Exhibition of Modern Decorative and Industrial Arts—this show of the "Arts Décoratifs" launched the celebrated movement today known as "art deco."

Then, it was simply called the "Style Moderne," and the exhibition was dedicated to the world's most beautiful and innovative objects, an "exquisite presentation of a few choice luxury commodities" by the world's most famous firms, in an opulent theatrical setting. To celebrate daring new architecture, entire buildings were erected for the exhibition, and showcase gardens were planted in parks along the river Seine. There were pavilions dedicated to the display of handcrafted textiles, the book arts, jewelry, and, of course, the entire world of Parisian high fashion. It was the first world exposition to include film, and "the promotion of cinema was a means of vaunt-ing the modernity of French industrial and cultural production," because film was, after all, originally a French invention. Fashion designers and interior decorators were already working to produce costumes and sets.

One of the most celebrated spectacles of the 1925 Paris exhibition was a lighted glass fountain, a staple of the postcards sent around the world to offer friends and family back home a glimpse of these modern marvels. It echoed the shape of the Eiffel Tower—itself the achievement of an earlier great exposition—but instead of lacy steel-work, it featured a column of brilliant arching crystal and streaming water. The fountain's designer was René Lalique, the man who had made a name designing fragrance bottles, and just beyond it stood a temple of the senses, the great perfume pavilion.

Inside the perfume pavilion were all the most famous names of the French fragrance industry, and the names that would soon become famous. Perfume, after all, was one of France's signa-ture luxury products. There were fanciful stalls hosted by firms like Houbigant, Parfums de Rosine, Lenthéric, D'Orsay, Roger et Gallet, Molyneux, and Coty. Parfum Delettrez trumpeted its new fragrance, a numbered perfume named simply XXIII (1923). Jacques Guerlain also understood the significance of the event and knew it was the perfect venue to launch his masterpiece Shalimar, still one of the world's great fragrances. Of course, there was also a beautiful display put on by Bourjois, the people who now produced and distributed Les Parfums Chanel.

The Exposition Internationale des Arts Décoratifs et Industriels Modernes—known at the time simply as the "expo"—was a cultural landmark that shaped the direction of style for another two decades, and it would have been the perfect opportunity to launch a scent as quintessentially modern as Chanel No. 5.

Indeed, the catalog for the exposition describes eloquently the coming of a new era of modernist fragrances that might have captured the spirit of Chanel No. 5 precisely. "Perfumery," those sixteen million visitors read,

> is an essentially modern art. . . . [and] the principle of perfume, like that of fashion, is always to make something new. It is the condition of its existence. . . . the discoveries of chemists . . . have opened unknown horizons, the synthetic perfumes with aldehydes, ionones, vanillin, coumarin, hydroxycitronnel-lol, and of course the living flower . . . [are] the synthesis of natural essences and these aromatic scents. . . . the mysterious harmony of ingredients . . . a seductive composition.

No fragrance aficionado in 1925 could read this description and not think of Chanel No. 5, a product that should have been singled out as one of modernity's great design achievements. While Chanel No. 5 wasn't the first perfume to use aldehydes and while it might not have been an entirely new invention, these materials were still rare in the fragrance industry until the late 1920s. The explosion of their popularity afterward owed a great deal to the astonishing commercial success of Ernest Beaux's creation and to the mad rush to create imitations. Just as Guerlain's Shalimar defined that year what it meant to use vanillin and coumarin in a fragrance and epito-mized the modern oriental perfume, Chanel No. 5, already a cult favorite with an enviable sales record, was the first perfume to make aldehydes famous.

Yet, amazingly, the partners at Les Parfums Chanel did not dis-play the fragrance. In fact, they didn't promote any of the Chanel perfumes, which is especially surprising since an entire salon in the pavilion was dedicated to the scents of Bourjois. It was a missed op-portunity to introduce millions of visitors to Chanel No. 5, and it can only have been deliberate. Perhaps the company simply believed that the real market for Chanel No. 5 would be on the other side of the Atlantic. Tellingly, the perfume wasn't advertised in France until as late as the 1940s. Even so, passing on such an easy chance to launch a perfume that was so much of the moment was a curious strategy.

Coco Chanel's design sense was part of what shaped this new Style Moderne, and nothing could have made more sense than that her signature couture scent should have been included. The very idea of the exhibition was to showcase the luxury products of France and to display them in a context that emphasized the decorative arts as personal identity—a concept she had helped to pioneer. It was a moment in history when "objects were defined as 'expressive' of the identity of the consumer" for the first time.

The Paris exposition of 1925 was the commercial highlight of the decade, and the exhibit was very near to the apex of Coco Chanel's celebrity. As one of her biographers writes, "The 1925 exhibition of decorative arts . . . saw her and her friends at the center of the excitement." Coco Chanel was the woman of the hour. Chanel No. 5 was conspicuously absent, however. Thinking about this new partnership, Coco Chanel was already beginning to feel the first twinges of regret.

Despite this missed opportunity at the Paris "expo," despite the conventional and rudimentary advertising during the 1920s, even despite the decision to market the perfume simply as part of a uniform line of Chanel fragrances, by 1925 Chanel No. 5 was flourishing in international markets. It was simply a word-of-mouth phenomenon, and those behind the department-store counters at places like Saks Fifth Avenue knew that it was a runaway favorite. Chanel No. 5 had been a popular perfume in Paris since Coco Chanel first launched it in 1921, and now it was quickly gaining a singularly important foothold in America, the world's largest market. When art deco swept the United States in the months and years that immediately followed, it only made Chanel No. 5—and Coco—more famous.

With that popularity came the inevitable imitations and a whole generation of new "number" perfumes. By 1927, it was clear to everyone in the world of fashion and perfumery that Chanel No. 5 was the scent to copy. That year, the designer Cristóbal Balenciaga launched his fragrance Le Dix—number ten—said to be a Chanel No. 5–type composition with the addition of violets. Before long, an advertisement in the French periodical *L'Illustration* flaunted another new perfume, Cadolle's Le No. 9. This one imitated Coco Chanel's signature bottle—and perversely her competitor had moved in just down the street at 14 rue Cambon.

The real competition, however, came from a familiar quarter. It was an obvious riposte in a long-standing, private industry battle that had been heating up dramatically in the 1920s. The competition between François Coty—whose loyalties had been with the Chiris family for the better part of a decade—and the partners at Bourjois and Les Parfums Chanel had begun to take on what looks like a bitter undercurrent.

Coty and the partners at Bourjois and Chanel were naturally in competition. These were the commercial giants of the fragrance industry, after all, and Les Parfums Chanel was attracting amazing talent—chief among them Ernest Beaux and, by the end of the decade, Jean Helleu, widely acknowledged to be among his generation's most gifted designers. At stake were also millions of dollars. So, when Coty bought out Chiris in 1926, he had his sights trained on Les Parfums Chanel and on directly challenging the popularity of Chanel No. 5.

It was a multifaceted strategy, and Coty had considerable resources at his disposal. He began by releasing a wave of new advertisements for the original Rallet No. 1, which he resolved to keep in production indefinitely. In a seemingly pointed allusion to the numbered perfumes of Chanel, Coty next relaunched a series of scents with names like Rallet No. 3 and Rallet No. 33. Then, he told perfumer Vincent Roubert to go back to the laboratory and the archives and to create something extra to challenge the competition. He wanted a fresh version of Chanel No. 5—a Coty version. He planned to make a splash on the world market with it. After all, he had the original Rallet formula.

Released in 1927, that perfume was L'Aimant—"the magnet"—and what Coty wanted to attract were some of the lucrative Chanel No. 5 sales. L'Aimant was an edgy and daring reinterpretation of Chanel No. 5 with a more intense dose of those famous aldehydes. Like Chanel No. 22 (1922)—also one of the original reformulations of Rallet No. 1 that Ernest Beaux had offered the designer, and even more strongly aldehydic—L'Aimant was the scent for women who wanted a lighter and more electric version. It had the advantage of also being considerably less expensive. Although never quite a blockbuster, L'Aimant did go on to be surprisingly successful.

If the goal had been to stem the sales of Chanel No. 5, however, Coty was disappointed. All the competition did was make Chanel No. 5 more desirable. In 1928, the department store of Jay Thorpe advertised the "light and sparkling" Chanel No. 5 as "the most famous" of the Chanel perfumes, and it was a colossal understatement. Chanel No. 5 was the most famous scent in the world. It had soared during the great economic bubble of the 1920s, and, in an era dedicated to the pursuit of incomparable luxuries, it had become one of the most coveted. That glorious ride, however, was almost over. In 1929, a wild and heady decade was coming to a close, and Chanel No. 5 had captured the spirit of it all effortlessly. That year it officially became the world's bestselling fragrance. What no one understood yet, though, was that the world was poised on the brink of an unimaginable financial disaster. What would matter in the decade to come was whether it was possible for Chanel No. 5 to hold on to its bestselling status.

ELEVEN
HOLLYWOOD AND
THE GREAT DEPRESSION

n New York and Paris at the end of the summer of 1929, it seemed as if nothing could stop the Roaring Twenties. Charles Lindbergh made his famous transatlantic flight, and the most daring women shocked the establishment by wearing trousers. Just the year before, Hollywood had produced the first talking feature film, *The Lights of New York*, creating a sensation. And Coco Chanel was an international celebrity, everywhere imitated. She passed the summer in luxury in Monte Carlo and at a new sprawling summer estate that she named La Pausa, in the company of dukes and princes and future British prime ministers. Sitting there in the warm breeze of the Riviera, surrounded by millionaires and their pleasures, the future seemed limitless.

Everyone, however, was on borrowed time—and soon there would be another generation of paupers to join her old friend and onetime lover, the prince Dmitri Pavlovich, in his genteel poverty. October 29, 1929 was a day few people of that generation would ever forget—especially the idle rich. It was the infamous Wall Street crash and the end of an exuberant era. That afternoon ended in panic amid the canyons of Manhattan's skyscrapers. In the days that followed, thirty billion dollars—the equivalent of $4,080,000,000,000—simply vanished. The Great Depression had begun, and the Roaring Twenties were categorically over.

That worldwide economic collapse would decimate the French luxury industry. The booming postwar American economy had fueled the sales of perfumes and Parisian high fashion, but many of the most prestigious houses were in precarious positions, living from season to season. Some of the small, elite designers had never fully recovered from the competitive extravagances of the art deco exhibit in 1925, where they had vied with one another to display the most fantastically opulent new kinds of modern artistry. More important, however, the devaluation of the French franc had been a boon to designers, making exported luxuries wonderfully—but artificially—affordable in America. The exchange rate was the reason that expatriates like Gertrude Stein and Ernest Hemingway and James Joyce could live in Paris so cheaply during the 1920s. Now came the collapse of the American economy—and of the dollar—and it brought the French luxury market in the United States down with it.

Within weeks, the most important luxury market in the world had all but evaporated. The numbers during those years are still breathtaking: from 1929 to 1941, more than a quarter of America's workforce were unemployed. For the fashion and fragrance industry, however, employment wasn't the crux of the problem. The trouble was that sales of "must-have" indulgences—and the daring new national experiment with buying things on credit—had been fueling the boom of the 1920s from the beginning.

Now, the transatlantic cruise ships were suddenly empty, as tourism ground to a halt. French exports during the Great Depression plummeted. Unsurprisingly, spending on advertising in the fragrance industry as a whole also dropped precipitously: from $3.4 billion in 1929 to $1.3 billion four years later. After all, there wasn't any point in saturating the press with advertisements for expensive French perfumes that most people couldn't afford to buy.

The partners at Les Parfums Chanel slashed their advertising budget. For three years—from 1929 to 1932—there was almost no marketing of any of the Chanel perfumes. While the company has never disclosed any of its sales records, even from the earliest decades, it's hard to imagine things back in Paris were looking entirely rosy. There was just one bright spot on the horizon: sales might be down, but that wasn't the same thing as share of the market. Chanel No. 5 remained a popular favorite.

So in 1932, the partners at Les Parfums Chanel launched a new concept. At least as early as 1928, they had marketed a small "pocket flacon" bottle for the entire line of Chanel fragrances. It was the perfect size for busy modern women—but it was also a clever way of encouraging consumers to sample a range of the perfume line, including all those numbers. Now, in a sign of the times, the company started marketing the small bottles aggressively—and they lowered the prices. In 1928, the "pocket flacon" had been offered at $3.75. In 1932, the company reintroduced the flacons as a "handbag" series and dropped the price to $2.25—the equivalent of less than twenty-five dollars a bottle, nearly a 40 percent discount. For the next several years, this was the almost exclusive focus of the marketing. Advertisements simply told readers that the fragrances were available "from $2.25." The larger, vanity-sized bottles of Chanel No. 5 and the other Chanel fragrances remained expensive and exclusive, but their prices went unmentioned. It was a sample-sized marketing teaser—and an invitation to an ever-broader group of women in the midst of an economic downturn to think of Coco Chanel's perfumes as a small luxury. What those women thought of, however, was Chanel No. 5.

• •

t may have been this small step toward marketing her fragrances for middle-class American consumers that gave Coco Chanel serious pause. As early as 1928, there were tensions brewing between the designer and the partners at Les Parfums Chanel, and later they would come to a head over the question of how to define luxury status. It can't have helped matters that, suddenly, fashion designers all around her were starting to launch signature perfumes and clearly imitating her strategy. Some of them were doing it in an opulent style—and offering their perfumes at a higher price point than Chanel No. 5. It was easy to wonder whether Chanel No. 5—and the house of Chanel—would remain the standard for exclusivity.

While Paul Poiret and Coco Chanel had been farsighted innovators when they launched their signature fragrances, throughout the 1920s designer perfumes had increasingly become the standard. It had been an era of perfumes by the letters as well as perfumes by the numbers. One couturier after another—each inspired by the astonishing commercial success of Chanel No. 5—released his or her own couture fragrance. Among this new wave of designers-turned-perfumers, Madeleine Vionnet and the house of Lenthéric had launched lines of fragrances named not after numbers but after letters as early as 1924. Vionnet's A, B, C, and D fragrances were marketed in futurist geometrical bottles. Designer Lucien Lelong, rather unoriginally, countered with A, B, C, J, and N (1924) fragrances of his own. Even the fashionable milliner J. Suzanne Talbot—in a nod to the famous Coco Chanel—came out with some letter perfumes, the J, S, and T fragrances, in 1925. By the early 1930s, designer perfumes were the norm, and each fashion house was looking for new and creative ways of promoting its scent.

Once again, Coco Chanel had changed the direction of the world of fashion, and it was all an extension of her initial intuition. From the beginning, the link between Chanel No. 5 and her atelier had been explicit. She had sprayed the perfume in the fitting rooms of her boutique as an essential part of her word-of-mouth marketing in 1921 and lauded it as *her* personal scent. Now that idea was coming to fruition in the luxury fragrance market. It meant new competition.

By the mid-1920s, the world of marketing was also experiencing a revolution. A new way of selling perfumes was emerging in Paris especially, and it didn't have much to do with the kind of depart-ment store-sponsored newspaper advertisements that the partners at Les Parfums Chanel used to promote Chanel No. 5 in those first few decades. These new trends, however, did owe a great deal to the history of the department store, which emerged as a powerful commercial institution in the early twentieth century. The owners of retail temples like the Galeries Lafayette in Paris "were pioneers in the art of enhancing and contextualizing commodities by using exotic backdrops." Théophile Bader at the Galeries Lafayette, in fact, had been the first retailer to sell Chanel No. 5 in the early days, and, in exchange for introducing Coco Chanel to the Wertheimer brothers, he still owned a 20 percent stake in Les Parfums Chanel—twice Coco Chanel's share in the fragrance she had created.

The great innovation of the 1930s, however, wasn't the department-store counter but the lush new scent salons being cre-ated by fragrance houses. In these extravagant boutiques, clients indulged their senses. It was a backward glance to the summer of 1911 and Paul Poiret's spectacular midnight launch of his Nuit Persane, which had inspired Coco Chanel to develop history's third couture fragrance. It was also part of a brand-new style of merchan-dising, one that emphasized "elaborate displays [and] the cultivation of the shopping experience."

The trend had begun with those perfume fountains of the 1925 art deco exhibition. "Perfume," visitors to the pavilion learned, "is a luxury naturally adapted . . . to feminine fantasy," and at the "expo" the retailers competed fiercely with one another to draw spectators into a perfumed world of the imagination. Those who saw it were delighted, and the perfume pavilion was such a success that perfume houses soon picked up on the idea and expanded upon it. It was the perfect way to make the point that fine fragrances were not the kind of thing you bought in a *prix unique*, the French equivalent of the five-and-dime. It was the birth of a certain kind of luxury marketing.

Designers began refitting their boutiques to showcase their perfumes and accessories, and the boutique created by the designer Jean Patou was a celebrated example. In 1930, Patou released his scent Joy, which was based on perfumer Henri Alméras's experiments with even more extravagant amounts of jasmine and rose than in the bestselling Chanel No. 5. Coco Chanel had told Ernest Beaux just a decade earlier that what she wanted to create was the most extravagant perfume in the world. Now, Joy had officially taken that title from her. It was not the kind of thing calculated to make Coco Chanel happy—especially combined with a series of newspaper advertisements touting her fragrances at remarkably modest prices.

In fact, Coco Chanel's aesthetics were far more in line with the marketing strategy that Jean Patou pursued to market his new fragrance. That tension—between heady exclusivity and the mass-market commercialization of a luxury product—was at the heart of much that came later. The early 1930s were a difficult time to introduce a new luxury product, even one with such a determinedly cheerful name as Joy, and Patou knew that selling this new scent in the aftermath of the stock market crash would require some creative efforts. Hoping to drum up some long-distance business, Patou sent bottles of Joy as a gift to cheer up his best clients in America, who were finding their European shopping trips hampered by the Great Depression. This perfume, he hoped, would keep the name of Patou in the minds of women as a designer at a moment when few people could afford haute couture.

Then, he did something else clever. In his boutique, he had long maintained a cocktail bar for the gentlemen who were kept waiting during those protracted feminine fittings. With a major redesign of his salon, he now gave his loyal clients—and the other women who frequented couturiers—an added incentive to make the effort to come to his salon in Paris. He added a glamorous perfume bar, where clients could sample not liquors but perfumes, several of which had clever new "cocktail" themes that year. Clients could even blend their own scents. Or they could buy his new ultra-exclusive interwar fragrance. It was the ultimate shopping experience. The combined result was that Joy became, despite the odds, a terrific success.

Before long, perfume showrooms and designer boutiques across Paris were opulent invitations to fantasy, more like movie sets than sales floors. The Hollywood connection wasn't coincidental, especially for Coco Chanel. In 1930, still enjoying great personal celebrity, she met the Hollywood producer Sam Goldwyn at a restaurant in Monte Carlo. Their collaboration would inspire new directions in fragrance marketing, bring Coco Chanel a fortune, and catapult Chanel No. 5 to even greater fame. It was a far cry from corner newspaper advertisements.

In these uncertain times, Hollywood producers were also looking for ways to reach audiences. It was the beginning of the golden age of Hollywood, and within just a few months the "Swedish Sphinx," Greta Garbo, would star in her first talkie, but the Great Depression was taking its toll even in sunny California. There were already other dark signs on the cultural horizon. Censorship, anti-communism, and anti-Semitism ran through those years in an ominous undercurrent. The surface, however, was glitter, and Hollywood moguls began experimenting with new ways of enticing audiences by bringing luxury products to consumers.

Those audiences were mostly female. Writes one film historian, "women were seen by Hollywood as the primary consumers of cinema." Everyone also knew that women found haute couture fascinating. So nothing could be more natural than to have films start borrowing from the conventions of the fashion show, which had been invented in the dressing rooms of Paris at the turn of the century.

It was the final logical marriage of the theatrical display of the 1925 art deco exhibition with costume and interior designing. Art deco was a phenomenon in America. The MGM artistic director Cedric Gibbons had attended the Paris exposition, and his interpretation of the new modernist style in the 1925 film *Our Dancing Daughters*, with Joan Crawford, set off a fashion in the United States for everything French and art deco. Despite the fact that Chanel No. 5—perhaps the quintessential art deco fragrance—had been curiously absent from the exposition, "Chanel" was already the epitome of this new Style Moderne in the minds of many.

When it came to marketing fashion, Sam Goldwyn also saw a golden opportunity. He would draw women to the movies by having his stars wear only the latest cutting-edge Parisian designs. In that world of couture, no one had more cachet and verve than Coco Chanel. Come to Hollywood, he said. Dress my starlets. And he offered her the staggering sum of a million dollars—the equivalent of over $75 million today—if she would take just two trips a year to California and design costumes for his stars.

Understanding a good business opportunity when she saw one, Coco Chanel took the contract and headed for the United States in the winter of 1931. For a second time in the history of Chanel No. 5, Dmitri Pavlovich had been behind an introduction crucial to Coco's success. According to an article in *Collier's* magazine in 1932, "The Grand Duke Dimitri, of the Romanoffs, quite casually introduced Samuel Goldwyn, of the movies, to [Mademoiselle] Gabrielle Chanel of Chanel. Pleasant talk, pleasant compliments, big inspiration, big contract—and the great Chanel has agreed to come to Hollywood to design clothes for the movies. Admittedly, it's a gamble, but on a million-dollar scale."

Still, Coco Chanel was dubious about the dazzle of the big screen and California. After all, she had once dreamed of a career on the stage, and she had determinedly left that life behind. But for a million dollars, she was willing to take a trip to "see what the pictures have to offer me and what I have to offer the pictures."

By then, Coco had another reason for being curious about the world of the movie industry. That winter, she had a new lover, and this time he was a man who had Hollywood connections. She had thrown herself into a liaison with the fashion illustrator, political satirist, and Hollywood set designer Paul Iribe, the illustrator and sometime-journalist who had famously sketched the dresses of her competitor Paul Poiret.

Coco Chanel and Paul Iribe had known each other for decades, and they had an entire circle of friends in common, including Misia Sert, Igor Stravinsky, Jean Cocteau, Sergei Diaghilev, and many of the Russian exiles associated with the Ballet Russes in the 1910s and 1920s. In fact, the connections between them went back even further. Paul Iribe's first wife, the famed vaudeville actress Jeanne Dirys, had worn hats created by her friend—another onetime showgirl—Coco Chanel.

To their friends, it was a bizarre connection, because, when it came to fashion, Coco Chanel and Paul Iribe had radically different sensibilities. In his polemical 1929 antimodern design treatise *Choix*, Iribe had attacked the revolutionary "emancipated" and international style her work epitomized, complaining that it was part of the degeneration of French culture. It hardly seems, then, that Paul Iribe would have been the person to turn to for career advice and supportive conversation. But he had worked for several years at some of the big studios, and, in advance of the Hollywood tour, Coco reconnected with her old acquaintance to get his perspective on the film industry. Sparks flew, and they quickly became lovers. In fact, as soon as he could get a divorce from his wife, an unlucky heiress named Maybelle, they planned to get married.

It all happened suddenly, and, within a year of beginning their liaison, things were serious. By Coco Chanel's own testimony, however, it was a strange and sometimes tortured relationship. "My nascent celebrity," she later told a friend,

> had eclipsed his declining glory. . . . I represented a Paris that he could never possess, dominate. . . . Iribe loved me . . . with the secret wish to destroy me. He longed for me to be crushed and humiliated, he wanted me to die. It would have given him great pleasure to see me belong to him totally, poor, reduced to helplessness, paralyzed. . . . He was a creature who was very perverse, very affectionate, very intelligent, very self-interested, with an extraordinary refinement. . . . My history tortured him.

Her celebrity at the beginning of the 1930s was hardly "nascent," but no one doubted that it was an astonishing attachment. Coco's friends thought Iribe was devilish and couldn't understand it. As always for Coco, her past troubled him. One thing that doesn't seem to have unsettled her about the love affair, however, was Iribe's politics, which flirted with a peculiar brand of proto-fascist nationalism. His views were only marginally less narrow than those of another former lover, the Duke of Westminster, and by now those narrow politics probably reflected her own. The history of Chanel No. 5 would soon become dangerously embroiled with them.

For Sam Goldwyn, bringing the famous Coco Chanel to America was all about the publicity, and he was delighted with the media blitz that surrounded her arrival in the United States. He had arranged for her to travel in high style—and very visibly—from New York to Los Angeles on a special white luxury train. Before she departed, *Time* magazine reported on March 16, 1931, "In Manhattan famed stylist Gabrielle ("Coco") Chanel, who is on her way from her Paris shops to Hollywood to design clothes for cinemactresses, received newsgatherers. She was attired in red sports clothes and wore a five-strand pearl necklace, ten bracelets." Cameras and admirers surrounded her. She had come to the great department stores of New York to see her designs on display and to give them her stamp of approval. And she stopped at the perfume counter to see that they had plenty of Chanel No. 5.

What words of wisdom did Coco Chanel have for American women about fashion? It wasn't hemlines or jersey suits that she mentioned. On her mind was perfume—a perfume that, technically, she had given up the right to control a half-decade earlier. Women, she once again told the press, should not wear floral scents. It was one of her stock lines about fragrances. They needed something modern, something composed, and she could recommend only Chanel No. 5. Not that anyone needed the recommendation. It was already a bestseller and one of the hallmarks of her fame.

The problems between Coco Chanel and the partners had been simmering in the background since as early as the mid-1920s, but in the aftermath of her trip to Hollywood her unhappiness intensified. From this point forward, a bitter—and sometimes explosive—resentment would define her relationship with the partners and with the product she had created. Having helped to establish the reputation of Chanel No. 5 and its position in the world market, having launched it and trusted the partners at Les Parfums Chanel to bring it to the attention of the world and nurtured it with her personal celebrity throughout the 1920s, she would spend the next several decades doing everything she could to wrest control of it from the investors.

By the early 1930s, Coco Chanel had also begun to feel that, in giving up control of Chanel No. 5, she had lost something terribly important. She had nagging doubts about the bargain she had brokered. She started to think that maybe she had even been tricked.

Now, having seen just how popular Chanel No. 5 had become in that vast American market, she was certain. This conviction signaled the end of whatever true partnership she had enjoyed with the men at Les Parfums Chanel. She wanted control over her fragrance.

If that didn't succeed, she was prepared to destroy it.

TWELVE

A BROKEN PARTNERSHIP

I t was the decade from 1925 to 1935 that first turned Chanel No. 5 into *the* signature Chanel perfume, although that's not the same as its becoming a cultural icon. That would come later. The success of the first decade, however, was by any account spectacular. Despite the confusing marketing and the plethora of Chanel perfumes with all those numbers, this one scent came to the foreground during the most profound economic crisis in modern history, and it has been the world's most famous fragrance ever since.

Notably, it was during these years that some of the first numbered perfumes finally began disappearing from the Chanel advertising, and in the mid-1930s—as a belated reflection of its already singular success—advertising for Chanel No. 5 consistently began to appear alone. By 1935, when the world was still in economic turmoil and political tragedy was looming dimly on the horizon, it was being hailed in casual advertising as the scent "worn by more smart women than any other perfume."

Finally the partners at Les Parfums Chanel seriously considered a campaign that would capitalize on the perfume's continued popularity, and the first true marketing blitz for Chanel No. 5 was planned for 1934 and 1935. This time, part of the strategy was to highlight Chanel No. 5 in some of the advertisements as a perfume with a unique brand identity, apart from the other numbered perfumes of the Chanel fragrance line. The first truly "solo" advertisement of Chanel No. 5, as the most important Chanel perfume, comparable only to her legend as a couturière, ran in the *New York Times* on June 10, 1934, ten years after Coco Chanel had signed her partnership with the investors at Les Parfums Chanel. In it, a model wearing a gown from the new collection poses, and someone has tucked into the frame a silhouetted bottle of Chanel No. 5 perfume. The tagline reads: "Both are Chanel. Equally they express that taste and originality that have won Chanel her high distinction. For perfume is Chanel's other life. And in her No. 5 she has triumphed as significantly as in the most inspired of her celebrated mode creations." By the time this advertising appeared, however, Chanel No. 5 had already triumphed for a decade.

Tensions between Coco Chanel and the partners had been steadily growing. By 1928 the partners had assigned an in-house lawyer to handle their prickly celebrity designer. Now, the conflict between Coco Chanel and the partners was about to intensify significantly. Her celebrity and the trip to Hollywood had only made matters worse. During 1935, suddenly Chanel No. 5 was everywhere. It was making Les Parfums Chanel more money than ever. Not coincidentally, Coco had been starting to feel that, in giving up control of it, she had lost something worth possessing.

Although Chanel had named her own terms for the initial partnership in the beginning, by the time Chanel No. 5 was the world's bestselling fragrance, she was convinced that she had been grossly cheated. From her perspective, Les Parfums Chanel—and the men to whom she had licensed her scents—was making a fortune off her name and fragrance, and, to the extent that her personal celebrity established the popularity of No. 5 apart from all those other early numbered perfumes, her frustration had some justification. She knew as well as anyone that the success of Chanel No. 5 didn't come down to those newspaper advertisements, and it had always seemed as though the partners should be doing more for their share of the money. Perhaps she also had concerns about how the tenor of those advertisements in the early 1930s had changed the idea of Chanel No. 5 as a luxury. Certainly, that was a bone of contention later. Ironically, it was the new marketing campaign—which focused on Chanel No. 5 as an exclusive product and which should have delighted her—that set off the controversy.

Part of the problem was a simple matter of dividends. Coco Chanel owned a minority 10 percent stake in Les Parfums Chanel—the right to receive a check, essentially, for 10 percent of the profits as a licensing agreement. This new publicity campaign, however, cost money, and that new advertising investment naturally meant a short-term reduction in her profits. While the benefit of this strategy seemed obvious to everyone else, all Coco saw was that the amount of money coming her way was decreasing when she knew for a certainty that sales were flourishing.

What prompted her outrage was ostensibly the extension of the Chanel cleansing-cream line, scheduled for 1934 as part of a larger effort to expand the sales of the fragrance further. Recognizing the potential for a broad range of Chanel No. 5 products, the partners saw that the product extension promised to bring in even more fabulous sales—all part of the new Chanel No. 5 marketing campaign.

Coco Chanel, however, had other ideas. Cleansing cream now struck her as not precisely luxurious. She had also reached the point where she wanted a bigger share of the profits before seeing her name used on any new project—and she felt certain that this was a new project for the company. Les Parfums Chanel saw that differently.

The language of the original contract she had signed licensing her products to the company in 1924 now struck her as ambiguous.

Les Parfums Chanel had the right to sell products associated with the perfume and beauty trades: that was manifestly clear. The terms of the licensing specifically included only "make-up," however, and she maintained that cleansing cream didn't fall under that category. "You don't have the right to make a cream," she told the partners; "I demand that you give me all the balance sheets, all the books, all the minutes and reports, all the profits and losses of the past ten years during which I have been president. [Or] else, I will go to court." Then Chanel—ever the suspicious businesswoman—sought a court order to prevent its production anyhow.

This launched a public battle that would last five years, and it was just the beginning of conflicts between Coco Chanel and Les Parfums Chanel that would result, as her lawyer René de Chambrun later ruefully remembered, in literally more than a ton of paperwork gathered in files in his offices. In fact, before the beginning of the Second World War alone, there would be three or four different lawsuits, all over minor—but important—contractual details of this sort.

Things heated up considerably in the autumn of 1933, when, rather than attend the board of directors meeting, Coco appointed her paramour Paul Iribe her representative. The result was disaster. The Wertheimers and the other men in the Parfums Chanel partnership were all from prominent Jewish families in France, and it can't have helped that Iribe spent his time privately—and sometimes publicly—railing against the "Judeo-Masonic Mafia." By 1931, the Nazis were already the second largest party in Germany, and its paramilitary branch, the S.A., had already begun openly attacking Jewish businesses. In 1933, Iribe launched a political magazine called *Le Témoin*—"The Witness"—and "In the first number, Iribe inscribed his journal in the line of far-right publications during the period."

It was an era of rising nationalism and anti-Semitism, and Coco Chanel's politics were also of the moment. Convinced that the partners were cheating her, she "developed a delusion that intensified her anti-Semitism." One of her relatives remembered Coco as an "appalling troublemaker" and told how she lumped the Jewish men with whom she did business—Samuel Goldwyn, of course, among them—into three categories. There were the "Israelites": the great Jewish families of France, among whom she counted the Rothschilds. In the 1930s and even the early 1940s, "Israelites" was still a religious category and not a racial one. Then, there were the ethnic "Jews," and, in racialized French slang, the "*youpins*" at the bottom. About those terms, there was nothing neutral. Depending on her mood, she counted the men who controlled Les Parfums Chanel in one of the last two categories.

In 1933, Chanel was the titular head of the company, but this had never been more than a matter of politeness. As long as she didn't interfere with the business of running the company, it was smart public relations. But with things souring rapidly between Coco Chanel and the partners, the advantages were suddenly less obvious. Now, as a show of pique, she refused to attend the board meetings. Instead, Iribe was there as her representative—with full power of attorney. He was obstreperous and stonewalled the agenda. Worse, he knew nothing about the perfume business and infuriated the partners—who included not just the Wertheimer brothers, who owned 70 percent of the company, but the sons-in-law of Théophile Bader at Galeries Lafayette, the Meyer and Heilbronn families, who controlled another 20 percent interest. At the end of the meeting, just to be difficult, Iribe refused to sign the minutes. Coco Chanel's strategy seems to have been simply to prevent business from getting done, and Iribe was using her position on the board to do it for her.

This resulted in the partners' immediate decision to vote Iribe—and by extension Coco Chanel—off the board of directors at the end of the meeting. The next step would be to remove her from the presidency. Since she was by far the minority partner, this was easily accomplished. The title had only ever been a courtesy, and her strategy had backfired disastrously.

Stripped of even symbolic control over the perfume company to which she had long ago signed away rights, Coco Chanel was incensed. Her relationship with the partners deteriorated further when, at the end of 1934, they replaced the management team. Coco was convinced that the sole object of this corporate reorganization was to cut her further out of the company, and she retaliated by hiring the team back on in the couture division just to make an embarrassing public spectacle of it all.

The timing of what came next also could not have been more emotionally complicated. The creation of Chanel No. 5 had represented an effort to contain the loss of Boy Capel. By the early 1930s, Coco Chanel's lack of control over the company and the perfume seemed like losing him all over. Now, she was in love again and for the first time planning to get married. Perhaps if that had happened, Chanel No. 5 gradually would have seemed less personally significant. Instead, in the middle of a tennis match one afternoon, on September 21, 1935, she watched Paul Iribe die in front of her from a heart attack, still in his early fifties. In the aftermath of sorrow, she threw herself again into scent and Chanel No. 5. This time, she wasn't intent on invention. She wanted control of the perfume, and she would do whatever she had to do to get it.

In the history of Chanel No. 5, the year 1935 was a decisive turning point. Les Parfums Chanel was taking a far more aggressive role in advertising this fragrance bestseller, and Coco had been removed from her figurehead position as president of the company. Everyone else was moving forward confidently with the business of marketing Chanel No. 5, but Coco Chanel was furious. She told René de Chambrun that she wanted to sue the partners at Les Parfums Chanel in a bid to regain control of the product.

Coco was sure that she would win her legal battles with the company and started a protracted series of tit-for-tat lawsuits on both sides of the Atlantic that were to drag on for more than a decade.

She sued to stop the development of the new beauty line and asked for the court's protection as a minority shareholder. The partners at Les Parfums Chanel counter-sued for breach of contract. Coco Chanel's position was that if the partners wanted to extend the Chanel No. 5 line to other beauty products, they would have to renegotiate the terms of the initial contract. The board of directors maintained that those rights had already been granted with the 1924 document. If they lost, Coco Chanel was determined to drive a hard bargain this time.

By the second part of the 1930s, life for Coco was also privately less satisfying. Paul Iribe was dead, and, astonishingly, he had been the first man she had loved who was prepared to marry her. The most important men in her life—her father, Boy Capel—had deserted her. Now, in his own way, Paul had deserted her too. Worse yet, she was also falling out of step for the first time with the world of fashion. Despite a 1937 advertisement for Chanel No. 5 that featured a full-length shot of Coco Chanel in front of the fireplace in her apartment at the Ritz Hotel and that lauded "Madame Gabrielle Chanel [as] above all an artist in living," times and fashions were changing. By the late 1930s, puffed sleeves, fitted waists, and shoulder pads were making the hourglass figure stylish, and the designers of the moment were Elsa Schiaparelli, Lucien Lelong, and Cristóbal Balenciaga. It was the antithesis of the classic Chanel style, which had always been suited to the boyish figure of Coco's youth. Add to these new tastes a decade-long economic crisis and a bitter strike with her workers, and it's no wonder she was frustrated and tired. At the end of the summer of 1939, after all, Coco Chanel was fifty-six.

So, when France declared war against fascist Germany that September, Coco closed her fashion house and retired. This, she said to those who criticized her, was no time for fashion. She didn't close her boutiques entirely, however. The shop at rue Cambon would remain open during the entire war. She planned to continue selling those famous fragrances and a line of costume jewelry and accessories, and, if anything, she became that much more invested in her perfume. She turned her attention back to Chanel No. 5 especially, blithely ignoring the fact that she had long ago sold its license. Already in America the perfume was becoming more famous than the designer. Suddenly, she was not prepared to count it among her losses.

The courts, however, had a different idea about the matter. During the first months of the Second World War, with other lawsuits still dragging on, she learned that the case launched five years earlier to stop the production of scented beauty creams had gone in favor of the partners at Les Parfums Chanel, whose right to produce and market the perfume was reconfirmed legally.

With this disappointing setback regarding Chanel No. 5 fresh on her mind, Coco Chanel just dug in her heels more doggedly. She was living at the Ritz Hotel in 1940. The back entrance looked out onto rue Cambon—where she still kept her showrooms and offices. By then Paris was occupied, and, if you were rich enough, rooms at the Ritz Hotel weren't a bad way to ride out the war in a city where daily life for many was a series of small and capricious horrors. At a time when thousands were losing their lives as well as their fortunes, the celebrated designer was still an immensely wealthy woman, and it was a life of relative comfort.

For many who lived in Paris during those years, it was life's small luxuries that helped to make those horrors bearable. There were already demeaning shortages. Coffee was replaced with chicory, and chocolate all but disappeared. Both became powerful objects of desire. Perhaps the only object more coveted was fine French perfume. It was the reminder of another time, when everything was not so brutal and so difficult, and it became an intoxicating indulgence. On the black market, its value was astronomical. Among all the French perfumes in the city, there was one that was famous beyond anything else. Sometimes one could still find it. Chanel No. 5. The scent was quickly becoming, in the crucible of those war years, an indomitable cultural icon.

THIRTEEN
IN THE SHADOW
OF THE RITZ

Sales of Coco Chanel's signature scent, the still wildly successful Chanel No. 5, were booming. To anyone who happened to stroll past her boutique on rue Cambon, the source of her riches was immediately obvious. During the war, the first floor of the shop was a sparkling trove of glass perfume bottles. Before long, it sold nothing else.

There, in the shadow of the Ritz Hotel, soldiers made orderly lines on the sidewalk as they waited to buy a bottle or two for someone back home or, far more often, a pretty French girl who, in these times of rationing and deprivation, didn't have Coco Chanel's advantages. "The ground-floor boutique," one historian writes, "was filled with German soldiers buying the only item on sale—Chanel No. 5. When the stocks ran out the Fritzes picked up the display bottles marked with the intertwined double C and paid for them. It was something to take back to the *Fraülein*, something that proved they had been in Paris." German generals didn't wait in line. They strode in and bought it by the armfuls. Coco told a friend that it was ridiculous: "During the war we could sell only about twenty bottles of perfume a day in the House of Chanel. People lined up long before opening time, chiefly German soldiers. I laughed when I saw them; I thought, you poor fools, most of you will go away empty-handed." Sold throughout the territories of the Third Reich, including Germany, of course, that singular scent was the reason she could afford to wait out the occupation in luxury.

For the partners at Les Parfums Chanel, waiting out the war in the Ritz Hotel was not an option. The Wertheimer brothers still owned 70 percent of the company. Théophile Bader had been in poor health since 1935, and his 20 percent stake had been entrusted to the management of his sons-in-law, Raoul Meyer and Max Heilbronn. Although from old French families, their backgrounds were Jewish, and they knew that they were in danger. The Wertheimer clan realized by the spring of 1940, in the weeks before the fall of France, that exile was the only protection. On May 13, as the German troops crossed the Meuse River and made their way to Paris, the family made a snap decision to flee France. They gathered at Pierre Wertheimer's house at 55, avenue Foch, and set out in a convoy of five cars, driving south to Bordeaux. From there, they crossed by train into Spain, where the borders still remained open for refugees. Then the family left immediately for South America, waiting only until visas for entry into the United States could be processed. By August 5, 1940, after nearly four months of travel and waiting, the Wertheimers had arrived in New York City. Meyer was later able to flee to the unoccupied territories. Heilbronn fought for the French resistance and ultimately survived the concentration camps at Buchenwald.

It was a narrow window, and, had the Wertheimer family not managed to flee France in the first days of the occupation, there would not be Chanel No. 5 as we know it, because it was during the Second World War that this fragrance went from being a bestseller to becoming an international cultural icon. From New York, the majority partners were determined to keep making Chanel No. 5 perfume, and they set out to dazzle once again the American market. Despite Coco Chanel's protestations and resentments, they had every right to do it. Les Parfums Chanel had been, for all intents and purposes, their business for almost twenty years.

Now in New York, the partners needed to find a way to produce the fragrance. So Pierre Wertheimer contacted an old friend, Arnold van Ameringen, who happened to be dating a lady named Josephine Esther Lauter—better known to the world as Estée Lauder. In order to keep Bourjois and Les Parfums Chanel running, the family would need a new production facility in the United States. They found one in Hoboken, New Jersey, but there was just one massive problem. They needed raw materials, especially those rare floral essences from Grasse that had always been part of Chanel No. 5's secret. Unless they moved quickly—and were willing to take a series of dangerous gambles—getting those supplies was going to be impossible.

They devised a daring plan: they would send someone back to France. The man they entrusted was named H. Gregory Thomas, a native New Yorker with law degrees from Paris and Salamanca, Spain. Thomas had been the president of the perfume house of Guerlain before the war, and he would go on to become the president of Chanel's fragrance operation in America. In 1940, while in his early thirties, he was sent on a complicated covert mission. Most urgently, someone needed to help Pierre Wertheimer's son, Jacques, escape from occupied France in advance of the deportations. After that, Thomas was charged with picking up the precious formula for Chanel No. 5 from the company offices in Paris, then going on to Grasse to purchase as much as possible of the rare botanical essences on which the perfume depended. Price was not an object.

Without the floral extracts from Grasse, the partners at Les Parfums Chanel knew that there could be no Chanel No. 5—at least not at the level of quality the world expected. Had Thomas failed, it might have been the end of Coco Chanel's famous perfume. Never had this celebrated fragrance been in such danger.

As times changed, tastes changed with them, and fifteen years was already a long time for any luxury product to remain at the height of international fashion. Even for a perfume as beloved and familiar as Chanel No. 5, an extended absence from the world stage would have been an incredibly risky proposition. Continued production was imperative—and that meant they needed jasmine. Amazingly, Thomas succeeded. Because the partners at Les Parfums Chanel had acted quickly, they would be among the only perfumers during the war to have access to these legendary and unique materials from Grasse—the scents at the heart of Chanel No. 5.

What was so crucial about these specific materials from Grasse? What made them worth sending someone to smuggle them out of France? It all goes back to the original formula. Coco Chanel once said that in Chanel No. 5 she wanted a perfume that was artificial, something composed—"like a dress"—and not something that made women smell like flowers. Ironically, however, it's the flowers that have largely made this perfume famous. Part of the secret of its beauty is the rare floral oils used to create it—what Ernest Beaux called the "first materials"—and especially the scents of roses and jasmine. At the moment when Chanel No. 5 was first being launched, these materials were used in many of the finest fragrances in France and could be obtained in Grasse.

Throughout the 1920s, in fact, the perfume industry made Grasse one of the most popular tourist destinations in the south of France, and visitors sent home postcards showing the rose harvest and the town's sprawling *usines*—its fragrance factories. Ernest Beaux's laboratory was among the area's most famously elite attractions. When

Coco Chanel threw herself into learning everything she could about the production of perfumes in 1918 and 1919, she visited Grasse.

The village was the world's epicenter of fragrance manufacturing and research, largely as a result of the stunning quality of the local natural materials. In fact, "in Grasse, where all flowers were called by their proper [Latin] names, jasmine was simply known [in the 1920s] as 'the flower,'" and vast plantations were given over to its cultivation. The jasmine, in particular, was unlike anything else in the world. The Côte d'Azur is the far northern limit of the natural climate for jasmine, and there is a truism in the world of aromatics that flowers take on the finest scents in the places where they struggle. Here the jasmine plants grow to only half their normal height, and they have lower proportions of those so-called indoles, which can give jasmine an intensely sweet physical odor. The result is a flower that smells subtler and less overpowering. It also has about it a distinct note that smells like tea.

Grasse was also home to large plantations of a particular variety of heirloom rose, the delicately floral *centifolia*. Often simply called the May rose of Grasse, the *centifolia* is grafted to the rootstock of the *indica major,* and when it blooms in the late spring its aroma is more complex than that of any other species of rose. Both were scents at the heart of Chanel No. 5. Ernest Beaux was simply using world-class local materials.

As her friends later remembered, though, Coco Chanel didn't just tour the flower gardens and plantations when she visited Grasse. She also visited the factories where natural plant materials were turned into the elements of a perfume. When Gregory Thomas negotiated those wartime supplies of rose and jasmine scents for Les Parfums Chanel, he, too, knew that what happened in the fields was only half the equation. The quality of a perfume depended on how carefully the flowers were processed in the distillery. The end result of that processing was to turn millions of blossoms into materials perfumers could use—either the waxy "raw" form of fragrance essence known as a concrete or the highly purified scent of an absolute.

Turning rose and jasmine petals to perfume is a delicate and laborious business, and this was the other thing that made the natural materials from Grasse superior in 1940. As the most important center of the fragrance industry for the better part of a century already, this was where many of France's great perfume companies had their research laboratories. In terms of technical innovation, Grasse was simply cutting edge, and the result was a superior level of quality.

It was the Chiris family who had pioneered at the end of the nineteenth century the essential process that freed Gregory Thomas from being forced to bring back to the United States sacks of flower petals. Heat is the enemy of aroma, and they had developed an efficient commercial process for distilling plant-based fragrance materials using organic solvents at low temperatures that freed the industry from the laborious alternate process called in French *enfleurage*, or "enflowering," where the blossoms were pressed into thin layers of fat over the course of days and weeks to extract their essences. By the turn of the century, "Louis Chiris had set up his first workshop based on solvent extraction," having wisely already secured "a patent on these techniques and created the first factory to employ chemicals." This discovery—along with the discovery of those new synthetic aromatic materials like aldehydes—is a large part of the reason the first decades of the twentieth century became the "golden age" of perfumery. For the first time, it was possible to obtain excellent-quality floral concrete and absolutes in larger and more affordable quantities.

While an absolute is the purest form of floral essence, what Gregory Thomas was looking to buy in 1940, anticipating a war that might drag on, was the less-refined material known as a concrete, a midstage product in the extraction process, where the scents remained blended with their natural vegetable waxes. Later, in New York, the concrete could be transformed into an even more intense absolute when the waxes were removed. There was a real advantage here. A fine concrete could last for several years, maybe even half a decade. Absolutes needed to be used far more quickly.

Today, a pound of jasmine absolute sells for more than $33,000. It was already fabulously expensive in the 1930s. The reason was the staggering number of flowers that it took to make it. Nearly 350 pounds of jasmine—over a half-million flowers—go into a pound of jasmine concrete, and in each small, thirty-milliliter bottle of Chanel No. 5 *parfum* is the essence of more than a thousand jasmine flowers and the bouquet of a dozen roses. Making Chanel No. 5 during the war was going to take all the raw materials they could get. The partners at Les Parfums Chanel, understanding what shortages would do to the perfume industry, were frantic to stockpile reserves of these essences.

Despite all the risks—and arrest for smuggling these rare ingredients out of France was a very real one—Gregory Thomas succeeded, returning with hundreds of pounds of rose and jasmine concrete from the finest fields in Grasse. In doing so, one might confidently argue he almost single-handedly saved Chanel No. 5 during the Second World War. Without those materials, production in the United States would not have been possible. No one knew whether the materials would be available in the months and years to come.

By sending Thomas at that critical juncture, the partners at Les Parfums Chanel had demonstrated a rare kind of entrepreneurial genius. Writes one historian:

> With a great deal of foresight, the Wertheimer brothers sent people to France to round up stocks while it was still possible to do so. Their exploits were worthy of James Bond: gold had

to be sent into France clandestinely, the jasmine taken out and brought into the United States. Some 700 pounds of jasmine were received, more precious than its weight in gold.

It was the essence of more than 350 million jasmine flowers. With stocks in hand, Les Parfums Chanel set up production during the war at the factory in New Jersey and carefully doled out the precious supply of French floral essences that were soon nearly impossible to obtain. What mattered most was that jasmine from Grasse, which naturally contained "eighty kinds of aldehydes, [and was] unique in the world." Without it, Chanel No. 5 simply would not have been the same.

The partners' daring coup in Grasse meant that Chanel No. 5 was poised to become even more famous. Crucially, it was one of the few—and perhaps the only—fabled French perfume of the 1930s still able to continue production at the highest levels of quality. At least as long as those supplies of jasmine lasted. Where the concrete to make Chanel No. 5 came from late in the war is another one of those tantalizing puzzles. Those seven hundred pounds were enough to produce perhaps 350,000 small bottles of the celebrated *parfum*, and sales figures of any kind remain a company secret. But given the immense celebrity that Chanel No. 5 had during the six years of the war, it's difficult to believe that the partners sold fewer than sixty thousand bottles a year. That means, of course, that the jasmine supplies somehow needed to be replenished. Perhaps it kept coming from those plantations in Grasse. The black market flourished across occupied Europe, and the truth is that anything could be obtained if someone were willing to pay enough for it—and to take a high-stakes gamble.

All we know for certain is that the prodigious sales of this perfume during the 1940s depended, according to someone who knew Coco Chanel, on one simple fact: that "No. 5 [was] probably the only perfume whose quality remained the same throughout the war." This, in turn, meant that Chanel No. 5 would become, in an era of rationing and making-do, the ultimate symbol of luxury.

T he future of No. 5 secure, at least for the moment, the partners did show fiscal restraint during the war. Importing hundreds of pounds of contraband jasmine and opening new factories in Hoboken took considerable resources, and the partners at Les Parfums Chanel understood that any resources they had left in France—especially real-estate properties—were almost certainly going to be confiscated. Expenses needed to be curtailed. One of the cuts they made was to the advertising budget.

The large-scale campaign that began in 1934—the first coordinated campaign to feature Chanel No. 5 as *the* Chanel fragrance— was scaled back in the early 1940s. Once again, it was a decision that leaves the marketing men wondering. It wasn't the industry norm at that moment. Perfume advertisements from the period show that other fragrance manufacturers were advertising aggressively, and companies like Yardley, Elizabeth Arden, Helena Rubenstein— and Coty—championed their products intensively during the war. Adding to the competition was a new breed of savvy American competitors. For the first time, fine fragrances were being manufactured in the United States, which still represented the world's largest luxury market.

There had been talk at the beginning of the war of how the partners were preparing to launch a "vast publicity campaign to showcase No. 5." In 1939 and 1940, there *had* been a flurry of significant advertising. By 1941, however, all that had been cut back dramatically, and the archives of 1943 and 1944 don't contain the record of even a single advertisement. Perhaps that was because the partners at Les Parfums Chanel soon realized that it simply wasn't necessary.

There was almost no print advertising. Yet, from 1940 to 1945, perfume sales in the United States increased tenfold; once again without a great deal of expensive advertising, Chanel No. 5 flourished.

That was because the partners at Les Parfums Chanel had a second stunning entrepreneurial insight that may have been the reason they decided pouring hundreds of thousands of advertising dollars into promoting Chanel No. 5 was superfluous. It was so simple. It was beautiful, really. One single brilliant insight, more than anything else, transformed Chanel No. 5 from being simply the world's best-selling perfume into a "goddamned cultural monument."

The partners' new plan in New York was to negotiate distribution of the fragrance through the United States Army, where it was sold tax-free through the military commissaries around the world during the war, along with other luxury products and basic supplies.

Selling a luxury product through the commissary post exchange—known to a generation of veterans simply as the "PX"—was a potentially risky strategy, however. The sales through the commissaries might easily have destroyed the prestige of the product, because Chanel No. 5 would be sitting there on the shelves with chocolate bars and soap powder. There was something five-and-dime about it.

In the beginning, however, that might have been part of the attraction to some of the partners at Les Parfums Chanel. Théophile Bader, who still held an important 20 percent share in the company, had won his immense fortune not in the fragrance business but as the owner of the prestigious Galeries Lafayette, one of France's largest department stores. By the early 1930s, he was leading the way in introducing a wider model to France with popular new *prix-unique* chains like Monoprix and the now-forgotten Lanoma. The world of consumer sales was changing, and the partners at Les Parfums Chanel weren't shy about embracing this new model of innovation. With the introduction of the small and less prohibitively expensive purse-sized flacons, they had been reaching out to the middle-class consumer since the late 1920s. It was the natural evolution of a strategy to do precisely what they had promised in the beginning: to bring the Chanel perfumes to a wide international market. But it was a risk. The trading-post style of the commissary didn't evoke the image of luxury and high fashion.

The partners at Les Parfums Chanel went ahead anyhow. And in the 1940s, they were proven right. Mass marketing Chanel No. 5 didn't destroy the prestige of the fragrance. Instead, it transformed Chanel No. 5 into a symbol of everything that had been lost and everything those soldiers and their girls at home, all those nurses on the front lines, hoped still might be saved. It was part of a world before the war, a world of glamour and beauty that somehow had survived. It became the ultimate symbol of France, part of what everyone was fighting for. In an oral history of World War II, one American wartime nurse later remembered that it was one of the few souvenirs she brought back home with her. "I couldn't bring back an awful lot," she said. But there was one thing she treasured: "Chanel, you know, the perfume."

In the end, No. 5's continued success was contingent upon some-how maintaining the quality of the perfume, and that depended, as the partners had known all along, on the rare plant materials from Grasse. It remained a luxury even as all other comforts of living vanished, and this status as a luxury—as something untouched by this era of losses—was part of the magic and the desire. It was this idea of making the perfume available through the United States Army, though, that catapulted the fragrance to a new level of cul-tural celebrity. Like the perfume itself—a balance of sexy florals and fresh-scrubbed aldehydes—it was the embodiment of an essential contradiction: something at once completely familiar and exclusively luxurious. At another moment, where and how Chanel No. 5 was sold might have mattered more. In fact, in time, it would matter crucially. During the chaotic years of the Second World War, how-ever, quality trumped venue effortlessly. No one expected to find opulent boutiques and glitzy showrooms in a war zone.

Given how expensive it had become to maintain Chanel No. 5's quality, however, the partners needed to raise funds to open that new production facility and resume advertising. Their competitor Estée Lauder in the beginning even helped the brothers—now busily developing their satellite American corporation called Chanel, Inc.—to finance it.

More than that, though, the partners were going to need to fight to retain control of Les Parfums Chanel. Before fleeing France in the spring of 1940, they had already taken important preparatory steps by doing something that demonstrated even greater powers of intuition. The Jewish partners of Les Parfums Chanel had sold their shares of the business to a daredevil pilot and industrialist named Félix Amiot. Needless to say, they hadn't asked Coco Chanel's permission. They had already been engaged in a private war with her for half a decade. They had no trouble imagining to what lengths she was prepared to go in Paris.

FOURTEEN
COCO AT WAR

Back in Paris, Coco Chanel was getting ready to play a deep and dirty game of business and politics. Determinedly at war with her exiled partners, she saw an opportunity.

Under the laws of the Third Reich, Jewish property was subject to confiscation, and her partners at Les Parfums Chanel were Jewish. It was her chance to break the contract she had signed giving up her rights to control the fragrance business. In fact, it was a chance to take over Les Parfums Chanel altogether.

She might have resorted to such tactics in time regardless, but it was the sale of Les Parfums Chanel in October of 1940 that set Coco Chanel hurtling into motion. The ownership of a 70 percent stake in the company—the controlling share, she couldn't help but notice—had now passed into the hands of Félix Amiot, who was both French and, more important, Aryan. She knew that sale was just an illusion.

The occupying German forces, along with their French administrative collaborators, suspected that it was just an illusion, too. Perhaps there were whispered rumors about the massive bribes Félix

Amiot reputedly paid to grease the wheels of this particular transaction. In the next few months there was a full-scale investigation, and it was in all the newspapers. Amiot was hauled in for questioning by storm troopers, who warned him bluntly what everyone suspected: "You have bought the Bourjois and Chanel perfumeries. But it's just a compliance sale. The Wertheimers are your friends and associates. You are their front man. This is naïve and dangerous for you."

Coco Chanel couldn't resist seizing the opportunity. On May 5, 1941, she wrote a letter, addressed to the provisional administrator—the man charged with determining who would receive business property left by anyone who had fled France. Parfums Chanel, she explained, was worth more than four million francs—over seventy million dollars in today's numbers—and "it is still the property of Jews." It had been, she claimed, legally "abandoned" by the owners.

She knew it had been abandoned under the terms of the statutes, because she had presided in the partners' absence over the Les Parfums Chanel board meeting where she had passed just such a resolution. She attempted to install a man named Georges Madoux as the temporary head of the company. He had worked until 1931 as the commercial director at Les Parfums Chanel and had later maintained close connections with Coco's couture house. Now, in his role as a government agent, Madoux had been charged with reassigning ownership of Jewish businesses. He was in her pocket, and, unsurprisingly, it was his assessment that "the company of Parfums Chanel is still a Jewish business." As one historian puts it, Coco Chanel and the administrator "appreciated each other."

Since the stated mission of the administrator's office was to cede property of this sort "to Aryan subjects," she was writing to ask for complete ownership of the company. "I have," she wrote, "an indisputable right of priority . . . the profits that I have received from my creations since the foundation of this business . . . are disproportionate . . . [and] you can help to repair in part the prejudices that I have suffered in the course of these last seventeen years." She still thought of Pierre Wertheimer, in particular, as "that bandit who screwed me."

What Coco Chanel sought was for the government of occupied France to annul the recent sale of the company to an Aryan other than herself. But the partners at Les Parfums Chanel were smart, and they were businessmen. They understood what the laws of wartime France meant, and, anticipating this maneuver before it was too late, they had worked out a solution. They had sold the company to Amiot before they ever left France, although Coco Chanel hadn't known that. He had agreed to hold it for them during the war. As early as May 1, 1940, "any presence of Pierre and Paul [Wertheimer] in the capital of the company had *officially* disappeared." In order to backdate the stock transfers that would "ma[k]e indisputable the purchase of the business," they probably had to bribe German officials, but they had managed it.

Félix Amiot was loyal to the partners at Les Parfums Chanel, but he was hardly a model of virtue either. As one historian summarizes it, the Wertheimer family:

> bought almost 50 percent of an airplane propeller company run by a French engineer (and an Aryan) named Félix Amiot. When Chanel betrayed them, the Wertheimers signed Les Parfums Chanel over to Amiot, a collaborator who sold arms to the Nazis. . . . When the war was over, Amiot gave the company back to the Wertheimers; helping them "saved his little neck" from the revenge-seeking Allies, Alain Wertheimer told *Forbes.*

In the end, the sale survived. The German investigator, a certain Herr Blanke, decided that Les Parfums Chanel could not be considered a Jewish business. Coco Chanel had lost another battle with her partners. The government—encouraged by a well-placed inducement or two, almost certainly—upheld the new ownership of the company, finding that "the perfume company of Bourjois [of which Les Parfums Chanel was a part] has passed to Aryan hands in a manner that is legal and correct." It was a transfer dated to to the first months of 1941. Even then, not everyone in occupied France was content to let the matter rest. In February of 1942, the case was reopened, and Félix Amiot was once again subjected to a long interrogation. In fact, his position throughout the war must have been precarious. He was allowed to run Les Parfums Chanel and to sell No. 5 throughout the Third Reich, despite suspicions. But who knows what was demanded of him. Perhaps unsurprisingly, that was the year Bourjois perfumes released in New York a new fragrance: Courage. Whatever his other sins, Amiot had stood by his old friends in America steadfastly.

Coco Chanel had tried to play dirty, and, surprisingly, given how the deck was rigged during those years, she still lost. The amazing thing is that she didn't lose a great deal more, because, as the war drew to a close in the summer of 1944, her position was growing increasingly tenuous also.

No one who lived in Paris in 1944 would ever forget how that summer ended, if only because the city's inhabitants could still remember the uninhibited, alcohol-soaked years before the war, when flappers danced the Charleston late into the night, women smoked cigarettes, and there were boozy drives along the winding back roads of the French Riviera. These years—the 1920s—had been known as *les années folles*—the crazy years—and they had seemed to promise so much at the time.

All that seemed like the distant past now, because the real crazy years had been the decades that followed. First had come the Great Depression, which had tempered the hedonism of the 1920s, and then a second terrible world conflict that destroyed it altogether. Here in the final year of that war, Paris remained occupied, and life under Nazi rule was cruel and unpredictable. Yet in the nightclubs, Édith Piaf still belted out sultry love songs, brothels were doing a fabulous business, and in the palatial Ritz Hotel on the Place Vendôme the party went on. Whatever else happened beyond its walls, at the Ritz there was still champagne on ice until it all ended.

By August of 1944, the wait was nearly over. The liberation began on August 19, Coco Chanel's sixty-first birthday. The week before, there had been rumors that the Allies were advancing on Paris, and, fearing an uprising of the local resistance, the Germans rounded up several thousand suspected French activists and loaded them on the final convoy of trains sent creeping from the industrial western suburbs of Pantin to the concentration camp at Buchenwald. The trains left not much more than a stone's throw from some of the city's renowned factories, including, coincidentally, the Bourjois factory where Chanel No. 5 had been produced for decades. In the last days of the war, Théophile Bader's son-in-law, Max Heilbronn, was on one of them. It was a cruel irony: Parfums Chanel was a company his family had helped to found, but under the laws of Nazi-occupied France it could no longer officially be theirs to manage. Its *usine* must have been one of the last things he saw that day in Paris.

Meanwhile, the battle in Paris began in the streets, fought by the other thousands of men and women of the French Résistance, part of the underground Forces of the French Interior—known colloquially as the FFI, or "fifi." For five days, Paris was an urban war zone. Finally, on the warm Thursday morning of August 25, the sound of gunfire stopped. Out of the silence, the ringing bells of the cathedral of Notre Dame echoed over the Seine. As the Allies gained control of one neighborhood after another, the other distant bells were added to the chorus. Soon everyone knew that the Germans had surrendered.

As those in Paris that night remembered, what came after was simply the world's greatest party, and the French "swept the [soldiers] into their arms, dancing, singing, often making love to them. . . . The lovemaking was so widespread that a Catholic group hastily ran off tracts addressed to Paris's young women," pleading with them to remember their virtue. It was all in vain. After years of living in an occupied city, restrained celebrations were the last thing on anyone's mind.

In fact, many of the city's inhabitants had long ago jettisoned sexual discretion. Only one-in-four Parisian residents had enough food during those years, but nobody could ration life's most simple pleasures. On the streets of occupied Paris throughout the war, Frenchwomen watched as scantily clad German soldiers performed daily calisthenics in the city's parks, and, small surprise, there were tens of thousands of war babies. Some have called the occupation not the crazy years but *les années érotiques*—the erotic years—instead.

Ernest Hemingway would always claim that he was among the soldiers who personally liberated the bar at the Ritz Hotel that summer day. He was there as a war correspondent, writing for *Collier's* magazine, and, when the bells began ringing throughout Paris, what he remembered was the hard-drinking life of youthful abandon, when he and F. Scott Fitzgerald and a generation of American expatriates had imagined the city as their playground. On this of all days, he wanted to celebrate with a cocktail at the Ritz. When he arrived, the Germans were already in retreat, however, so he fired a few rounds of gunfire from the roof, freed from their imprisonment in the cellars several good bottles of Bordeaux, and made his way to the bar, where he greeted his old friend Bertin, the bartender, whose dry martinis were legendary.

From the bar at the Ritz Hotel, the view faced onto rue Cambon, where, at number 31, everyone knew they could find one of France's most famous landmarks: the flagship boutique of Coco Chanel. In those heady days, as soldiers poured into the capital and the American troops liberated Paris, "there was one souvenir of the city they all wanted. An average G.I. only had to enter a perfumery and hold up five fingers, to buy Chanel's classic." Later, one British newspaper journalist claimed, "Not only was it the only French perfume the American G.I. had ever heard of, it was the only one he could pronounce." At the end of the First World War, French perfume had first become a souvenir symbolizing victory and elegance. At the end of the Second World War, it was simply Chanel No. 5 that everyone wanted. A year later, even the American president, Harry S. Truman, went looking for it. In a letter to his wife, Bess, written from Potsdam, Germany, in 1945, he wrote that he had purchased for her many pretty souvenirs—but he was sorry, he couldn't find her anywhere a bottle of Chanel No. 5.

In the months to come, Coco would discover why Chanel No. 5 had become something even an American First Lady coveted. The reason would make her wildly furious. That night, however, she had other things on her mind. At the Ritz Hotel in the days after the liberation, it was a scene of joy and wine and drunken celebration. Although she lived upstairs, Coco Chanel was not among the revelers. She hated the war and was glad that it was over. She loved France and its culture. But she was also proud, and, like a good number of other women in Paris, she had reason to be just a little bit worried.

Before the celebrations had even ended, *les épurations*—the purges—began, and from the beginning it was a kind of wild and indiscriminate vigilante justice. Those who had helped the Germans during the occupation were attacked by mobs and sometimes summarily executed in the streets. In those weeks after the war ended, as many as twenty thousand women were accused of "horizontal collaboration"—of having slept with the enemy. As punishment, their heads were shaved, and their identity cards were revised to list their occupation as prostitutes. They were then forced to walk, barefoot and often stripped naked, through the streets of Paris, reviled and ridiculed, with swastikas marked on their foreheads.

It was whispered that Christiane, the daughter of Coco Chanel's old friend and now archrival, François Coty, was among those brutalized. Although Coty's grandson, Henri, had fought for the

French resistance and was deported to the camp at Buchenwald at the end of the war for his efforts, what people remembered were the politics of her father. Before his death in the 1930s, François Coty had purchased controlling shares in two newspapers, *L'Ami du Peuple* and *Le Figaro*, and he used both as bully pulpits for his pro-fascist and anti-Semitic principles. They were painful times, and Christiane Coty was just one among thousands targeted.

You could have seen much of it from the windows of the Ritz Hotel, and Coco Chanel, whether she wanted to believe it yet or not, had a problem. Christiane Coty had been humiliated on the grounds that she had simply socialized with German officers—not unlikely, since the Coty mansion on Avenue Raphaël in Paris had been requisitioned as the personal residence of one of Hitler's generals, Hans von Boineburg, during the war.

If Christiane Coty had appeared too tolerant of the occupiers, Coco Chanel had fallen in love with one of them, an elegant and well-connected gentleman. His name was Hans Günther von Dincklage, and he was a German officer of the fascist regime and probably a spy, and, of course, also Coco Chanel's wartime companion. Some say they met by chance in the lobby of the Ritz Hotel in the summer of 1941, which had already been taken over by the Germans, and that the affair had begun when she asked him to help to arrange the safety of one of her nephews. Others insist that she had known him for years and been his lover before the war began. Whatever the case, she was in the good graces of the Germans, and Chanel No. 5 was sold freely throughout the Third Reich.

Now, after the liberation, Coco Chanel had no idea where Hans von Dincklage was, and all she could think to do in the days that followed was to ask a German-American soldier if perhaps he would help her. He was a fresh-faced G.I., and she guessed that his knowledge of the German language might mean he would be assigned in the coming days to intelligence and interrogation. She was looking for someone, a friend, she told him. If he ever found him among the prisoners of war, would he be kind enough to let her know. All the young man ever needed to do was to send a postcard. Address it simply to Coco Chanel, The Ritz Hotel, Paris. It would reach her. As thanks, she did the only thing she could imagine. She filled his duffel bag with bottle after bottle of her Chanel No. 5 perfume. With it, he could buy anything on the black markets. It was as good as giving him gold and worth a small fortune.

For days, Coco kept to herself, and all was quiet. Then, one day in early September came the inevitable knock on the door of her room at the Ritz. There were officers waiting, agents of the purges. She was, in the idiom of the time, a suspected *collabo*, and they asked that she come along for interrogation. When friends had warned her that the liaison with von Dincklage was dangerous, she had indignantly dismissed them. His mother, she insisted, was English. If he were a double agent, that might have mattered. All that mattered now at the end of the war was that von Dincklage was a German and an officer. What if he was German, she insisted. She couldn't see how it mattered. At her age, she wryly announced, when she had the chance of a lover she was hardly going to inspect a man's passport. About his politics, she never commented.

The possibility of being paraded through the streets as a collaborator and whore was grim enough, but Chanel was, in fact, in far greater danger. She had done more during those years than simply carry on a romance with a German officer in Nazi-occupied Paris. Just that past spring, in April of 1943, when there were whispers of talks between Germany and the Allies, she had traveled to Berlin with von Dincklage and played a high-stakes game of what she considered covert diplomacy. There she met with Theodore Mumm, an S.S. officer named Schiebe, and Walter Friedrich Schellenberg—the powerful German officer best known to history for his memoirs of Nazi Germany, written after his conviction for war crimes. Declassified documents show that Coco returned to Berlin again in December of 1943. Remembering those meetings, Mumm later declared that she had "a drop of the blood of Joan of Arc in her veins." From her perspective, she was trying to help broker a separate peace between Germany and Britain. With emotions running high in Paris, a wartime trip to Berlin might have looked to others like treason.

And even that wasn't everything. There had also been that spring an ugly complication involving the German gestapo and Coco's former employee Vera Lombardi, an Englishwoman with connections to the royal Windsor family. Vera's husband was an Italian colonel now in fascist custody, and, thinking she would help the situation, Coco Chanel worked some high-level German contacts and—according to top secret memos sent between the United States government and the office of Winston Churchill—deliberately exaggerated her old friend's use to German intelligence. Coco may have seen this as assistance, but, after her interrogation at the hands of the Gestapo, Vera saw things in a starkly different light. She wrote to Churchill, a family relation, that summer protesting Coco's treachery.

All this seems to have caused a lot of trouble. And it's hard to know precisely who was playing whom. Vera might have had some good reasons for wondering if she was a pawn in a larger game. Or perhaps she was involved in some ugly covert "diplomacy" herself. The British and American governments wondered about it and her possible fascist sympathies in some of those memos. At any rate, in order to establish contact with Churchill, Coco had the idea that Vera would help, and it seems that, when Vera refused, von Dincklage may have been the one who thought to have her arrested. It was a diplomatic and personal disaster.

Undoubtedly, this was part of what those officers on her doorstep wanted to ask Coco about in the weeks after the liberation of Paris. The United States and British governments both wanted to get to the bottom of the matter, too, but the final report was never more than ambiguous. Vera's own politics, the Americans decided, were dubious. But she did have a good reason to be angry with her old friend Coco: "Madame Chanel," the report reads, "apparently instigated the special facilities afforded by the German Gestapo to Madame Lombardi."

In the end, Coco Chanel was questioned and released. In fact, the officers of the purges got an extraordinary instruction. Mademoiselle Chanel was to be allowed to leave immediately. It was an order from the highest level. At the time, no one ever quite understood how it happened. For many years, there were two stories that told how she managed her release. Files in the British Foreign Office were mistakenly declassified for a brief window, and those who saw them say they hint that Coco Chanel knew dangerous and embarrassing state secrets about aristocratic British collaboration. There were said to be grim secrets about the political compromises made by the Windsor family, in particular. Some say that it was Winston Churchill himself who negotiated Chanel's freedom. A decade later, people in Paris also speculated that Churchill—Coco Chanel's next-door neighbor during summers on the Riviera—had sent a chauffeured limousine to police headquarters personally to fetch her, and the driver headed straight for the Swiss border. There was even a story that he made sure that Hans von Dincklage was in that car with her.

It is actually all quite likely. That autumn after the end of the war, Churchill followed the investigation into Coco's wartime imbroglio carefully, and, in the end, despite the "suspicious circumstances"— her meeting with Nazi leaders in Berlin and the Vera Lombardi fiasco included—he seems to have believed that she was not an active collaborator.

The other story of Coco's escape from the purges, however, is almost as astonishing, and there is also likely to be some truth in it. In the words of one British intelligence officer with the government's notoriously secretive M16 division, Coco Chanel did something even cannier. With her legendary sense of timing, it seems that she had hedged her bets thoroughly in the first hours of the purges. "By one of those majestically simple strokes which made Napoleon [sic] so successful as a general," the anonymous agent reported, "she just put an announcement in the window of her emporium that scent was free for G.I.s, who thereupon queued up to get bottles of Chanel No. 5, and would have been outraged if the French police had touched a hair of her head." It was a time of vastly complicated loyalties—and desires.

After her release from interrogation, Coco had the sense to hedge her bets further. She set up a new life for herself in Swiss exile, where one way or another Hans von Dincklage—known to friends by the nickname Spatz, or "sparrow"—joined her. There, in Switzerland's famously neutral banks, some of her wartime profits from Chanel No. 5 were safely deposited.

Despite the fact that Coco Chanel's personal reputation at the end of the war was pretty well in tatters, Chanel No. 5 had become, in the space of less than four or five years, one of the most potent icons of the century. More than just a popular and bestselling perfume, it became during the Second World War a powerful cultural symbol. That, after all, is the story behind the words of that British intelligence officer. It is what the duffel bag of that young German-American G.I. also tells us. It is what Harry S. Truman's letter to Bess testifies. Long before the end of the war, Chanel No. 5 was a commodity exchangeable for anything.

Consider how deeply that irony also resonates. Chanel No. 5 encapsulates some of the last century's most complex tensions. It was a perfume produced and distributed by a partnership of Jewish families living as entrepreneurial refugees in New York City. It bore the name of an apparently anti-Semitic fashion designer who spent the war living with a German lover and who tried to use the laws of Nazi-occupied France to strip her partners of their investment. It was a luxury coveted by fascist officers and American G.I.s alike, and neither side cared much about the story of its origins, because in so many ways it had already slipped free of its inventor. It was sold in army commissaries and everywhere on the black market, and it lost none of its glamour and allure. It was as valuable as gold or whiskey

American soldiers in front of 31 rue Cambon in 1945
to buy the perfume Chanel No. 5.

or cigarettes all across Europe, and it emerged from the war with a new identity. This was all largely thanks to those countless young soldiers on both sides of the conflict.

n fact, of all the images that speak to what Chanel No. 5 had become by the end of the Second World War, the most articulate is an old snapshot. It's a black-and-white photograph, taken in the days after the liberation of Paris. In it, some of those fresh-faced young men, in their crisp uniforms, smile shyly at the camera. They are waiting—as German and American and British young men waited all throughout the war—in a long line on a narrow sidewalk along rue Cambon. Their destination is the Chanel boutique in Paris, and the soldiers—by 1945, they are, of course, American—are there to buy just one thing: a bottle of No. 5. It didn't matter if they didn't speak even a single word of French that summer. All it took was raising five fingers. It had always been the perfume with the famous number.

What the photograph says is only this: a generation of consumers had mapped onto the perfume the essence of their hopes and desires, which gave it an intensely personal meaning. Chanel No. 5 had a life of its own precisely because it had an intimate place in the lives of others. Oddly, though, the one person to struggle with a connection to the perfume was the woman whose identity was perhaps most inextricably tied to it. Despite everything that had happened during the war, no one paid much attention to what Coco Chanel was doing because her signature scent had broken free from her. What had begun as something deeply personal had become a broad cultural icon that told the story of millions. Symbolically, as well as literally, it just wasn't her business anymore. For Coco Chanel this was a crucial psychological turning point.

Recognizing that Chanel No. 5 had a life of its own didn't mean Coco Chanel stopped taking her conflict with the partners at Les Parfums Chanel personally, however. Coco identified deeply with the perfume, and part of her loved it. After the war, though, she came to see the entire situation as monstrous. She now understood that she had lost control of it for good—and she was prepared to change her strategy dramatically. She might not have the right to manage the product, but that didn't mean she couldn't harm it. It was the only power left to her, and, by the beginning of 1945, she was in a white fury and prepared to cause no end of trouble.

FIFTEEN

COCO PLAYS THE NUMBERS

Her hope was to market mass confusion.

There are rumors in the world of fragrance collecting, every so often, of something special coming up for auction: a bottle of vintage Chanel perfume with a bright red label. Most often it's Chanel No. 1. Sometimes it's a bottle of Chanel No. 2 or No. 31. New initiates each time ask the same question: Is it authentic? The answer comes back that, yes, those bottles are real. And Coco Chanel was behind them.

From her exile in Switzerland, Coco Chanel started making plans for a new line of signature perfumes, provocatively sold with names that were numbers. One scent deliberately replicated her world-famous iconic formula. It was the fame of Chanel No. 5 that she was after. Not only did she plan to launch her own new formulas, she also began a whisper campaign among her well-placed friends and the denizens of high society, running down the reputation of her famous fragrance. Her object: "to create total confusion among her haute-couture clients, her friends, and the distributors of the authentic Chanel No. 5."

That was the only way, after all, that she could think to force the partners at Les Parfums Chanel to renegotiate. She was furious when she learned, belatedly, that *her* signature fragrance—the scent of her youth and memories and private history—had been produced during the war in the United States.

Now, it seems astonishing that she didn't know it, but, then again, during the occupation, the German government had encouraged the continued production of some French luxury goods as part of an effort to put a positive spin on life in Nazi France. Joseph Goebbels, in charge of Hitler's propaganda efforts, put out a directive: Paris would be "gay and animated," filled with art, music, and entertainment. The fashion houses, in particular, would remain open. Surprisingly, Coco Chanel was one of the few designers who refused to cooperate.

She obviously knew that Chanel No. 5 was for sale. She sold it from her boutique on rue Cambon, presumably from stocks provided by the "new" Parfums Chanel operation, under the Aryan directorship of Félix Amiot. During his tenure, Chanel No. 5 was legally sold and distributed in all territories under the control of the Third Reich, and it remained a bestseller.

She knew that there were production facilities throughout the war in Britain, even after the Bourjois factory on Queen's Way in Croydon was destroyed in a terrible air raid in the summer of 1940. She knew that the production of her signature perfume continued, although on a reduced wartime scale, in Pantin. Perhaps the factory in Pantin even managed to get its own supplies of that rare jasmine from Grasse. During the war, the production of prestigious luxury goods was especially encouraged, as a simple matter of pleasure and propaganda. After all, "after the defeat of France," writes one historian, "Germany received a supply of luxury goods such as she had not seen for years. Soldiers on leave in Paris and other French towns sent home silk stockings, perfumes, wines, and women's clothing of a far superior quality to anything that German austerity had produced."

Coco Chanel learned of the American manufacture of Chanel

No. 5 through the profits. When the partners returned to France after the war to reclaim their business properties and resume production, they also brought back a souvenir for Coco Chanel: the passbook to a Swiss bank account, where they had deposited her share of the wartime profits for sales of Chanel No. 5 perfume, distributed from the United States through the branch corporation, Chanel, Inc. It was $15,000—today worth a cool million dollars.

Coco Chanel, now living in exile with Hans von Dincklage, was not happy. Not only did the complex arrangement between Les Parfums Chanel and Chanel Inc. mean that from the sales of Chanel No. 5 in the United States she received only 10 percent of a 10 percent dividend, but she hadn't been aware of the American production of the perfume at all. This fact alone infuriated her. "It is monstrous," she insisted. "They produced it in Hoboken!" It made no difference to her that the materials had come from France. Or perhaps she simply didn't believe it.

Despite the fabulous sales that it generated, Coco Chanel was also horrified to learn that the partners at Les Parfums Chanel had arranged distribution through the United States Army. To her, it didn't seem appropriately exclusive. The problem was one of commoditization: "From Miami to Anchorage, from Naples to Berlin, from Manila to Tokyo, next to milk chocolate, cigarettes, and pantyhose, No. 5 attracted the G.I.s when they made their tax-free purchases in the exchange posts and military department stores." It was the beginning of the duty-free business model that today sustains fragrance sales internationally, and it had made Coco Chanel a very rich woman. In her private war with the Wertheimers, though, she now declared, "We need to get our weapons . . . and I have some!"

The weapons she meant were some new perfumes. At first, she threatened to produce a scent simply called Mademoiselle Chanel No. 5, and she planned to launch new versions as well of Ernest Beaux's scents Bois des Îles (1926) and Cuir de Russie (1928), which she would market with the words "Mademoiselle Chanel" simply added in front of them. Her lawyers advised her that this was entirely illegal under the terms of her contract with Les Parfums Chanel. So, she produced instead perfumes that she called Mademoiselle Chanel No. 1, No. 2, and No. 31.

She may have first started producing these Mademoiselle Chanel scents before the war had ended. Faced with shortages of Chanel No. 5—a mere twenty bottles a day—and an insatiable demand among the German soldiers in occupied Paris, any savvy entrepreneur would have begun looking for ways to augment her product line. Why not add some new Chanel perfumes to the offerings at the boutique on rue Cambon?

Under the terms of the contract with the partners at Les Parfums Chanel, she had always reserved the right to sell other fragrance products from her shops; so as long as there was no distribution it was technically legal. While perfume production in France during the war was difficult—and Félix Amiot is unlikely to have helped her—some of the factories in Switzerland continued to fabricate fragrance materials in the 1940s. Just outside Zürich, for example, in the village of Dübendorf, a small perfumery called Chemische Fabrik Flora stayed open, and it produced some of the same materials that were used in Chanel No. 5. Whether or not Coco Chanel worked with Flora directly, she had contact with someone in the perfume industry near Zürich, because her right to produce the fragrances there later became a bone of contention.

At any rate, by the autumn of 1945 the Mademoiselle Chanel perfumes were readily available for sale in her elegant salon on rue Cambon. An American G.I. named Steven Summers bought bottles of the red-label perfumes—and of the original Chanel No. 5—on a series of weekend leaves in Paris. They were gifts for his girl back home, and they were relatively expensive gifts, too. He paid about five dollars each—more than sixty dollars a bottle—for flasks of what he listed indiscriminately simply as Chanel No. 5, Chanel No. 22, Chanel No. 1, and Chanel No. 31.

Mademoiselle Chanel No. 31 was one of Coco Chanel's personal favorites, and—jettisoning for the first time Chanel No. 5 as her signature scent—became the perfume she reserved for private use. This mossy, green scent with jasmine and roses went on to become, after some reformulation by perfumer Henri Robert, "the celebrated No. 19" fragrance, named after the date of her birthday in August and launched commercially by Les Parfums Chanel just before her death in the early 1970s. Smelling it, the scent once prompted Coco Chanel to remark, "A perfume ought to punch you right on the nose . . . I'm not going to sniff for three days to see if it smells or not? It has to have body, and what gives a perfume body is the most expensive thing there is." She meant, of course, the heavy doses of those exquisite and expensive floral materials from Grasse, the heart of her perfumes.

Abandoning Chanel No. 5 as her signature scent was a key turning point for the woman who had created it. She needed to think of herself as free of it, and she had found an important way of signaling this. The first of these new perfumes—Mademoiselle Chanel No. 1—was a direct assault on Chanel No. 5. She boasted that it was the scent of Chanel No. 5—"but even better."

Coco Chanel knew perfectly well that distributing these red-label perfumes—even without the number five on them—was illegal. The terms of the 1924 contract had stipulated clearly that she reserved the right to sell the perfumes bearing her name from her boutiques only. She could have those scents made privately, but she was the only one who could carry them. That meant there was no point in advertising, at least not in the normal way. If the only place that she was free to sell these new scents was from her boutique in Paris, then she just wasn't going to be able to cause the kind of uproar she desired. And by 1945, she was definitely looking to bring matters with the partners at Les Parfums Chanel to a point of crisis.

The other option, of course, was simple. She could distribute her new red-label scents in defiance of her contract with Les Parfums

Chanel. Let them sue her, she thought. She welcomed the publicity. In fact, Coco Chanel was counting on the fact that, even if she lost the inevitable lawsuit, she would be able to do massive damage to the perfume's reputation. Selling her Mademoiselle fragrance collection was only a secondary goal in any of this. Her first concern was undermining Chanel No. 5 and the partners at Les Parfums Chanel, with an eye toward forcing them to revisit the terms of that contract.

The assault started one afternoon in the office of René de Chambrun, when she arrived with a collection of bottles and informed him that they were for Madame de Chambrun. Remembering the success of her whisper-campaign launch of Chanel No. 5 from her fashion house in 1922, she wanted to know what his fashionable wife, Josée, thought of them. She planned to start by creating some high-society buzz about Coco Chanel's new perfumes, and she would tell everyone that Chanel No. 5 was poor quality and that these were better Chanel fragrances, more authentic. She also planned to start international distribution.

Knowing something was afoot, Chambrun's first response was to call an unnamed Russian chemist and perfumer at Coty to find out what Coco Chanel had been up to. "When he came in," the lawyer remembered, "I showed him the samples. He smelled and went into a trance; overcome with emotion, he shouted: 'Fabulous! Wonder of wonders! It is No. 5, but even better!'" Coco Chanel was happy to confirm it—and to raise the price point accordingly.

She wanted to have the perfumes made in Switzerland, and she planned to sell them from her boutique in Paris. She also fully intended to sell them in America. It wasn't legal, but this wasn't a point that much concerned her. She considered that the partners at Les Parfums Chanel had already voided the initial terms of the contract. There had also been a clause guaranteeing that only perfumes that she deemed sufficiently luxurious could be sold under her name, and, although Chanel No. 5 was, in fact, one of the rare

French perfumes that managed to maintain its quality during those years, thanks in part to the partners' foresight in stockpiling materials from Grasse, that certainly wasn't her opinion of their wartime manufacture at a plant in New Jersey. As far as she was concerned, the entire deal would have to be renegotiated. Obviously, she expected it would be to her advantage, and these new perfumes were a way of forcing the partners' hand. Essentially, they would need to pay to stop her from damaging the reputation of Chanel No. 5.

What Coco Chanel planned to do was wreak utter havoc on the ability of Les Parfums Chanel to market Chanel No. 5 effectively. Her goal was to create as much uncertainty as possible in the mind of the consumer, and, if it meant smearing the reputation of Chanel No. 5, she had no hesitation about doing so. In fact, she wanted it to be spread widely that Mademoiselle was unhappy with the quality of *her* fragrance being produced by the distributors and that she recommended no one buy it. She was producing them herself instead, for the most discriminating clients.

To get the word out, she began by working her old contacts in New York—all those friends she had made in the department store and fragrance industries during her trip to the United States in the 1930s. She had friends at Saks Fifth Avenue; she knew people like her old acquaintance Stanley Marcus, the entrepreneurial genius behind Neiman Marcus. These were the kind of men who ran businesses where postwar sales were flourishing. She had started at the Galeries Lafayette, and she knew how the game was played. She sent over shipments of the red-label perfumes, and the scents were briefly distributed and sold. As soon as the partners at Les Parfums Chanel learned what she was up to, however, they had the fragrances confiscated in the ports on arrival. So, instead, she started sending all her contacts in the New York business world free "samples."

She also filed a lawsuit, which was covered in papers around the world. The *New York Times* on June 3, 1946 reported, "The suit asks that the French parent concern [Les Parfums Chanel] be ordered to cease manufacture and sale of all products bearing the name and to restore to her the ownership and sole rights over the products, formulae and manufacturing process" on the grounds of "inferior quality." At stake, the journalist noted, were said to be annual sales of more than eight million dollars—$240 million today. It was a marketing nightmare. Here was the woman everyone thought of— legal contracts and business deals aside—as the creative force behind Chanel No. 5, saying the perfume was shoddy. There was no positive spin to put on it.

Her strategy was remarkably effective, but it was only because she was publicly attacking the quality of Chanel No. 5 and not because anyone imagined these red-label fragrances would ever compete with the original. Coco Chanel certainly didn't have the resources or expertise to compete with Bourjois, which had long been one of the largest fragrance companies in the world.

But the release of a "super Chanel No. 5" was bound to cause a stir, and a new version might easily have generated some serious interest. No. 5 was a scent that held great fascination for many. The relationship between Chanel No. 5 and Mademoiselle Chanel No. 1, however, was a tricky one. Coco Chanel knew that her new No. 1 was "super Chanel No. 5" for one simple reason. She'd convinced someone with access to the old Rallet No. 1 formula to create it.

Who was that rogue perfumer? Several sources speculate that it must have been Ernest Beaux. Like artists or musicians, perfumers leave silent signatures in a formula, and many fragrance experts believe that the similarities between Mademoiselle Chanel No. 1 and Chanel No. 5 are simply too close for it to be the work of anyone else. Chanel headquarters in Paris is certain, however, that whoever this person was, it simply wasn't their perfumer. It's a fair point, too: Ernest Beaux worked for Les Parfums Chanel and for Bourjois as the chief "nose," and, no matter how much he respected Coco Chanel for her savvy, his loyalties should have been to the company whose entire line of fragrances he managed—because Bourjois remained one of the industry's great powerhouses. Gilberte Beaux, Ernest's daughter-in-law, is equally confident that he wasn't the nose behind those fragrances, and her observation is also a good one. She remembers intimately, she says, how proud Ernest Beaux always was of his creation of Chanel No. 5 during the years that she knew him. He never would have done anything to harm the reputation of the scent that he considered his masterpiece. And undermining Chanel No. 5 was always part of Coco's threat behind those lawsuits and the red-label perfumes.

In the mid-1940s, however, only a handful of other people could have created Mademoiselle Chanel No. 1. The chemical analysis comparing the fragrance with Ernest Beaux's original scent, Rallet No. 1, is very straightforward. Someone definitely went back to the old formula—a formula that had been used to create at least one other "super Chanel No. 5"—Coty's L'Aimant. Although more modern than the original Rallet No. 1, Mademoiselle Chanel No. 1 was identifiably of the same concept, with the same floral heart of jasmine, May rose, and lily of the valley. Instead of the heady aldehydes, though, it had an overdose of the luscious powdery notes of synthetic orris—or iris-root powder.

Where was Ernest Beaux during the Second World War? That's the question that leaves curious perfume historians wondering. His friend Léon Givaudan—one of history's great innovators in the science of fragrance chemistry—was based in Zürich, Coco Chanel's home after the war, when she was filled with plans for those red labels. In fact, she was already having the perfumes manufactured there. That coincidence has given rise to a good deal of speculation. But Gilberte Beaux says that the answer to that question is a simple one: Ernest passed the war with his daughter and his wife in southern France, in the Vendée—a part of the country that remained unoccupied territory.

The other obvious candidate is a man named Vincent Roubert—or someone in his laboratory. He had created in 1946 one of the great orris fragrances in history, the long-discontinued and much-lamented Iris Gris. Since Roubert, the head perfumer at Coty, had also created L'Aimant, he would have been one of the few other men capable of creating a fragrance like Mademoiselle Chanel No. 1. The experts say, however, that the scent just doesn't bear his signature. Gilberte Beaux suggests one other possibility. Those years were difficult and complicated. It is not impossible that the formula for Chanel No. 5 simply found its way into circulation. The mystery of who created Coco Chanel's red-label perfumes has never been solved conclusively, but it is hard to imagine that Ernest Beaux would have willingly participated in any plan that tore down the prestige of a cherished accomplishment. Whoever crafted it, Mademoiselle Chanel No. 1 was a scent that won many admirers.

The curious thing is that, by 1946, Mademoiselle Chanel No. 1 wasn't the only version of Chanel No. 5 on the market. Its precursor, Rallet No. 1, was still in production as late as the end of the 1940s. Coty was still producing L'Aimant, the scent based on some version of Ernest Beaux's original formula, found in the archives when the Coty firm acquired Rallet in the 1920s. There was also, if the legend is true, Guerlain's Liù, developed in 1929 when the celebrated perfumer Jacques Guerlain was chagrined to learn that his wife was wearing Chanel No. 5. Plus, Les Parfums Chanel still sold its Chanel No. 22, that intensely aldehydic variation on the No. 5 theme. Now, with Mademoiselle Chanel No. 1, Coco Chanel had simply presented another option—the sixth scent like No. 5.

In late 1945 or early 1946, the partners at Les Parfums Chanel introduced a seventh version of the scent. Known as Chanel No. 46, it was released during that emblematic year of victory celebrations. It looked a lot like a return to the old strategy of proliferating fragrance options in the Parfums Chanel numbered lineup. This time, however, there were other complications to consider. Perhaps it was a clever hedge against Coco Chanel's wartime behavior. No one knew quite how the public would feel about Chanel No. 5 in light of Coco Chanel's politics and her choice, even now, of German romantic partners. For anyone who wanted the scent of the world's most famous perfume, Chanel No. 46 was the new postwar option. Among all the variations, it was another scent that imitated Chanel No. 5 very precisely. In the end, however, it existed only briefly.

None of these fragrances was, of course, an exact replica of Chanel No. 5. Each perfumer had taken the concept and worked to improve and reimagine it. Even with Chanel No. 46 there were significant modifications. Yet if they had been simple knockoffs, it hardly would have mattered. What all these new Chanel No. 5 versions testify to is the terrific celebrity of the original product. By the end of the Second World War, Chanel No. 5 was no longer just a perfume. It was a cultural icon, rich with a meaning and symbolism that had little to do any longer with the scent itself or with the woman who had first been inspired to produce it.

The partners at Les Parfums Chanel weren't worried, then, that Coco Chanel's red-label perfumes would compete with Chanel No. 5. It was already obvious that nothing could rival the fragrance. What they were worried about was Coco Chanel tearing down the prestige of the name. Part of that concern was for the damage she could do by stirring up worries about its quality. But the bigger part of their concern, it was said, was the damage she could do to the name of Chanel itself if her wartime story were laid bare to the international press. Said her friend and biographer Marcel Haedrich, "If one took seriously the few disclosures that Mademoiselle Chanel allowed herself to make about those black years of the occupation, one's teeth would be set on edge."

It was all too easy to imagine Coco Chanel becoming infamous. It would be far better for everyone that she just retire quietly. *Forbes* magazine reported later that Pierre Wertheimer's worry was how "a legal fight might illuminate Chanel's wartime activities and wreck her image—and his business." By the late 1950s, even Coco Chanel realized that it would be wiser to pass over the war in silence, and she reputedly paid Walter Schellenberg, one of the principal operatives in the failed diplomatic mission to Berlin, to suppress any mention of her in his prison-house memoirs. For Coco, however, what Chanel No. 5 represented made letting go of the scent emotionally difficult. Losing control of the fragrance evoked too viscerally the pain and desire tangled up with all those earlier losses. What she needed was to feel that she had conquered a whole set of demons, and Chanel No. 5 was a symbol of it all.

By 1946, both sides were suing each other in courts on two continents, with cases in New York, London, and Paris all moving along inexorably. The partners at Les Parfums Chanel blinked first. They decided that it was better to make peace, at almost any cost. In early May of 1947, the lawyer for Les Parfums Chanel, Claude Lewy, placed a transatlantic telephone call from New York to Paris. "Pierre [Wertheimer]," he told Coco Chanel's lawyer, "is standing here next to me. He is ready to make a trip with me. We can start by seeing you on Saturday, the 17th in the afternoon. We'll have dinner together. He wants with all his heart to conclude a total and definitive peace with Coco." On May 17, they did meet in an office on the Champs Elysées, but nothing got resolved by the dinner hour. The negotiations went on late into the night. After an epic eight-hour conference, throughout which Coco Chanel remained insistent, a peace treaty in one of the century's great entrepreneurial battles was signed.

By the end of the meeting, just as Coco Chanel wanted, they had renegotiated the contract. She would have the right to sell her new line of perfumes in Switzerland, where she was now living. But that wasn't what had ever really mattered. What mattered was the settlement. The partners at Les Parfums Chanel would give Coco Chanel $350,000—a sum today worth nearly nine million dollars—as payment for the wartime sales of Chanel No. 5, and in the future not just 10 percent of the profits but 2 percent of the perfume *sales* worldwide, a vast increase in her income. In exchange, she agreed not to use the number five in any of her marketing. Her estimated annual income would be over a million dollars—today's equivalent of $25 million a year, using conservative estimates. Before the ink was dry, she had become, at the age of sixty-five, one of the richest women in the world.

Unmoored from her signature perfume, without a fashion house, and living in a kind of half-exile between Zürich and Paris as some version of a pampered mistress, Coco Chanel now became, in the world of fashion and fragrance during the final years of the 1940s, a kind of ghostly presence. Chanel No. 5, however, was still living large.

PART III

THE LIFE
OF AN ICON

SIXTEEN

AN ICON OF THE 1950S

During the winter of 1947, it wasn't Paris that was occupied but Berlin, as the Allies took administrative control of the city that Coco Chanel had visited quietly in the final days of the Second World War on her unlucky diplomatic mission. Now, President Truman would not have had the same troubles finding a bottle of Chanel No. 5 as a souvenir for Bess.

One of the popular entertainments in Berlin that year testifies to just how famous Chanel No. 5 had become—to the way in which this perfume had become a powerful and truly international cultural icon. Coco's signature scent had plenty of admirers in Germany. Chanel No. 5 was also part of what the Americans in the city were celebrating. The show tunes that the G.I.s were singing that winter came from a light "boy-meets-girls" comic opera called *Chanel No. 5*. "We know the ladies," one of the catchy tunes went,

> the blond and blue-black [haired] ones, the large and the slender ones. They love the bottles with the jingly names: l'Arpège, Schiaparelli, Mitsouko, Scandal. They choose the

becoming scents for their type, the scents by Coty, Lanvin, Houbigant, and von Weill; it has an effect like slinking poison and costs many a man his sanity. The wildest man becomes like a lamb, the tame one becomes crazy, all because of the scent of a woman. When a beautiful woman passes by, then a scent of pefume follows her. And every man standing nearby asks himself, Was that Chanel, was that Guerlain? . . . Madame without *quelques fleurs* would be like a flower without its scent. When a beautiful woman passes by, her perfume discreetly does her talking for her: Non, non, monsieur! Peut-être mon ami! Oui, oui, mon chéri! [No, no, sir! Maybe, my dear! Yes, yes, my darling!]

For men who had served in France and lined up on streets to find bottles of a favorite fragrance after the liberation, a tune about perfumes was amusing and contemporary. What is fascinating about this long list of popular scents is the simple fact that Chanel No. 5 was the one that stood in for them all: the ladies might like Mitsouko and Scandal, but the title of the opera was Coco Chanel's signature perfume. On the cover of the score, what everyone saw was a huge bottle of Chanel No. 5 and a sultry woman standing next to it. It wasn't just the American G.I.s who loved it, either. It had been a favorite scent of the German troops in Paris, too. Fragrance crossed all those complicated borders during the 1940s.

By the late 1940s, Coco Chanel was also crossing borders again and traveling between France and Switzerland, and in the end her relationship with von Dincklage seems to have simply fizzled. By 1950, she was once again alone, and 1953 found her back in Paris permanently and dissatisfied. Her wartime sins, a decade later, had been largely forgotten, but the world of fashion had forgotten her too. After all, her couture house had been closed for fifteen years. It was only Chanel No. 5 that everyone remembered, and, in her second deal with the partners at Les Parfums Chanel, it seemed that she had let go of that part of her past. Her relationship with Pierre Wertheimer, though, was still a deeply complicated one, and René de Chambrun believed that it was "based on a businessman's passion for a woman who felt exploited by him." In the mid-1950s, he remembered how "Pierre returned to Paris full of pride and excitement [after one of his horses won the English Derby]. . . . He rushed to Coco, expecting congratulations and praise. But she refused to kiss him. She resented him, you see, all her life." To those who knew Coco Chanel, however, the relationship she constructed with him looked distinctly like the relationships in which she had spent her twenties.

Chanel No. 5 was over for her. Having given up even a minority role in the company that she had struggled to reassert control over in the long decades of the 1920s, '30s, and '40s, she wasn't sure she was ready to be done with perfume entirely, however. One afternoon in a café, she proposed to Pierre Wertheimer that perhaps they should launch a new fragrance, and she would play a role in designing it. "Pierre," she said, "let's launch a new perfume." "A new perfume," he countered, "why?" Conveniently forgetting her forays into the red-label fragrances, Coco responded that she hadn't created a new one since 1924. "Don't even think of it," Wertheimer responded. "It's too risky. Launching a new perfume now would take an enormous investment in publicity. And why bother? One can live on No. 5. The Americans don't want something new. They want No. 5." Anything they released, he explained to her, would only compete with the sales of Chanel No. 5, and that scent, he reminded her, was the reason she was living in the lap of luxury, with money in the bank. Finally—after decades of the company creating its own competition—it was all about Chanel No. 5.

Sometime in late 1953 or early 1954, Coco Chanel and Pierre Wertheimer settled instead on a different arrangement. She would reopen the fashion house, and he would pay for everything associated with this business venture. There was one last thing, too. She

gave up in the new settlement the right to use her own name in exchange for a huge monthly income from him. With the death of his
brother and the decision to buy out the Bader family interests in the
late 1940s, he was now the only partner left at Les Parfums Chanel.
He would pay all her bills—everything from her rent at the Ritz
Hotel to the cost of her postage stamps. Later, offended at being
taxed under French law as a "spinster," she would even insist that
Pierre pay her taxes. In giving up Chanel No. 5 for a second time,
she was even more fundamentally giving up rights to her persona
and her public identity.

It was a scent that had been born out of her conflicted relationship with her sexuality and her history as a rich man's mistress. Curiously, what made her happy in the end was something that looked
a lot like becoming, once again, a kept woman. Perhaps that had
been part of their long conflict.

As her acquaintance Edmonde Charles-Roux wondered later,
"Pierre Wertheimer, you see, had been one of those *entreteneurs* (like
Balsan) of a type that no longer existed, whence Gabrielle's attraction for him. How could he have regarded her as anything but an
irrégulière?" An *entreteneur* translates, quite simply, into a man who
kept mistresses. Wertheimer was:

> a man who had had many mistresses in his day, [and he] was
> used to paying women's personal expenses. Coco, in fact,
> could never make up her mind whether she wanted Pierre to
> treat her as a businessperson or as a woman, with the result
> that he treated her with the listless forebearance a lover ex-
> hibits toward a mistress who has outstayed her welcome.

Pierre Wertheimer was used to paying for a mistress, and, for
Coco Chanel, there was also something about this that was comforting and familiar. In the end, what made her happy was to formalize
their arrangement.

Adding to the sense of *déjà vu* surrounding her relationship with Pierre, it was an odd replay of the way in which Étienne Balsan and Boy Capel had funded her millinery shop in the beginning. Coco would now give up the rights to everything. In a curious kind of entrepreneurial marriage, she would give Pierre, in fact, her name. The Wertheimer interest would include not just ownership of the Chanel brand in the fragrance industry but rights to the fashion house as well. Coco Chanel would have complete license as designer and artistic director, but it would be, in all other respects, once again someone else's business.

It sounds like a hard deal to accept, but once again it was also Coco Chanel's idea. This time, she was happy with it. She was vastly wealthy already, and she had the funds to launch any new and daring enterprise she could imagine. If she had wanted to go solo with a relaunch of the fashion house, there was nothing stopping her. She had 2 percent of Chanel No. 5's sales coming in year after year and could count on it for decades. Someone else would pay all her bills on top of it. The truth was that retaining control over the Chanel name simply wasn't what she wanted. Pierre Wertheimer now controlled the entire Chanel business operation, and Coco Chanel was his only real partner.

Considering everything that had happened between them during the Second World War—including the Wertheimers' exile as Jewish refugees and Coco's efforts to use the laws of Nazi-occupied France to strip the partners of this contested possession—it is an astonishing story. Despite their curious love-hate relationship, Pierre Wertheimer had cut through the Gordian knot of their legal battles with Coco Chanel simply by agreeing to pay for anything she ever wanted, forever. She seemed to have finally found some lasting closure.

Coco Chanel had given up her name entirely, and, having disentangled herself from her signature fragrance, she returned to a private life that was, despite all her riches, oddly monastic. She lived in a simply decorated room at the Ritz Hotel and took to writing, in her Catholic schoolgirl hand, a book of aphorisms that she imagined one day publishing.

But the story of Chanel No. 5 didn't end with her retreat from the world of perfume. If it had, Chanel No. 5 would have gone down in history as one of the great scents of the early twentieth century, but it never would have become the fragrance industry's *monstre*. Its greatest success was still in front of it. In the 1950s, the perfume took on a life of its own, and it would need to live and die on its own value and on the basis of how others saw it. Artists and celebrities would become increasingly important arbiters of its fame—but the celebrity of Coco Chanel would no longer be the driving force behind the perfume.

During those grim years of the Second World War, Chanel No. 5 had become embedded in the cultural imagination. It had become as much about the idea of mystery and feminine sexuality as about the scent contained in the bottle. Like only a handful of other brand names in history, Chanel No. 5 represented more than just a famous product. In many respects, the 1950s—its first decade as an icon—was the first moment of its true glory.

What was iconic about Chanel No. 5 in the 1950s still wasn't the bottle, though, and that's a claim that would seem to fly in the face of reason. After all, it's widely known that pop art guru Andy Warhol used the Chanel No. 5 bottle as the basis of a series of silk screens, placing it in the company of mass-culture icons such as Marilyn Monroe, Mao Tse-Tung, and Campbell's Soup cans.

It's all part of the familiar Chanel No. 5 story, and, like so much of the legend, it's fantasy mixed with fact. True, Andy Warhol did use the image of the famous square-cut bottle as one of his commercial icons, and he based his art on a series of advertisements that appeared briefly, from 1954 to 1956, in fashion magazines. The reality, however, is that Warhol didn't create the Chanel No. 5 silk screens until the mid-1980s. What happened is perfectly simple. In the early 1960s, Warhol had placed an outdated women's magazine containing one of those mid-1950s advertisements into a time capsule and then went on busily creating his pop art renditions of the era's great icons. The bottle for Chanel No. 5 was not yet among them.

It is also a generally accepted part of the legend that in 1959 Chanel No. 5's bottle was famously featured in a special exhibit on "The Package" at the Museum of Modern Art in New York—one that would feature items "removed from their conventional context of advertising and sales" and selected "for excellence of structure and shape, color, texture, proportion, and the suitability of these qualities to functional performance"—and added to the permanent collection. Not quite so, it turns out. While Chanel No. 5 *was* included in that famous exhibit, what captured the attention of those curators was the paper packaging, not the bottle.

Item number 22 in the catalog is "Box for Chanel No. 5," with a note reading, "This is a most sophisticated use of bold black lettering on a white ground. Bounded by thick black borders, this package becomes elegant through understatement." It was the monastic simplicity of the white box in which it was sold that seemed distinctively modern in the late 1950s—a shape that Coco Chanel had first discovered in the twelfth-century convent of her childhood. What that catalog doesn't point out is that the design is also funereal: white paper bordered in black was associated with death and mourning, and everyone who had lived through the casualties of the Second World War knew it. Also featured among the collection were exhibits highlighting the perfection of the egg, an aluminum bottle for the Fragonard perfume Zizanie (1949), and plasticine perfume vials created by the Nips Company (1948–50)—but not the iconic Chanel No. 5 bottle.

This Museum of Modern Art exhibit featuring Chanel No. 5's packaging also dovetailed nicely with an important economic trend that had been emerging throughout the 1950s. With the postwar boom in the United States and the massive increase in the sales of domestic goods came the explosion of advertising, and it was the golden age of packaging in America. In the fifteen years from 1940 to 1955, the gross national product in the United States—always Chanel No. 5's key market—soared 400 percent, and the average American had a discretionary income now five times that of 1940. For the first time, "The package became an independent communicator of its own brand personality."

What happened to Chanel No. 5 in the 1950s is also a curious example of a larger phenomenon that characterized the decade. After an era of rationing and "making do," in which denying oneself consumer pleasures was lauded as a form of patriotism, now Americans threw themselves into the pleasures of material comforts and cozy domesticity. In postwar America, the mass-market commodity reigned supreme. Nothing was so tantalizing after years of war and destruction as normalcy, homogenization, and the pleasures of shared middle-class luxuries. Once again, Chanel No. 5 fit the mood of the moment precisely. It became not just a famous and successful perfume but also a symbol of the times—a cultural icon that captured something universal.

Creating a common cultural framework for those domestic, intimate narratives was the whole point of the marketing for Chanel No. 5 in the 1950s. During the first decade of its status as an icon, the advertising perceptively focused on the women who wore Chanel No. 5 and less intently on the product. The idea was to find a way to explain to women how they could enjoy mass-market luxuries and all the pleasures of a homogenized middle-class cultural experience but still express their individuality. The 1950s, after all, also saw the full expression of advertising directed at persuading people to identify themselves with the products around them in far more intimate and personal ways. This was especially true of the beauty industry. Writes one historian, "In 1955, $9,000,000,000 was poured into United States advertising, up a billion from 1954 and up three billion from 1950. . . . Some cosmetic firms began spending a fourth of all their income from sales on advertising and promotion. A cosmetics tycoon, probably mythical, was quoted as saying: 'We don't sell lipstick, we buy customers.'"

Psychologists in the 1950s began working for advertising firms, and the mainstream view became "any product not only must be good but must appeal to our feelings." It was a period in which marketers first identified the goal of brand loyalty and the idea that what mattered to consumers were images—especially self-images. One 1950s advertiser claimed, "Infatuation with one's own body . . . and sex [were] now used differently to sell products."

The early postwar Chanel No. 5 advertisements were very much of the moment. During 1959, the campaign for Chanel No. 5 featured the tagline "Chanel *becomes* the woman you are"—with the text below explaining how "A perfume is different on different women because every woman has a skin chemistry all her own. Chanel No. 5 is subtly created to blend with your own delicate essence—to be like Chanel No. 5, yet deliciously like you alone. Chanel *becomes* you because it becomes *you*." It was always chic because it was always Chanel No. 5. *You* are what makes it extra unique and special, the ads told women. Thus the popular—but largely unfounded—legend that a perfume smells different on each woman was invented.

While the campaign to remind women how "Chanel *becomes* the woman you are" was aimed at creating a personal, even intimate connection with what was already the world's most ubiquitous fragrance, the company had taken a different tack in introducing its first television advertisements in the United States in 1953. Bourjois had been using radio commercials successfully since the 1930s, and, by embracing this new mass media, Chanel No. 5 was the first fragrance ever advertised on television. Intended to reach an even wider audience, the scene showed a handsome man in a tuxedo and a woman being transformed—through the power of a fine perfume—into a princess in a fairy-tale fantasy. It was a predictable narrative but one that satisfied. More important, it was a return to Chanel No. 5's long associations with cinematography and the glamour of Hollywood, which had started back as early as Coco Chanel's trip in 1931 to the MGM studios.

That connection had been confirmed in the minds of millions of Chanel No. 5 enthusiasts in 1952, when rising starlet Marilyn Monroe revealed that when she wanted to feel sexy, she turned to No. 5. Memorably, an impertinent reporter once asked what Monroe wore to bed, and the coy response came: "Nothing but a few drops of Chanel No. 5." Today, it is still one of her best-remembered quips. Later, Marilyn Monroe said about that interview, "People are funny. They ask you questions, and when you're honest they're shocked."

In the spring of 1955, she agreed to pose for a shoot in the Ambassador Hotel in New York City with a bottle of the scent, which she was applying generously to her ample cleavage. It was a sensation. For Marilyn Monroe, keen to give a response that wouldn't look like a shameless commercial endorsement, Chanel No. 5—already an unassailable classic—was a response no one could criticize. It wasn't bad press for Chanel No. 5, either. The company had nothing to do with her saying it, however. They didn't need to. It was a testament to the legendary status this perfume had already achieved that even Marilyn Monroe wanted to wear it.

As a postwar icon being heavily marketed to consumers in a booming postwar economy, by the end of the 1950s Chanel No. 5 should have been riding high; its fame had never been greater. There was just one problem. For some reason, the fashion for Chanel No. 5 was fading. Even more important, "In France, in Europe, in the United States, the sales outlets exploded." With the expansion, "the price [of a bottle] went lower, lower, lower." In 1960, the company may have accelerated the decline in popularity by launching a new campaign with the tagline "every woman *alive* wants *Chanel No. 5*." That was precisely the dilemma. Every woman wanted it, and it wasn't hard to come by. It was for sale in discount drugstore chains everywhere. It was becoming inexpensive—and common.

It was a thin line between a coveted icon and a tired cliché. That had been the danger during the Second World War of selling the perfume through the commissary. At the time, the extraordinary value of the perfume had been more important than the venue in which it was sold. Now, it began to seem that Chanel No. 5 had crossed into the realm of the mass commodity. Marketing didn't make this perfume famous, but it looked as if brand management—combined with overdistribution—just might be capable of under-mining its prestige.

SEVENTEEN

THE ART OF BUSINESS

A product like Chanel No. 5 always had a problem. The balance between being an elite cultural icon and an object of mass-market appeal is a delicate business. Luxury demands exclusivity. For other twentieth-century commercial icons—Coca-Cola or McDonald's, for example—things were inherently simpler. They made their fame as everyday products in which there could be a communal rite of participation, and more people buying what they were selling didn't run the risk of contaminating their popularity.

When Andy Warhol began creating his pop art lithographs in the late 1950s and early 1960s, this was part of the cultural moment to which he was responding. The whole idea behind pop art was to use mass-cultural imagery playfully and to reduce objects to the disembodied circulation of images and surfaces. "Being good in business is the most fascinating kind of art," as he once put it, and his work played with those boundaries.

Prestige, however, is a slippery business. In her book *Deluxe: How Luxury Lost Its Luster,* fashion journalist Dana Thomas pins the slow decline of the real luxury product on the idea that everyone should be able to buy it. When Coco Chanel found the idea of selling Chanel No. 5 at the commissary warehouse "monstrous," she understood something essential about exclusivity. Average people writing onto Chanel No. 5 the story of their own hopes and desires turned the perfume into a cult commodity, but too many average people wearing it could also cut the other way.

When, in the boom years of the postwar period, people found those desires being satisfied, and when Chanel No. 5 was every-where, the world's bestselling perfume ran the risk of seeming ho-hum. By the early 1960s, it was suffering from a potentially disastrous overexposure and was widely available throughout the United States in discount drugstores and at chain outlets like Wool-worth's. It was becoming associated with the kind of scent that was worn by an older generation of women who were out of step with fashion. During the countercultural decade of the 1960s, Chanel No. 5 became essentially unmoored.

Brand management had created the problem, and the challenges of the 1960s had their roots in the strategies—and in the phenom-enal success—of the 1950s. The marketing of the 1960s only exac-erbated the trouble. Combining the unfortunate "every woman *alive* wants Chanel No. 5" campaign with a massive new one in *Seven-teen* magazine, which showed images of love-struck and hopelessly naïve-looking young couples blissfully gazing into each other's eyes, looks now like an essential miscalculation.

What made Chanel No. 5 famous wasn't that it was innocently alluring. If Coco Chanel had wanted that, she would have stuck with the scent of those traditional soliflores in the beginning. People fell in love with the perfume because it was unabashedly and confi-dently sexy. It wasn't a perfume for teenage girls; it was a scent for women—and especially women who dared to be a bit dramatic.

The mid-1960s also held other dangers for the company. Pierre Wertheimer died in 1965, and his son, Jacques, took over manage-ment of the partnership. While Jacques was, by all accounts, brilliant at raising racehorses, there were reports that he had less passionate interests in the daily management of the company. Coco Chanel simply called him "the kid." Still designing beautiful collections for her couture line, Chanel was in her eighties, and her final settlement with Pierre Wertheimer had freed her from that lifelong obsession with the fragrance.

Meanwhile, a new problem was brewing in the south of France. Jasmine production was in decline. The war had taken a heavy toll on the perfume plantations, and bumper crops in the mid-1950s had driven prices to an unsustainable rock bottom. Just as the market recovered, new and cheaper sources of jasmine from Italy, Spain, and Holland—and a new generation of vastly improved and inexpensive synthetics—began flooding into the market during the 1960s. Soon, the flower plantations of Grasse, where the art of perfume-making had begun in modern Europe, would disappear, foreshadowing bad news for Chanel No. 5, which depended on large doses of that exquisite scent to uphold its expensive reputation.

Coco Chanel had been railing for years against the erosion of Chanel No. 5 as a supremely luxurious fragrance. She had wanted to create the most expensive perfume in the world, and in the original contract in 1924 that was one thing that she had specified insistently—that she would be the sole arbiter of what it took to preserve the prestige of her name and products. In her long battles with the partners at Les Parfums Chanel, she had used and abused this clause indiscriminately, but her reasons were sometimes good ones. Chanel No. 5 had emerged from the Second World War as one of the world's most coveted and most recognizable indulgences. Like any product, though, it held only a tenuous grasp on its status as a must-have luxury item. By the 1960s, it seemed to some that the partners had finally overplayed their hand, and Coco Chanel was there to say she had told them so. But it was a hollow victory for her.

Coco was no longer a young woman dancing to titillating tunes in the dance halls of Moulins sur Allier. She wasn't even a middle-aged woman, procuring one lover after another during *les années folles*. In 1971, she was eighty-seven. Time was running short for one of the twentieth century's greatest celebrities, and she had put those battles about her signature scent behind her.

During the second week of January that year, Coco Chanel complained that she was feeling poorly but went to work in her atelier despite it—as she usually did. She was working to prepare the spring collection, and there was no time to spare. On January 10, the day passed uneventfully. She went for a long Sunday drive and, feeling tired, went to bed early. That evening, in the quiet and simply decorated room at the Ritz Hotel that she had made her home in Paris since before the Second World War, Coco Chanel passed away quietly.

The next morning around the world, newspapers carried the headlines: "Chanel, the Couturier, Dead in Paris." The obituary in the *New York Times* noted that "Chanel dominated the Paris fashion world in the nineteen-twenties and at the height of her career was running four business enterprises—a fashion house, a textile business, perfume laboratories and a workshop for costume jewelry—that altogether employed 3,500 workers." This wasn't strictly accurate. During the height of her fame, it was always someone else—the partners—running the perfume business; that was always part of the complexity of Coco Chanel's relationship to Chanel No. 5. However, the obituary had this detail about the perfume correct: "It was," the column read, "perhaps her perfume more than her fashions that made the name Chanel famous around the world. Called simply 'Chanel No. 5'—she had been told by a fortune-teller that five was her lucky number—it made Coco a millionaire."

Ironically, Coco Chanel's death came at a precarious moment for her signature scent. For the second time in its long history, Chanel No. 5 was in danger. During the Second World War, the partners had smuggled supplies of jasmine out of France and enchanted a generation of American soldiers. Now, Chanel No. 5's share in the all-important American market had slipped to under 5 percent. It was a strange and unlucky coincidence. As Alain Wertheimer, Jacques's son, once said in an interview, by the early 1970s "Chanel was dead. . . . Nothing was happening." It was a statement that was both literal and figurative. The perfume had been launched as an expression of the passionately opposed forces of Coco Chanel's experience, and—despite the autonomous life of her creation and the conflict that she had felt over that separation—it seemed to be coming to the end of its life cycle with her. Chanel No. 5 would have to rise or fall according to its own destiny, and perhaps it had had its moment.

C hanel No. 5, however, was not beyond resuscitation; in fact, it was far from it. Despite the dip in market share and a loss of brand-management direction, the perfume was far from any kind of deathbed. It was still a bestselling fragrance, even if its prestige was sliding.

This time, it really was the magic of marketing and the combined vision of a few key company figures that gave it new life and transformed it, in the words of Chandler Burr's anonymous industry insider, into the perfume business's *monstre*. The genius behind the modern transformation of the Chanel No. 5 advertising—that updating of the story of the fragrance that helped another generation of women to imagine how it was part of their sensuality—was Jacques Helleu, the young artistic director. He was the son of Jean Helleu, the celebrated marketing designer who had worked for Chanel since the 1930s. During the early 1970s, Chanel scaled back its work with outside advertising agencies in marketing the perfume and instead gave control to a man who had more or less grown up in what is still, despite its international prominence, a family company. The marketing of Chanel—the marketing that everyone assumes first made it famous—was his personal vision of the scent and what made its allure timeless. "From the age of eighteen, when he first joined

Chanel, [Jacques Helleu] focused his efforts on turning the signature black-and-white packaging"—and especially the trademark bottle—"into a universally recognized brand." Surprisingly, it was, in the history of the company, an essentially new direction.

Helleu's early insight, to put it simply, was to return to the glamour of the movies. Marilyn Monroe, as the perfume critic Tania Sanchez puts it, wore Chanel No. 5 because it was sexy. She was always the kind of woman to whom the scent appealed. It was the same reason Chanel No. 5 was adored by those risqué flappers in the 1920s. To transform the story of Chanel No. 5 again, Helleu hired Catherine Deneuve as fragrance spokes-model. According to the company legend, it was a simple decision. Helleu was in New York City and a devoted *cinéphile*—a "film buff"—and, there on the cover of *Look* magazine, he read the caption "Most Beautiful Woman in the World" alongside the image of the young French actress. That, so the story goes, was when he made the decision.

The choice was far savvier than any chance encounter, though. "Chanel," Laurence Benaïm has perceptively noted, "chooses its models as carefully as any harvest of May roses or jasmine from Grasse," and Jacques Helleu was the man behind those decisions. In 1968, the year Catherine Deneuve began representing Chanel No. 5, she was best known for starring in two recent and decidedly racy films, Roman Polanski's *Repulsion* (1965) and especially Luis Buñuel's *Belle de Jour* (1967), the celebrated story of an otherwise respectable young woman who lives out her fantasies through afternoons of illicit sexual adventure. It was a return to what had always been the central narrative that Chanel No. 5 told from the moment Coco Chanel began imagining it. It was once again the story of how a fragrance could reconcile the scent of fresh-scrubbed bodies with the open enjoyment of a liberated sexuality.

As an advertising campaign, it was fabulously successful during the 1970s, and the glamour of Chanel No. 5 turned Deneuve into one of her generation's most famous actresses. Deneuve's beauty and quintessential sexuality also made this iconic perfume more legendary than ever and was the necessary antidote to a decade of advertising that had mistakenly defused the eroticism of Chanel No. 5 during the countercultural years of the 1960s and even the early 1970s, as a scent for sweetly proper co-eds reading *Seventeen*.

The advertising for the perfume became even more daring as the 1970s progressed. The focus stayed on renewing the long associations of Chanel No. 5 with movie-star glamour—associations that had begun with Coco Chanel's trip to Hollywood in the 1930s. In fact, at the end of the Deneuve campaign, Helleu began commissioning not just television commercials for the fragrance but a series of inventive, even surrealistic ad-length films, all with that same *Belle de Jour* theme of sensual fantasy. Directed during the 1970s and 1980s by Ridley Scott, some including Carole Bouquet, the "face" of Chanel No. 5 during the 1980s, these short promotional films invited viewers into an atmosphere of seductive mystery. Best remembered today are Chanel No. 5 shorts such as *La Piscine* (1979), *L'invitation au rêve* (1982), *Monument* (1986), and *La Star* (1990).

The advertisements of the 1970s in the crucial American market, however, featured simply Deneuve and the Chanel No. 5 bottle in photograph after photograph. It was a simple iconography. Suddenly, Les Parfums Chanel was all about No. 5—and specifically about the bottle. The Ridley Scott films played on the same visual imagery, with the silhouette of the bottle part of the fantasy, and it was these new advertisements, as much as the photographs from the fashion magazines of the late 1950s, that inspired Andy Warhol in the mid-1980s to celebrate the Chanel No. 5 bottle as officially iconic. The title of his silk screens, "Ads: Chanel," in fact, is suggestively plural, gesturing to both their mass-market reproducibility and the historical evolution of this famous image.

The combination of these two successful advertising campaigns

during the 1970s and into the 1980s counteracted the overdistribution of the 1960s, which had threatened to cheapen the name of the
fragrance. At a moment when the perfume and fashion industry as
a whole was moving toward the commercialism that Dana Thomas
calls "new luxury," Chanel made a decision to recommit itself to an
older—more art deco—philosophy: to the idea that a certain class
of consumer goods could be artistry. Only a "handful of major
brands—Hermès and Chanel in particular—strive to maintain and
seem to achieve true luxury," Thomas claims. "The quality comes
through in their products . . . and in their philosophies."

Many credit this revitalization of Chanel during the 1970s to the
new, energetic leadership of Pierre's grandson, Alain Wertheimer,
who stepped in to lead the company in 1974. One of his first actions
as head of the company was to reduce dramatically the number of
outlets carrying the perfume in the United States and to take it out
of the drugstores. Even the act of buying a fine fragrance, after all,
is a form of seduction, and Chanel No. 5 was always about there
being nothing cheap about being sexy.

Since the 1970s, the marketing of Chanel No. 5 has been remarkably consistent, periodically reviving this same theme of fantasy and
Hollywood-inflected sensuality that teases consumers with the idea
of something implicitly just a little bit naughty. Director Jean-Paul
Goude became what the company calls "Chanel's master storyteller"
during the 1980s and early 1990s, and his short film *Marilyn* (1995)
reimagined that early photo shoot at the Ambassador Hotel. The
advertisement featured playfully edited footage and computer-
generated images of the candidly sexual starlet in her first—and
only—"official" Chanel appearance.

While Catherine Deneuve had evoked fantasies of female desire
and Marilyn Monroe was nothing less than cultural shorthand for
sexy, by the 1990s, the film advertisements were becoming even
more daring. Estella Warren starred in the memorable *Little Red
Riding Hood* shorts and print layouts produced by Luc Besson (1998,

1999). They were an adult retelling of the old fairy tale—and they harkened back to precisely the kind of schoolgirl sexuality that had made Coco Chanel an alluring young mistress during the 1910s and 1920s. The "green girl" wears red was the essential message.

In fact, in the history of Chanel No. 5 advertising in the last several decades, the women who have represented the perfume have often evoked something of the *irrégulière*, the courtesan, or the mistress. In the first decade of the new millennium, the face of Chanel No. 5 was movie star Nicole Kidman—spotlighted in a 2004 short film, directed by Baz Lurhmann, that echoed the blockbuster success of her role in his Oscar-winning *Moulin Rouge* (2001). The film, of course, is the story of a showgirl and *grande horizontale* and of a dangerously illicit love triangle that pits true romance against the desires of a powerful and rich aristocrat. It is hard not to think of Coco Chanel's time on the vaudeville stage in Moulins—or that complicated relationship with Boy Capel and Étienne Balsan and the private history that Chanel No. 5 was created to capture.

Little surprise, then, that the most recent face of Chanel No. 5 during the second decade of the new century is the girlishly sexy Audrey Tautou, who first came to international fame as the title character in *Le Fabuleux Destin d'Amélie Poulain* (2001; released in English as *Amélie*), director Jean-Pierre Jeunet's story of a charming Parisian waitress at the Café des Deux Moulins. Tautou appeared in short films advertising Chanel No. 5—directed again by Jeunet (2009)—and in the feature-length film by Anne Fontaine *Coco Avant Chanel* (2009), where she plays the young Coco Chanel during her years as a showgirl and "green-girl" mistress. Those first links with Hollywood that Coco Chanel explored in the 1930s had once again come full circle.

The same is true of the fragrances. Since the 1970s, the new perfumes have also been a nod to tradition and that earlier age of glamour—even as they have been designed to appeal to a new generation of women. In fact, in some ways, the scents since the

1970s have been a series of creative refashionings of *le monstre* and a return to the legacy of those early Chanel numbers. The most celebrated new fragrance has been Jacques Polge's Coco (1984) and the updated version of it released in 2001 as Coco Mademoiselle, both inspired by the baroque aesthetics of Coco Chanel's private Paris salon. The scents are entirely distinct from Chanel No. 5. Both Coco and Coco Mademoiselle—rather unusually—are sold, though, in the signature No. 5 bottle, an appeal to young women who want the luxury status of the iconic bottle but don't yet want the iconic fragrance.

Other new scents have eschewed the signature art deco flacon, but there has been a return since the 1970s to the renewed pro-liferation of multiple Chanel numbered fragrances. The modern reintroduction of the numbers began with the release in 1970 of Chanel No. 19—reputedly the reformulated version of Coco's il-licit red-label Mademoiselle Chanel No. 1, the scent that she called her "super Chanel No. 5." A return to the numbers is largely a very recent campaign, however. In 2007, several new numbered perfumes appeared, all part of the boutique-only range of ultrapremium Chanel fragrances marketed as Les Exclusifs—"the exclusives." As one journalist notes, these are all fragrances "based on the compli-cated trajectory of the founder's difficult and flamboyant life . . . scents she cherished, outdoors and at home."

Some of these scents were entirely fresh "address-inspired" per-fumes like 31 rue Cambon, 28 La Pausa, and now a Chanel No. 18—which takes its name from the Chanel jewelry boutique at 18 Place Vendôme in Paris. Many of the scents were updated re-releases of the original and much-loved scents in the Chanel perfume range of the 1920s and 1930s, however. The company returned to produc-tion once-famous early Chanel fragrances such as Bois des Îles and Cuir de Russie. And it relaunched Chanel No. 22, one of Ernest Beaux's original ten samples and always a fragrance closely tied to the history and to the innovative aldehydic scents of Chanel No. 5.

Then, there has also been Jacques Polge's consciously modern up-dating of Chanel No. 5 itself—Eau Première. According to Polge, it is the scent of Chanel No. 5 and nothing else, but for each accord he has added more ingredients, working with innovative new scent materials discovered since the 1920s. Eau Première is an attempt to imagine the Chanel No. 5 that Ernest Beaux would have crafted if he had lived at the beginning of the twenty-first century.

For much of its early history, the scent of Chanel No. 5 circulated on the world's fragrance market in different versions, from Coco Chanel's red-label perfumes to Chanel No. 22 or Chanel No. 46, Rallet No. 1 or Coty's L'Aimant. Today, that trend has once again come full circle, too. This time, however, the marketing has been innovative and ingenious. It has been a coordinated and evolving campaign that has made Chanel No. 5 more famous than ever, but it has worked for the same reason the Second World War made it an icon: these films and fragrances are an invitation to mystery and fantasy.

While Chanel's marketing, distribution, and brand man-agement breathed new life into Chanel No. 5 those last critical decades of the twentieth century, its future as the world's most famous perfume has never been a certainty. The per-fume has simply faced new dangers from different quarters. After all, even the best marketing and most ingenious, decadent advertis-ing ultimately mean nothing if there is no product to sell. And in the fall of 2009, the press was reporting that it looked like Chanel No. 5 was in serious danger of disappearing altogether.

EIGHTEEN

THE END OF
MODERN PERFUMERY

n September of 2009, newspapers around the world carried headlines announcing, "Rules put famous perfumes 'at risk'" and "Allergen rules may alter scents of great perfumes." The blogosphere was buzzing with the news that the end of Chanel No. 5 was near and that "twentieth-century perfumery [is] history." The source of the controversy was a new set of amendments from the perfume industry's self-regulatory body, the International Fragrance Association, usually known simply as IFRA, which for the first time added jasmine to its list of restricted materials—that rare and coveted jasmine from Grasse included.

Word spread that the notorious forty-third IFRA amendment would limit jasmine to 0.7 percent of any perfume, and this proposed restriction led to immediate fears about the demise of the world's most famous jasmine fragrance, the iconic Chanel No. 5 *parfum*. Massive proportions of the natural jasmine of Grasse, counterbalanced by the overdose of aldehydes, was the tightrope act at the heart of Ernest Beaux's genius scent. Decrease the jasmine, and the whole thing was ruined.

Not since the beginning of the war, when Gregory Thomas was attempting to smuggle precious supplies out of France, had Chanel No. 5 itself been in this kind of jeopardy. Without that stockpile of roses and jasmine, it would have been a different scent—with a different quality and a different history. Had its ingredients been stopped on their way to the United States, the partners would have needed to reformulate the perfume using synthetics, and it would have been a massive—and demoralizing—project. Producing Chanel No. 5 in New Jersey would have been less feasible, the opportunity to distribute the fragrance through the commissaries less brilliantly timed. Those key factors allowed the perfume to permeate the American market. Now, having triumphed for nearly ninety years as the world's most famous fragrance—having weathered the Great Depression and a world war, the changes of the 1960s and overexposure—it seemed from the headlines that here at last was an insurmountable obstacle.

At stake was the thorny issue of perfumes and allergies, and the restrictions on "naturals" like jasmine remain the topic of one of the perfume industry's most intense debates. IFRA instituted these recommendations on jasmine—the natural floral essence, not the synthetic accord—because it can be a skin irritant for some unlucky people. Specifically, the problem, from an allergist's perspective, is that people are far more likely to be sensitive to natural plant materials than to a single, isolated scent molecule. Accordingly, from the scientific and industry-safety perspective, hand-harvested naturals—not ones created in laboratories—pose the greatest risk.

In this case, the disaster Chanel No. 5 faced was a nightmare narrowly averted. In a statement to the press, in-house deputy perfumer Christopher Sheldrake assured Chanel No. 5 enthusiasts, "When the new IFRA standards were issued we immediately checked the percentages of *jasmine grandiflora* and [*jasmine*] *sambac* in our finished products, and in none of our fragrances is the recommended level exceeded." There would be, the company promised, no changes to Chanel No. 5.

In the back of everyone's mind, however, was the thought that, when IFRA revisits the question, further restrictions on jasmine are possible. Next time, perhaps modern perfumery wouldn't be so lucky. For now, though, Chanel No. 5 was spared. Its scent would stay the same.

The question is: Chanel No. 5 would stay precisely the same as what? While the jasmine regulations posed an undeniable threat to the perfume's future, one of the keys to understanding Chanel No. 5's lasting success is to recognize something fundamental about the perfume itself: the scent that enticed those passing by Coco Chanel's table in Cannes back on that late summer evening in 1920 wasn't precisely the same as a bottle of Chanel No. 5 perfume on the market today. That was always going to be impossible, and, over the course of so many decades, government and industry regulations have banned more than one of the ingredients in Ernest Beaux's original formula.

The amazing thing isn't those changes—it's the fact that Chanel No. 5 smells as close to the 1920 original as it does despite them. Remarkably close. So close that very few of us would ever notice the difference. That has been the goal of Chanel's in-house perfumers. Unlike some of the other great perfumes of the early part of the twentieth century, changes in Chanel No. 5 have been only minor and only when absolutely required, at least since the 1950s. Long before the new IFRA announcement, moreover, concerns about maintaining No. 5's integrity were already on the minds of Chanel's perfumers. For decades they have been negotiating the end of the use of certain ingredients.

Among the ingredients at risk by the end of the 1970s were the sultry musks that grounded Chanel No. 5's scent. These are only marginally less important than the jasmine at its heart and those effervescent aldehydes that lift the perfume's opulent aromas. It was clear by the time Catherine Deneuve became the celebrated "face" of Chanel No. 5 that some of the most important musks would soon have to be abandoned.

Natural animal materials smell rich and wonderful, and *muscone*— the term for the aromatic core of the musk taken from the *Moschus moschiferus*, a deer native to the Tonquin region of Tibet and China that is widely recognized as of superior quality—is the scent of warm, clean skin. Other musks came from the glands of civet cats and beavers, and their scents are undeniably sexy. Those aromas were always part of the perfume that Coco Chanel imagined. The methods for obtaining these reproductive fluids, however, are understandably delicate—and that fact, along with overharvesting, has meant that all of the natural musk scents have always been fabulously expensive.

Toward the end of the nineteenth century, with the development of organic chemistry in the world of fragrance, perfumers started looking for the new effects and notes that were to revolutionize perfumery. In the 1880s, when a chemist named Albert Bauer was working with explosives, including the derivatives of TNT (trinitrotoluene), he noticed in the test tube a compound that smelled startlingly like deer musk. Recognizing a marketing opportunity, he began selling the molecule to perfumers as "Musk Bauer," and it was the world's first "nitro-musk," the name for the category of nitrogen-and-oxygen-based molecules that imitated the smells of natural musk.

The first bottles of Chanel No. 5 used generous doses of these nitro-musks, and perfumers loved their scent. In fact, they still lament their loss. It turned out, though, that, as beautiful as they smelled, they posed a number of hazards. Based around molecules that were essentially explosive, they were chemically unstable, and this was true especially if they were exposed to sunlight, when they tended to degrade and react in ways that were sometimes neurologically toxic.

With the sole exception of musk ketone, which was the only nitro-musk to meet the tough new international safety standards, they were banned during the 1980s. Today musk ketone is still permitted only with strict limitations. The perfumes that used them had to be re-formulated. Chanel No. 5 was among them.

Finding a way to replace the depth and richness of these nitro-musks required a good deal of commitment. The suppression of nitro-musks heralded the end for some of the revered fragrances of the 1970s and 1980s. Unfortunately, the ways of harvesting natural animal musk from the nether glands of some unfortunate fellow creatures made using them too unpalatable. There have been no natural musks in Chanel No. 5 since sometime in the early 1990s.

Chanel No. 5 fans need not worry, though, because Chanel No. 5 still has those rich, warm scents of skin and that note of intense sensuality that Coco Chanel always wanted. As Christopher Shel-drake explains, while those nitro-musks were wonderful, powerful, and inexpensive, they were not irreplaceable. There are ways to re-create their warmth and powdery textures in a perfume. It's just that they can't be replaced on the cheap, and most fragrance houses aren't prepared to spend the money. And, as perfumer Virginia Bonofiglio quips, "You can't make cheap that smells like Chanel No. 5."

Staying true to the original fragrance is the great challenge of any historically important perfume. Allowing the scent of Chanel No. 5 to change with the decades would have been far simpler. Even without evolving regulations, it is remarkably difficult to make any expensive perfume—one made with those complex sub-scents of naturals—smell consistent from one year to the next. Yet good perfumers manage it year after year and, in the cases of legacy scents like Shalimar or Joy or Chanel No. 5, decade after decade, despite the fact that, as in wines, the natural materials that go into a fra-grance are always affected by vintages. At the most essential level, flowers also change their aromas from year to year, from place to place, sometimes dramatically.

The skill of a perfumer, then, is not only in innovation and invention, but in taking into account the ever-shifting changes in the floral components and finding the right proportions needed to re-create a scent that is somehow timeless. It is always the search to create again and to preserve in nuance and complexity the essence of something fleeting. Above all, as Coco Chanel knew, perfume is an act of memory.

Jacques Polge is only the third chief perfumer in the history of Les Parfums Chanel, so the chain of olfactory memory and tradition is unbroken in Chanel No. 5's case. Illustrating the importance perfumers attach to this process, Polge tells a story about how his predecessor, Henri Robert, used to watch Ernest Beaux correct an entire batch of Chanel No. 5 perfume in the production facility by inhaling deeply and adding just a few drops of some particular essence or another to make it smell like his original creation.

When Jacques Polge became perfumer in 1978, he faced a similar task of maintaining the scent's legacy, and the problem Chanel faced then wasn't just one of the soon-to-be-banned nitro-musks. It was—as always with this scent—one of flowers. The production of jasmine from Grasse was declining, and Polge went to the south of France to meet the farmers who grew this unique jasmine, hoping to convince them to grow more of it at the finest level of quality. What he discovered was that the plantations were dying. Less expensive exotic jasmines were flooding the world markets, making it not worthwhile for the farmers to try to save them. Without jasmine— much of it from the fields of Grasse—in large quantities, however, Chanel No. 5 would be compromised.

Responding to this threat, in the early 1980s Chanel brokered an exclusive long-term agreement with the Mul family—which has been growing flowers for the perfume industry in Grasse for five generations—to save the last commercial jasmine plantations from destruction. For this project, a resistant jasmine stock was found onto which could be grafted the traditional jasmine of Grasse.

Today, at least 99 percent of the production of jasmine from Grasse, universally agreed to be the finest quality in the world, goes into just one perfume: Chanel No. 5.

New IFRA allergy restrictions won't threaten the perfume either, because for several years researchers at Chanel have been committed to finding a permanent solution. Among those hundreds of molecules in natural jasmine, it is only one or two that have the potential to cause even the most sensitive among us any problems. Creating a synthetic jasmine as nuanced and subtle as the natural jasmine of Grasse would be an impossible undertaking, but breeding just one or two molecules out of a plant or finding a technique to remove one or two molecules from an extract is entirely possible. Soon, Chanel hopes simply to have resolved the problem of jasmine sensitivity entirely. They hope that, eventually, the jasmine from Grasse will be something anyone can wear without hesitation—no matter how daringly high the doses.

For now, the legacy of the perfume is safe. Despite changes around it, the world's most famous fragrance remains essentially unchanged and timeless.

In the history of Chanel No. 5, there have been a series of moments like this: moments where it could have failed to keep pace with cultural changes or where its changes might have been too dramatic. The greatest temptation with any product over a ninety-odd-year history is the one to alter it beyond recognition in the name of progress. Indeed, reformulation is a great temptation in the face of slipping sales or marketing missteps, and many perfume houses have been unable to resist this kind of updating. At that moment in the 1970s when the brand management for Chanel No. 5 was being fundamentally reimagined—a moment when, for the first time, Chanel No. 5 ran the risk of seeming mass-market and outdated—it would have been easy to experiment with the formula and relaunch it as a "new" No. 5. It might even have seemed a logical extension of the strategy that first led the partners at Les Parfums Chanel to introduce alternative versions of the scent with Chanel No. 22 and Chanel No. 46 in the 1920s and 1940s.

Today, the scent of Chanel No. 5—particularly at the luxurious *parfum* concentration considered the ultimate version—remains true to the original 1920 fragrance. It's the scent that the perfumers at Chanel work to preserve, and that has meant, in the face of changes, finding ways to adapt without compromise.

And this commitment to reinventing itself—in order to remain itself—at any cost is the reason why, generation after generation, Chanel No. 5 has persisted as a perfume and as a symbol. At any number of critical moments in the history of this fragrance, the scent that first enticed diners on a warm night in the south of France might have disappeared. It might have faded into obscurity like so many of the other great scents of that golden age of perfumery. It might have ended with the death in the 1970s of the complicated woman whose name it carried or have quietly disappeared from the cultural imagination.

Instead, Chanel No. 5 has proven astonishingly resilient. An enduring monument, it has escaped the dangers of ossification. Now nearly ninety years old, Chanel No. 5 is poised to remain the world's most famous perfume for a second century.

AFTERWORD

The title of this book is not meant to be coy or provocative. In the history of Chanel No. 5, there is a real secret here to be unraveled, an untold story that explains so many decades of fabulous success. That real secret isn't about the origins of this famously original perfume in a lost fragrance from imperial Russia. There is a reason one survived and the other didn't. Nor is it a secret about how Chanel No. 5 became a bestseller because of some ingenious and aggressive marketing push in the 1920s. It's certainly not that. Chanel No. 5 succeeded *despite* a campaign that was at best uninspired and, at worst, confounding. More to the point, had those early advertisements been responsible for No. 5's rapid ascent, they would have turned those other numbered perfumes into the same kind of smashing success. Yet only Chanel No. 5 became a commercial triumph. Only Chanel No. 5 became a monument.

As beautiful as it was—and as it remains—the scent isn't the secret either. Today, it doesn't take dusty company archives or stolen formulas to produce knockoff copies of any of the world's great perfumes, just some moderately expensive equipment and a decent laboratory.

Generic versions of Chanel No. 5 are for sale internationally in cheap drugstores and on websites. Versions of Chanel No. 5, in fact, were readily available to consumers by the 1920s. It never made any difference. It was always Chanel No. 5 that women wanted. By the same token, there are also half a dozen great perfumes from the golden age of the 1930s and 1940s, once found on dressing-room tables around the world, that have long since disappeared, although their dazzling scents should have made them classics. Perfume aficionados are still saddened by their loss. But a great product has never been, in the world of business, a guarantee of anything.

The secret isn't even found in the story of the perfume's imperfect creator, her ill-considered wartime love affairs, or her calculating and distressingly opportunistic business tactics, although Chanel No. 5 was at the heart of those years and what came after. Nor, even, is it in the story of the partners who quietly triumphed. Long before the Second World War, Chanel No. 5 had slipped free of the life of the woman who had invented it and had become a product with its own destiny.

Instead, the secret at the heart of Chanel No. 5 and its continued success is us and our relationship to it. It's the wonderful and curious fact of our collective fascination with this singular perfume for nearly a century and the story of how a scent has been—and remains—capable of producing in so many of us the wish to possess it. Think of that number: a bottle sold every thirty seconds. It is an astounding economy of desire.

Chanel No. 5 is arguably *the* most coveted consumer luxury product of the twentieth—and twenty-first—centuries. But it hasn't changed in any of the essentials; rather, decade after decade, we have reinvented it in our minds. At moments, primarily since the 1980s, brilliant marketing has been part of what has guided us. But Chanel No. 5 was never the creature of crass commercialism. Instead, something larger, something more timeless, almost immediately made it an unprecedented success.

All along, we have been willing participants in the production and reproduction of its legend. Indeed, we have been the principal agents of it. It's part of the reason stories about Chanel No. 5 proliferate. We have sometimes invented and dreamed our way to those legends, so the true history of the world's most famous fragrance comes to us at moments as a surprise. And it's not just with the invention of "new luxury" in the 1990s that we began to map onto it the narratives of our own hopes and desires and sometimes even our losses. Chanel No. 5 has been about the stories we tell of ourselves from the beginning, and that includes all the people who have shaped its history.

Some of those people are the characters whose lives were tangled up intimately with the history of this perfume—the characters whose lives this book touches upon. All of them found ways to connect personally and privately with this scent that they helped to make famous, and, of course, no one was as tightly bound to the fragrance as Coco Chanel. It was part of her history and her story. Its contradictory scents would capture something essential about what she loved and hated—and, at moments, the fragrance would become her *bête noire* long before it became the industry's glorious *monstre*. For Dmitri Pavlovich, it was the familiar scent of a privileged life that had faded with the Russian empire and the remembered fragrance of an ultimately cruel imperial aunt and a well-loved fellow exile and sister. Even the unsentimental Ernest Beaux invested it with private meaning, with the memory of scents that seemed to capture the freshness of snow melting on rich, black earth at the northern reaches of the world.

It has been the same for the generations of nameless and faceless men and women who have made this perfume the world's bestselling and most famous fragrance for generations. It is our story—and in some fundamental way the story of the last complicated century. With no thought for the family histories behind Chanel No. 5 and heedless of the ugly newspaper controversies in occupied France that the sale of the company to Félix Amiot generated, German soldiers only knew that they loved it. So did the British. The American troops shared that passion, too.

When the G.I.s arrived to liberate Paris, Coco Chanel's famous boutique was the most beautiful perfume salon in a still beautiful city. The entire first floor was given over to the display of sparkling cut-glass bottles, their light reflected in mirrors. Chanel No. 5 was everything one imagined when dreaming of Paris. It was scent and sex: something to contain the years of losses, something promising the hope of something lovely surviving. Those soldiers lined up on rue Cambon in that photograph each had their own story. But the name of the girl back home, the mother or sister or lover, isn't what mattered for the history of this perfume. It's the fact that there were so many of these stories, each with private resonance and meaning.

Who knows precisely what those American G.I.s were each thinking that day on the street behind the Ritz Hotel? Part of the brilliance of the partners' commissary-based sales strategy during the war was that Chanel No. 5 became not just the most recognizable French perfume on the market but one implicitly approved by the United States Army as an appropriate object of desire in the midst of a time that was terrible and ugly. The thoughts of those soldiers were never recorded, but in the 1950s a young American woman named Ann Montgomery traveled to Paris to become a fashion model, and she remembers the meaning of Chanel No. 5 clearly.

Ann—now Ann Montgomery Brower—remembers that when she was in college in the 1940s, Chanel No. 5 symbolized Paris and glamour. Today, Paris perhaps is not so far. Then, she muses, it seemed a great distance. Her first trip after the war took ten days by boat on a Holland America liner. Paris was still exotic and a symbol of luxury and splendor. And it was during the war, she says, that Chanel No. 5 became the perfume everyone coveted.

By the end of the Second World War, to say "No. 5" was to conjure a narrative that was both culturally universal and deliciously private, and Coco Chanel always knew there was a kind of magic and a uniquely human destiny in that special number. Today, the charm remains as powerful as ever. Women wear Chanel No. 5 because it is still capable of that same invitation to—as the current company slogan puts it—"share the fantasy." Young women wear it to feel rich and sophisticated. Rich and sophisticated women wear it to feel sexy. Sexy women know precisely why Marilyn Monroe made it her signature perfume.

Or perhaps they wear it for some other reason—some reason that is almost certainly personal. But that is what has always been at the heart of the Chanel No. 5 legend. This is the biography of that scent, and the story of our collective participation in its production—participation that has made Chanel No. 5 a perfume with a life of its own.

ACKNOWLEDGMENTS

N ever, I believe, have I written anything that depended so much on the kindness of friends and on the generosity of so many new acquaintances.

Among those friends, thanks to Noelle Baker, Bill Hare, Roberta Maguire, Jeff Cox, Mark Lussier, Paul Youngquist, Christine Renaudin, Graham Lawler, Michael Gamer, Elise Bruhl, Michael Eberle-Sinatra, Tim Fulford, Paula Torgeson, Noelle Oxenhandler, Adrian Blevins, Nate Rudy, Lydia Moland, Axel Witte, the late Susanne Kröck, Matt and Erica Mazzeo, Dave Suchoff, Carleen Mandolfo, Lisa Arellano, Anindyo Roy, Liz Vella, Hannah Holmes, Shari Broder, Bruce Redford, Dennis Crowley, Mark Lee, Joyce Hackett, Jeremy and Paula Lowe, Michael Buss, Anna-Lisa Cox, Abby and Jon Hardy, Jérémie Fant, Jeffery McLain, Sam Hoyt Lindgren, Don Lindgren, Victor Hartmann, and Elizabeth Morse. Richard Wendorf offered perceptive advice on the manuscript at a crucial juncture. Jim Wendorf and Barbara Fiorino were guardian angels in New York, and my thanks to Mark Anderson for assistance with last-minute research in Berlin. Hillary Rockwell Cahn and Charles Cahn steered me in the right direction at the outset. My mother, Charlene Mazzeo, was once again my last and best reader, and my thanks to Pierre Guyomard and Simon Pittaway of La Maison de Léontine in Aubazine for putting me up, showing me around, and—along with so many others in the village that night—helping me haul a rental car out of a snowy ditch in the middle of a French blizzard.

I am also grateful to Chanel for having given me invaluable assistance in the research for this book, although Chanel was clear with me in indicating that it could not confirm many of the facts that are set forth herein. I have relied throughout this book on the many—and occasionally contradictory—published sources on the life of Coco Chanel and on the Chanel No. 5 legend. Also in the world of perfume, Christophe de Villeplee and Nicholas Mirzayantz welcomed me at International Flavors and Fragrances (IFF), and I am grateful to Subha Patel and Ron Winnegrad of IFF and to Virginia Bonofiglio at the Fashion Institute of Technology for everything they shared. Linda Gerlach also shared her experience creating Love, the Key to Life, and, at the Osmothèque de Versailles, Jean Kerléo and Yves Tanguy offered freely time and expertise. Marie-Christine Grasse introduced me to the Museum of Perfume in Grasse. Thanks, too, to Philip Kraft at Givaudan; Walter Zvonchenko at the Library of Congress; and Bradley Hart at the University of Cambridge for his research assistance in the Churchill Archive Centre and in the National Archives in London. At Aubazine, Michèle Millas and Jean-Louis Sol were superb guides to Coco Chanel's childhood home. Thanks to odor artist and researcher Sissel Tolaas for olfactory conversations and other pleasant diversions and to Luca Turin and Tania Sanchez for taking the time to speak in Boston. Memoirist and former model

Ann Montgomery Brower generously recollected her days at the house of Chanel in the 1950s.

Last—but certainly not least—at HarperCollins, Matt Inman was, as always, the kind of editor most authors only ever dream about, and I could not have written this book without him. A warm thanks goes, as well, to my agent, Stacey Glick, for the fine art of making everything possible. Finally, I am grateful to my colleagues in the English Department at Colby College and to Dean of Faculty Edward Yeterian, particularly, for the gift of time and for their patience as I completed this book.

NOTES

PREFACE

xiii *"Chanel No. 5 rated 'most seductive scent' in poll of women":* Sherryl Connelly, "Chanel No. 5 perfume rated 'most seductive scent' in poll of women," *New York Daily News*, December 2, 2009, www.nydailynews.com/lifestyle/ shopping_guide/2009/12/02/2009–12–02_chanel_no_5_perfume_is_tops_ with_women.html.

xiv *"Marilyn Monroe never had trouble attracting men":* "The Secret to Bagging Your Dream Man? Why, Chanel No. 5, Of Course . . . One in Ten Were Wearing Seductive Fragrance When They 'Met the One,'" *Daily Mail*, December 1, 2009, www.dailymail.co.uk/femail/article–1232047/ The-secret-bagging-dream-man-Why-Chanel-No5-course—One-wearing- seductive-fragrance-met-one.html#ixzz0fQVxXLʟʙ.

xiv *"it appear[ed] her colourful love life may have been down to a simple choice":* "The Secret to Bagging Your Dream Man?" *Daily Mail*, December 1, 2009.

xiv *the starlet famously quipped that all she wore to bed at night were a few drops of Chanel No. 5:* Paul Kremmel, ed., *Marilyn Monroe and the Camera* (London: Schirmer Art Books, 1989), 15; "Something for the Boys," *Time*, Monday, August 11, 1952. Other versions of the quote say "A drop of Chanel No. 5."

xiv *"for getting beyond it to boyfriend status":* "The Secret to Bagging Your Dream Man," *Daily Mail*, December 1, 2009.

xiv *One in ten claimed they met Mr. Right while wearing the iconic perfume:* Ibid.

xiv *according to the French government, a bottle of the world's most famous per-fume sells:* "News From France," *Ambassade de France aux États Unis* 6, no. 12 (December 6, 2006), http://ambafrance-us.org/IMG/pdf/nff/News FromFrance%2006_12.pdf; other sources claim that sales are closer to one bottle of the fragrance every fifty-five seconds, e.g., "Chanel No. 5 Most Iconic Perfume," *The Telegraph,* November 27, 2008, www.telegraph.co.uk/news/uknews/3530343/Chanel-No.-5-most-iconic-perfume.html.

xiv *A few years later, the ranks of the super rich had swelled by more than 700 percent:* On the rising concentration of wealth in the United States during the 1920s, see, for example, Larry Samuel, *Rich: The Rise and Fall of American Wealth Culture* (New York: ACOM, 2009).

xv *department stores, another phenomenon of this enticing new commercial era:* On the history of the department store, see Richard Longstreath, *The American Department Store Transformed, 1920–1960* (New Haven, CT: Yale University Press, 2010); Jan Whitaker, *Service and Style: How the American Department Store Fashioned the Middle Class* (New York: St. Martin's, 2006); Jacques du Closal, *Les Grands Magasins: Cent Ans Après* (Paris: Clotard et Associés, 1989).

xv *Babe Ruth led the New York Yankees to three World Series titles:* For the cultural history of the 1920s, see Lucy Moore, *Anything Goes: A Biography of the 1920s* (New York, Overlook Press, 2010); Edmund Wilson, *The American Earth-quake: A Chronicle of the Roaring Twenties, the Great Depression, and the Dawn of the New Deal* (New York: DaCapo Press, 1996); Malcolm Cowley, *Exile's Return: A Literary Odyssey of the 1920s* (New York: Penguin, 1994); Jean-Claude Baker, *Josephine Baker: The Hungry Heart* (New York: Cooper Square, 2001); and Michael K. Bohn, *Heroes and Ballyhoo: How the Golden Age of the 1920s Transformed American Sports* (Dulles, VA: Potomac Books, 2009).

xvii *Chandler Burr reminds us . . . spoken of in reverent tones simply as* le monstre—*the monster:* Chandler Burr, *The Perfect Scent: A Year Inside the Perfume Indus-try in Paris and New York* (New York: Henry Holt, 2007), 143.

xvii *"It's unbelievable! It's not a fragrance; it's a goddamn cultural monument, like Coke":* Ibid.

CHAPTER ONE

3 *at nearly four hundred dollars an ounce:* At the time of press, a .25-ounce bottle of Chanel No. 5 retails for $95, www.chanel.com/en_US/fragrance-beauty/Fragrance-N°5-N°5-PARFUM–88173.

4 *Gabrielle Chanel's peasant roots:* Several biographies explore the details of Coco Chanel's early life, and I have drawn on the following source material throughout this book: Pierre Galante, *Mademoiselle Chanel,* trans. Eileen Geist and Jessie Wood (Chicago: Henry Regnery Company, 1973); Axel Madsen, *Chanel: A Woman of Her Own* (New York: Henry Holt, 1990); Frances Kennett, *Coco: The Life and Loves of Gabrielle Chanel* (London: Victor Gollancz, 1989); Edmonde Charles-Roux, *Chanel,* trans. Nancy

Amphoux (London: Harvill Press, 1995); Claude Baillén, *Chanel Solitaire,* trans. Barbara Bray (New York: Quadrangle, 1973); Misia Sert, *Misia and the Muses: The Memoirs of Misia Sert* (New York: John Day Company, 1953); and Isabelle Fiemeyer, *Coco Chanel: Un Parfun* [sic] *de Mystère* (Payot: Paris, 1999).

5 *saint Étienne d'Obazine: La Vie de Saint Étienne Fondateur et Premier Abbé du Monastère d'Obazine,* ed. Monsignor Denéchau (Tulle, France: Jean Mazeyrie, 1881).

5 *Coco Chanel once later said that fashion was architecture:* Haedrich, *Coco Chanel,* 252.

6 *Charles-Roux always believed that: "Whenever [Coco] began yearning for austerity, for the ultimate in cleanliness":* Charles-Roux, *Chanel,* 43.

6 *Bernard of Clairvaux, who founded the Cistercian movement:* See Bernard of Clairvaux, *Sermons on the Song of Songs,* trans. Kilian Walsh (Collegeville, MN: Cistercian Publications / Liturgical Press, 1976).

7 *Étienne had made a mission of planting richly scented flowers everywhere in the empty ravines and wastes around his abbeys:* See *La Vie de Saint Étienne Fondateur et Premier Abbé du Monastère d'Obazine;* the life specifies that Étienne planted the hills with "flowers yellow and rose," 233.

7 *stone staircase at Aubazine that led to the children's bedchambers:* Madsen, *Chanel: A Woman of Her Own,* 17.

7 *It was a desperately unhappy childhood:* Baillén, *Chanel Solitaire,* 167.

7 *it remained a guarded and shameful secret:* Charles-Roux, *Chanel,* 43.

8 *the aroma of sheets boiled in copper pots sweetened with dried root of iris:* Ibid.

8 *Aubazine was also filled with symbols and the mysterious power of numbers:* Fiemeyer, *Coco Chanel,* 74; my thanks to Madame Michèle Millas and to the staff and sisters at the abbey of Aubazine for their hospitality and assistance.

8 *Double columns reflected the duality of body and spirit, earth and heaven:* Aubazine, local historical information sheet, courtesy Michèle Millas; the information on the symbolic importance of architectural numerology that follows also refers to this source material.

8 *these are the churches most closely associated with the occult mysteries of the Knights Templar:* See Walid Amine Salhab, *The Knights Templar of the Middle East* (San Francisco: Red Wheel, 2006).

8 *"Cistercian cathedrals, churches, and abbeys . . . are built on measures . . . which equal more or less [the] Golden Ratio of Pythagoras":* Salhab, *The Knights Templar of the Middle East,* 158.

9 *"No. 5 was her fetishistic number from childhood":* Fiemeyer, *Coco Chanel,* 74.

9 *"she engraved it in the earth . . . with a branch she had picked up":* Ibid.

10 *name "'Cistercian,' and that of [its] first monastery, Citeaux, both come from the word cistus, of the Cistaceae rockrose":* Karen Ralls, *Knights Templar Encyclopedia: The Essential Guide to the People, Places, Events, and Symbols of the Order of the Temple* (Franklin Lakes, NJ: New Page Books, 2007), 54.

10 *Alexandre Dumas brought them to the popular vaudeville stage a generation*

later: Alexandre Dumas, *La Dame aux Camélias* (1847) (New York: Oxford University Press, 2000); Giuseppe Verdi, *La Traviata* (1853) (New York: G. Schirmer, 1986), libretto; Beverly Seaton, *The Language of Flowers: A History* (Charlottesville: University of Virginia, 1995).

10 "La Dame aux Camélias," *she once said, "was my life, all the trashy novels I'd fed on":* Baillén, *Chanel Solitare,* 180.

10 *It was the shape, she always said, of infinite possibility:* Linda Grant, "Coco Chanel, la dame aux camélias," *London Telegraph,* July 29, 2007, www .telegraph.co.uk/fashion/stellamagazine/3360675/Coco-Chanel-la-dame-aux-camelias.html.

CHAPTER TWO

13 *In just another few months, the painter Henri Matisse and his compatriots:* See Pat Shipman, *Femme Fatale: Love, Lies, and the Unknown Life of Mata Hari* (New York: Harper Perennial, 2008); Rachel Shteir, *Striptease: The Untold History of the Girlie Show* (Oxford, UK: Oxford University Press, 2005); Alfred Marquet, *From Fauvism to Impressionism* (New York: Rizzoli, 2002).

14 *dance halls like La Rotonde:* Charles-Roux, *Chanel,* 82.

14 *selling lingerie and hosiery at a boutique called* À Sainte Marie *in Moulins*: Charles-Roux, *Chanel,* 56.

15 *Called simply* La Jolie Parfumeuse—*"the pretty perfumer":* Charles-Roux, *Chanel,* 53, 78; Hector Jonathan Crémieux and Ernest Blum, La Jolie Parfumeuse, *An Opera-Comique in Three Acts* (New York: Metropolitan Print, 1875).

16 *What had occurred to her was—as she put it herself years later—that she had "a hot little body":* Judith Thurman, "Scenes from a Marriage: The House of Chanel at the Met," *The New Yorker,* May 23, 2005, www.newyorker.com/ archive/2005/05/23/050523crat_atlarge1?currentPage=all.

16 *the tunes of "Qui qu'a vu Coco" and "Ko Ko Ri Ko":* "Ko Ko Ri Ko" was a song from the popular turn-of-the-century one-act opera *Ba-Ta-Clan* (1855), by Jacques Offenbach—the man behind *La Jolie Parfumeuse*—and librettist Ludovic Halévy. Ko Ko Ri Ko (baritone) is a French colonialist plotting a coup d'état against the Chinese emperor; the plot involves humorous political machinations, rousing songs, and jokes about Frenchmen meeting abroad. The character may have later been an inspiration for Ko Ko in Gilbert and Sullivan's *Mikado* (1885). Mary E. Davis notes that it was made famous as a piece of boulevard music in 1897 by the stage star Émilie Marie Bouchaud, better known as Polaire; see Mary E. Davis, *Classic Chic: Music, Fashion, Modernism* (Berkeley: University of California Press, 2006), 154.

The other song that gave Coco her nickname was also a popular stage number. Davis writes that "Qui qu'a vu Coco dans le Trocadero" was a "'canine complaint' recounting the adventures of a lost dog, which was composed by Elise Faure in 1889," 154. The lyrics translate to "Who has seen Coco on the Trocadero, / Haven't you seen Coco? / Coco on the Trocadero, / Co on the Tro, / Co on the Tro, / Coco on the Trocadero, / Who, oh, who has seen Coco? / Eh! Coco! / Eh! Coco! / Who, oh, who has seen Coco? / Eh! Coco!"

16 *"For a large section of society, the similarities between the actress's life and the prostitute's or* demi-mondaine's *were unforgettable and overruled all other evidence of respectability":* Tracy C. Davis, *Actresses as Working Women: Their Social Identity in Victorian Culture* (London: Routledge, 1991), 69.

17 *She had consented to "be 'hired' for amusement":* Davis, *Actresses as Working Women,* 69.

17 *what her biographers believe was a botched abortion:* Madsen, *Chanel,* 27.

17 *"I've already had one protector named Étienne, and he performed miracles too":* Charles-Roux, *Chanel,* 73.

18 *She had been mistress to the king of Belgium:* See Claude Dufresne, *Trois Grâces de la Belle Époque* (Paris: Bartillat, 2003); Cornelia Otis Skinner, *Elegant Wits and Grand Horizontals* (New York: Houghton Mifflin, 1962); Florence Tamagne, *A History of Homosexuality in Europe: Berlin, London, Paris, 1919–1939* (New York: Algora Publishing, 2006); and Marcel Proust, *À la recherche du temps perdu* (Paris: Gallimard, 2002).

18 *there was a notable difference between the scent of a courtesan and the scent of a nice girl:* Richard Stamelman, *Perfume: Joy, Obsession, Scandal, Sin* (New York: Rizzoli, 2006), 29, 93; see also Edwin Morris, *Fragrance: The Story of Perfume from Cleopatra to Chanel* (New York: Charles Scribner's, 1984).

19 *the world's oldest perfume was made on the Mediterranean island of Cyprus:* John Roach, "Oldest Perfumes in History Found on Aphrodite's Island," *National Geographic News,* March 29, 2007.

19 *the ancient world's most famous cults dedicated to sacred prostitution:* Stephanie Budin, *The Myth of Sacred Prostitution* (Cambridge, UK: Cambridge University Press, 2008), 50.

19 *a plant resin from the Cistercians' cistus or rockrose, known as labdanum—is inherently sexy:* See, for example, Manfred Milinski and Claus Wedekind, "Evidence for MHC-Correlated Perfume Preferences in Humans," *Behavioral Ecology* 12, no. 2 (2001): 140–49; for more on the origins of this material, see H. Greche, N. Mrabet, and S. Zrira, "The Volatiles of the Leaf Oil of *Cistus ladanifer L. var. albiflorus* and Labdanum Extracts of Moroccan Origin and Their Antimicrobial Activities," *Journal of Essential Oil Research* 21, no. 2 (2009), 166–73.

19 *the "floating gold" known as ambergris or "gray amber":* See Cynthia Graber, "Strange but True, Whale Waste Is Extremely Valuable," *Scientific American,* April 26, 2007; Corey Kilgannon, "Gift of Petrified Whale Vomit Could Be Worth Its Weight in Gold," *San Francisco Chronicle,* December 25, 2006, A22.

19 *Jeanne Bécu, better known to history as the celebrated royal courtesan Madame du Barry:* See Joan Haslip, *Madame du Barry: The Wages of Beauty* (London: Tauris Parke, 2005); Corey Kilgannon, "Please Let It Be Whale Vomit, and Not Just Sea Junk," *New York Times,* December 18, 2006, http://www

.nytimes.com/2006/12/18/nyregion/18whale.html?pagewanted=print; Kilgannon, "Gift of Petrified Whale Vomit." See also Cynthia Graber, "Strange but True, Whale Waste Is Extremely Valuable," *Scientific American*, April 26, 2007, www.scientificamerican.com/article.cfm?id=strange-but-true-whale-waste-is-valuable.

20 *Joséphine doused everything in the palace at Versailles in the intimate smells of animal musk:* Stamelman, *Perfume*, 120.

20 *"the* 'odor di femina' *of prostitutes and other women of easy virtue":* Stamelman, *Perfume*, 95.

20 *"were marked as belonging to the marginal world of prostitutes and courtesans":* Stamelman, *Perfume*, 29.

20 *Women "of good taste and standing" wore "only [the] simple floral scents":* Stamelman, *Perfume*, 95.

20 *So keen was her nose . . . the way some of those other kept women smelled made her nauseous:* Madsen, *Chanel*, 38.

21 *women with the childish bodies known as* fruits verts—*green fruits:* Madsen, *Chanel*, 36; for its origins in erotic literature of the period, see, for example, Alphonse Momas, *Green Girls* (Paris: Renaudie, 1899); or the pseudonymous "Donewell," *Green Girls* (Paris: Bouillant, 1899), cited in Peter Mendes, *Clandestine Fiction in English 1800–1930, A Bibliographical Study*, Scolar [*sic*] Press (Aldershot, UK, 1993), 312; thanks to Stephen Halliwell, Christine Roth, and the Victoria listserv for this reference.

21 *what was titillating wasn't women who looked like men, "but rather like children":* Alison Laurie, *The Language of Clothes* (New York: Random House, 1981), quoted in Davis, *Classic Chic*, 163.

21 *Victor Margueritte's scandalously erotic novel* La Garçonne*:* Victor Margueritte, *La Garçonne* (New York: A. Knopf, 1923; Paris: E. Flammarion, 1922; with illustrations by Kees van Dongen).

CHAPTER THREE

24 *She liked that Boy smelled of "leather, horses, forest, and saddle soap":* Madsen, *Chanel*, 49; details of Coco Chanel's early life here and following drawn from the various biographies cited above.

24 *Virginia Woolf would make the bold assertion that "On or about December 1910 human character changed," bringing along with it sweeping changes in "religion, conduct, politics, and literature":* Virginia Woolf, "Mr. Bennett and Mrs. Brown," in Mitchell A. Leaska, ed., *The Virginia Woolf Reader* (San Diego: Harcourt, 1984), 194.

24 *the initial lease on her boutique on rue Cambon had in it a clause:* Galante, *Mademoiselle Chanel*, 30.

25 *Fragrance had already made the young Corsican entrepreneur François Coty . . . one of France's richest men:* Roulhac B. Toledano and Elizabeth Z. Coty, *François Coty: Fragrance, Power, Money* (Gretna, LA: Pelican Publishing, 2009), 24.

25 *Inspired by the "heavily perfumed odalisques in* Scheherazade," *it was a sultan's*

fantasy: Christine Mayer Lefkowith, *Paul Poiret and His Rosine Perfumes* (New York: Editions Stylissimo, 2007), 36; also the source of details on the launch of Parfums de Rosine below. Dana Thomas, speaking with perfumer Jean Kerléo, reports that Poiret may have developed before Nuit Persanes a fragrance called Coupe d'Or (Golden Cup), also suggestive of oriental fantasy. See Dana Thomas, *Deluxe: How Luxury Lost Its Luster* (New York: Penguin, 2007), 141.

25 *That summer evening, on June, 24, 1911, the warm air was alive with the sound of low Persian music:* The party is described by Paul Poiret in his memoirs; see Paul Poiret, *The King of Fashion: The Autobiography of Paul Poiret* (London: V & A Publishing), 2009.

27 *Maurice Babani became the second couturier to launch a signature scent:* Marie-Christine Grasse, Elisabeth de Feydeau, and Freddy Ghozland, *L'un des sens. Le Parfum au XXème siècle* (Toulouse: Éditions Milan, 2001), page for 1921.

27 *bestselling book,* Modern Dancing, *written by the couple of the hour, Verne and Irene Castle:* Vernon and Irene Castle, *Modern Dancing* (New York: Harper, 1914); see also Eve Golden, *Vernon and Irene's Ragtime Revolution* (Lexington: University Press of Kentucky, 2007).

28 *just because he and Coco were in love didn't mean that Boy didn't have a stable of mistresses:* Baillén, *Mademoiselle Chanel*, 20; Haedrich, *Coco Chanel*, 76.

28 *she could afford to treat herself to a seaside villa in the south of France and a "little blue Rolls":* Davis, *Classic Chic*, 169.

29 *"The war helped me," Chanel later remembered. "Catastrophes show . . . I woke up famous":* Haedrich, *Coco Chanel*, 95.

29 *the city was still filled with many of the two million American soldiers:* Toledano and Coty, *François Coty*, 24.

29 *large fragrance companies like Bourjois and Coty had begun setting up offices in the United States by the 1910s:* On the history of the French perfume industry and the American markets, see Toledano and Coty, *François Coty*; Geneviève Fontan, *Générations Bourjois* (Toulouse, France: Arfon, 2005); Morris, *Fragrance*; Harvey Levenstein, *We'll Always Have Paris: American Tourists in France Since 1930* (Chicago: University of Chicago Press, 2004); and Helen M. Caldwell, "1920–29: The Decade of the French Mystique in the American Perfume Market," http://faculty.quinnipiac.edu/charm/CHARM%20proceedings/CHARM%20article%20archive%20pdf%20format/Volume%204%201989/259%20caldwell.pdf.

30 *François Coty, who in 1919 became France's first billionaire . . . wife Yvonne, who had also made her start as a fellow milliner in Paris:* Details here and following from Toledano and Coty, *François Coty*, 24, 50, *passim*; Coty had earned his first billion by 1919.

30 *Coco Chanel received an excited visit from a friend, the bohemian socialite Misia Sert:* See Arthur Gold, *Misia: The Life of Misia Sert* (New York: Vintage, 1992).

31 *They had talked about it already, debated bottle designs, and even planned how Coco*

would market it to her couture clients: According to Misia Sert, "Together we studied the packaging, a solemn, ultra-simple, quasi-pharmaceutical bottle, but in the Chanel taste and wrapped in . . . elegance," Madsen, *Chanel*, 133.

31 *It was a formula for the lost "miraculous perfume" of the Medici queens:* Charles-Roux, *Chanel*, 164.

31 *After all, the history of perfume-making in France began at the court of the Medici queens:* See Nigel Groom, *The New Perfume Handbook* (London: Chapman and Hall, 1997).

31 *"set up a laboratory in Grasse for the study of perfume-making in order to rival the fashionable Arab perfumes":* Groom, *The New Perfume Handbook*, 143.

32 *She paid six thousand francs—the equivalent of nearly $10,000 today:* Determining the relative value of historical currency is a notoriously imprecise science; all contemporary figures given here are based on the calculators developed by Professors Lawrence H. Officer and Samuel H. Williamson at www.measuring worth.com/uscompare/. The value of all commodities are calculated using consumer-price-index measures; other measures are as noted.

32 *Misia Sert would later claim that this was the origin of Chanel No. 5:* Madsen, *Chanel*, 133; see also Dominque Laty, *Misia Sert et Coco Chanel* (Paris: Jacob, 2009); Misia Sert, *Misia par Misia* (Paris: Gallimard, 1952); Gold, *Misia*.

32 *His wife, Yvonne, always claimed that . . . François offered to let her use his laboratory for the development:* Toledano and Coty, *François Coty*; the authors claim that, as late as 1960, there were people who saw the original bill, "presented on old brown paper with the company watermark," 86.

34 *"We were in love," she later remembered, "we could have gotten married":* Madsen, *Chanel*, 91.

35 *"For a woman," Coco Chanel would later say, "betrayal has just one sense: that of the senses":* Baillén, *Chanel Solitaire*, 69.

CHAPTER FOUR

38 *These were favorite summer retreats for artists, intellectuals, and impoverished foreign princes:* Marie-Christine Grasse, interview, 2009.

39 *Lady Abdy remembered, "When she decided on something, she followed her idea to the end. In order to bring it off and succeed she brought everything into play":* Kennett, *Coco*, 49.

39 *Today, there are at least a half-dozen different rubrics for diagramming all the possible categories of perfume:* Perhaps the most widely used—but also rather complex—is the twelve-part fragrance wheel developed by Michael Edwards in the 1980s. For more on the topic, see also Luca Turin and Tania Sanchez, *Perfumes: The Guide* (New York: Viking, 2008); Stamelman, *Perfume*; Charles Sell, *The Chemistry of Fragrances: From Perfumer to Consumer* (London: Royal Society of Chemistry Publishing, 2005); David J. Rowe and Philip Kraft, *Chemistry and Technology of Flavours and Fragrances* (Oxford, UK: Blackwell, 2004); Jonathan Pereira, *The Elements of Materia Medica and Therapeutics* (Philadelphia: Blanchard and Lea, 1854); Morris, *Fragrance*; La Société

Française des Parfumeurs, Osmothèque, *La Mémoire Vivante des Parfums,* Brochure Historique (Versailles: Osmothèque, n.d.); and Groom, *The New Perfume Handbook.*

40 *When Cleopatra famously set sail to meet Mark Anthony:* See Lisa Manniche, *Sacred Luxuries: Fragrance, Aromatherapy, and Cosmetics in Ancient Egypt* (Ithaca, NY: Cornell University Press, 1999); also Stamelman, *Perfume.*

40 *Aimé Guerlain's "ferociously modern" scent Jicky . . . the classical oriental perfume Shalimar:* Stamelman, *Perfume,* 97; on the history of vanilla, see Patricia Rain, *Vanilla: The Cultural History of the World's Favorite Flavor and Fragrance* (New York: Penguin, 2004).

41 *traditional perfumery relied on perhaps as few as a hundred natural scent materials:* See Milinski and Wedekind, "Evidence for MHC-Correlated Perfume Preferences in Humans"; also Lyall Watson, *Jacobson's Organ and the Remarkable Nature of Smell* (New York: Plume, 2001).

41 *the first scent to use a synthetic aromatic, the compound coumarin . . . new scent materials known as quinolines:* First synthesized in 1868; Stamelman, *Perfume,* 96–97.

42 *In 1895, the fragrance-industry giant Bourjois introduced a chypre . . . Chypre de Limassol:* Fontan, *Générations Bourjois,* 48; see also *Perfume Intelligence: A Comprehensive Illustrated Encyclopedia of Perfume,* http://www.perfume intelligence.co.uk/library/index.htm.

44 *At the turn of the century, the runaway bestseller was François Coty's La Rose Jacqueminot (1903):* Toledano and Coty, *François Coty,* 60.

44 *A special formulation called Violetta di Parma (1870) was the signature fragrance of the empress Marie Louise Bonaparte:* See Francesca Sandrini, et al., *Maria Luigia e le Violette di Parma* (Parma, Italy: Pubblicazioni del Museo Glauco Lombardi, 2008).

45 *"dreamed of imitating nature but of transforming the real," with a new "emotive perfumery":* Stamelman, *Perfume,* 98.

46 *"[T]he perfume many women use . . . is not mysterious. . . . I don't want a woman to smell like a rose":* "People, March 16, 1931," *Time,* March 16, 1931, L7, www .time.com/time/magazine/article/0,9171,769528,00.html; also quoted in Galante, *Mademoiselle Chanel,* 26.

46 *"I want," she had decided, "to give women an artificial perfume":* Pierre Galante, *Les années Chanel* (Paris: *Paris-Match* / Mercure de France, 1972), 79–80.

46 *A woman, she thought, "should smell like a woman and not like a flower":* Various sources, including, for example, Galante, *Mademoiselle Chanel,* 67.

46 *"A badly perfumed woman . . . is a woman without a future":* Interview with Jacques Chazot, produced as "Dim Dam Dom," directed by Guy Job, 1969.

CHAPTER FIVE

47 *The musical references in both cases are telling:* Ernest Beaux later said, "It is like writing music. Each component has a definite tonal value . . . I can compose a waltz or a funeral march," "Business Abroad: King of Perfume," *Time,* Sep-

tember 14, 1953, www.time.com/time/magazine/article/0,9171,858285,00
.htm.

48 *Women sunbathed on the beaches wearing ropes of pearls:* For a cultural history of
the 1920s, see, for example, William Wiser, *Crazy Years: The Twenties in Paris*
(London: Thames and Hudson, 1990); Carol Mann, *Paris Between the Wars*
(New York: Vendome Press, 1996).

48 *"It was a whole race going hedonistic, deciding on pleasure":* F. Scott Fitzgerald,
The Jazz Age (New York: New Directions, 1996), 6.

48 *Soviet Russia after the revolution of 1917:* On the history of this period in
Russia, see Sheila Fitzpatrick, *The Russian Revolution* (Oxford: Oxford University Press, 2008).

49 *"While in his cups," Rasputin it seems told the two young noblemen about the
czarina's "fixed intention":* *Russian Diary of an Englishman, Petrograd, 1915–
1917* (London: William Heinemann, 1919), 5. Details also drawn from Felix
Youssoupoff, *Lost Splendor: The Amazing Memoirs of the Man Who Killed Rasputin* (New York: Helen Marx Books, 2007); Evard Radzinsky, *The Rasputin
File* (New York: Anchor, 2001).

50 *When Dmitri's part in the murder was discovered:* See *Russian Diary of an Englishman*; the anonymous civil servant writes, "All the Imperial Family are off
their heads at the Grand Duke Dmitri's arrest, for even the Emperor has not
the right to arrest his family. . . . it was for threatening to arrest the Tzesarvich [Alexander I] that the Emperor Paul was killed," 87–88.

50 *"the confines of the Empire [at] the Persian border":* See *Russian Diary of an Englishman*, 79.

51 *in the* New York Times *that "Rumors spread he was traveling in fetters":* "The
German Propaganda: How It Spread in Russia and Roused Popular Indignation," *New York Times*, March 16, 1917.

51 *We "implore you," they wrote in their petition, "to reconsider your harsh decision":*
See *Russian Diary of an Englishman*, 211.

51 *"The past, our past, still held the most important part of our lives":* Marie Pavlovna, *A Princess in Exile* (New York: Viking Press, 1932), 70–71.

51 *one of Paris's most famous textile and embroidery houses, Kitmir:* See Marion
Mienert, *Maria Pavlovna: A Romanov Grand Duchess in Russia and in Exile*
(Mainz, Germany: Lennart-Bernadotte-Stiftung, 2004).

52 *known as Rallet O-De-Kolon No. 1 Vesovoi—or simply Rallet No. 1 perfume:*
Philip Kraft, Christine Ledard, and Philip Goutell, "From *Rallet No. 1* to
Chanel No. 5 versus *Mademoiselle Chanel No. 1*," *Perfume and Flavorist*, October 2007, 36–41, 37–38. This seminal article is the source for information
throughout on the chemical structures of Rallet No. 5, Mademoiselle Chanel
No. 1, and Chanel No. 5-like perfumes.

52 *Among the personal possessions looted from the Romanov royal family's prison
chambers were vials of some unnamed perfumes:* "List of Valuables Taken by
Yurovsky from the Romanovs," www.alexanderpalace.org/palace/Yurovsky
List.html.

53 *They may have met in Venice that first winter after Boy's death, in early 1920:* Charles-Roux, *Chanel*, 199.

54 *Fabergé, the Russian-French jewelry firm . . . fled to exile in Switzerland:* Toby Faber, *Fabergé's Eggs: The Extraordinary Story of the Masterpieces That Outlived an Empire* (New York: Random House, 2008); Eric Onstad, "Revived Fabergé to Create First Egg Since 1917," *USA Today*, May 23, 2008, www.usatoday.com/money/industries/retail/2008-05-23-faberge-eggs_N.htm.

54 *which had been purchased in 1898 by a prominent French family of perfume distributors:* Kraft, Ledard, and Goutell, "From *Rallet No. 1* to *Chanel No. 5*," 39.

55 *as he later remembered, it "became an incredible success":* Interview with Ernest Beaux, in S. Samuels, "Souvenirs d'un Parfumeur," *Industrie de la Parfumerie* 1, no. 7 (October 1947), 228–31; Beaux's recollections are the source of other details in this chapter.

56 *interrogating Bolshevik prisoners in Arkangelsk, at the infamous Mudyug Island prison:* Pavel P. Rasskavov, *Notes of a Prisoner* (Arkhangel: Sevkraigiz, 1935).

56 *It has since been called modern history's first concentration camp:* Robert C. Toth, "Diplomats Say TV Show Instigates Hatred, Soviets Blame 'Amerika' for Vandalism," *Los Angeles Times*, February 18, 1987, http://articles.latimes.com/1987-02-18/news/mn-2723_1.

56 *These alliances—and the many wartime decorations that he earned for his service to France and Britain and in the cause of the White Russians:* Gilberte Beaux, interview, 2010.

56 *Bolshevik prisoners at the camp in Arkangelsk later remembered a Lieutenant Beaux:* Rasskavov, *Notes of a Prisoner*, transliterated in Russian to "Bo." See also Beaux, "Souvenirs."

57 *Misia Sert and Paul Morand both believed that Dmitri was the one:* Madsen, *Chanel*, 132; as Madsen notes, some people have also suggested that the French novelist Colette might have made the introduction. However, since Coco Chanel and Colette didn't become friends until sometime after 1922, that scenario is impossible.

CHAPTER SIX

59 *Ernest was hesitant:* Galante, *Mademoiselle Chanel*, 74.

60 *The gap in the numbers reflected the fact that these were scents in two different—but complementary—series:* Beaux, in "Souvenirs," explains, "I created in 1919–1920, in addition to No. 5 of which I have spoken, No. 22 and a series of other different perfumes." See also "Business Abroad," *Time*, 1953.

60 *"that is what I was waiting for. A perfume like nothing else. A woman's perfume, with the scent of a woman":* Galante, *Les années Chanel*, 85.

61 *It had been Boy Capel's magic number, too, something else they shared:* Boy Capel introduced Coco Chanel to the new spiritualist movement known as theosophism, of which he was an enthusiastic member, and, as one of Chanel's biographers writes: "Boy also had a penchant for the number five, speaking of divinities with five heads in Hinduism, the five horizons, the five visions of

the Buddha, the mystique of the number five in China, the number five in alchemy also, and the other uses of this sacred and magical number," Fiemeyer, *Coco Chanel*, 74; see also Haedrich, *Coco Chanel*, 138.

Theosophism was a blend of these different spiritual traditions. It was a religion of mediums and séances, popular in the first decades of the twentieth century with fashionable bohemians, a blend of ancient yogic philosophy and the Russian mysticism of its founder, the celebrated psychic Madame Blavatsky. It was also, unfortunately, not entirely free of those rising currents of European anti-Semitism. Writes one historian, "The semites were in Blavatsky's scheme. . . . 'later' Aryans—degenerate in spirituality, and perfected in 'materiality,'" Colin Kidd, *The Forging of Races: Race and Scripture in the Protestant Atlantic World* (Cambridge: Cambridge University Press, 2006), 244.

Among the central beliefs of theosophism—familiar ground for Coco Chanel—was a faith in numerology and, especially, in the magic of quintessence. "*Quintessence* or the *fifth dimension*," the theosophists believe,

> is . . . of a metaphysical nature [and] leads us to consider the number five, a most sacred Pythagorean number, associated in ancient symbolism with the mysteries of Life. It evokes especially the five-fold nature of man, the microcosm, whose symbol is the five-pointed star. Nature aims visibly at the production of beautiful shapes. . . . All the kingdoms are teeming with masterpieces of creation. . . . witnesses of the finest kind of aesthetic imagination. [Hermine Sabetay, "Creative Asymmetry," *The Theosophist Magazine*, August 1962, 301–308; 304–305.]

As Coco Chanel once said, "I believe in the fourth, fifth, sixth dimensions." It comes, she explained, "from the need for reassurance, for a belief that one never loses everything." All her life, Coco Chanel believed that Boy Capel communicated with her from beyond this world of substance; see Haedrich, *Coco Chanel*, 138.

For further information on these "dimensions" as Coco Chanel understood them, see also Herbert Radcliffe, "Is There a Fourth Dimension?" *World Theosophy*, February–June 1931, 293–296; Helena Petrovna Blavatsky, *The Secret Doctrine* (Wheaton, IL: Theosophical Publishing House, 1993).

61 *A fortune-teller had told her that it was the number of her special destiny:* "Chanel, the Couturier, Dead in Paris," *New York Times*, January 11, 1971.

61 *"I present my dress collections on the fifth of May, the fifth month of the year," she told him, "and so . . . it will bring good luck":* Beaux, "Souvenirs."

61 *A perfume, she once sermonized, "should resemble the person wearing it":* Interview with Jacques Chazot, produced as "Dim Dam Dom."

62 *chemists Georges Darzens and E. E. Blaise . . . found ways to separate and synthesize a large group of fragrance molecules:* Darzens directed the perfume research

laboratory at L. T. Piver from 1897–1920; see Michael Edwards, *Perfume Legends* (Levallois: H.M. Editions, 1996), 43, 83.

62 *A chemist would say that the hydrogen in the ethanol, the kind of alcohol in wine, combines with the oxygen in the air:* Technically, ethanol oxidizes to acetic acid, with acetaldehyde as an intermediary stage; acetaldehyde is also the result of the fermentation process; see S. Q. Liu and G. J. Pilone, "An Overview of Formation and Roles of Acetaldehyde in Winemaking with Emphasis on Microbiological Implications," *International Journal of Food Science and Technology* 35 (2000), 49–61.

63 *Aldehydes have the smell of many things:* For the best general discussion, see Luca Turin, *The Secret of Scent: Adventures in Perfume and the Science of Smell* (New York: Harper Perennial, 2006), 54.

63 *The "unblemished whiteness of [these] aldehydes," writes one fragrance expert, is the smell of "powder snow":* Jim Drobnick, ed., *The Smell Culture Reader* (Oxford, UK: Berg Publishers, 2006), 226, writing here about Estée Lauder's strongly aldehydic fragrance White Linen, based on the almost equally aldehydic Chanel No. 22, based on Chanel No. 5; see also Turin, *The Secret of Scent*, 54, for the role of aldehydes in White Linen.

64 *They are part of what gives a fine wine its heady bouquet and smooth tannins:* On the role of aldehydes in wine, see Siss Frivik and Susan Ebeler, "Influence of Sulfur Dioxide on the Formation of Aldehydes in White Wine," *American Journal of Viticulture and Enology* 54, no. 1 (2003): 31–38; Laura Culleré, Jaun Cacho, and Vincente Ferreira, "Analysis for Wine C5-C8 Aldehydes through the Determination of Their O-(2,3,4,5,6-pentafluorobenzyl)oximes Formed Directly in the Solid Phrase Extraction Cartridge," *Analytica Chimica Acta* 523, no. 1–2 (2004): 201–206.

64 *One of the earliest aldehydes discovered, cinnamaldehyde:* For details on aldehydes, my thanks to Ron Winnegrad and Subha Patel at International Flavors and Fragrances and to conservator Elizabeth Morse.

64 *adding aldehydes to the rich scents of florals is very much like what happens when a cook drizzles fresh lemon over strawberries:* Jacques Polge, Chanel, interview, 2009.

64 *Chemists will also argue that aldehydes have the effect of stimulating what is known as the trigeminal nerve:* Luca Turin, interview, 2009; see also Ron S. Jackson, *Wine Tasting: A Professional Handbook* (San Diego: Elsevier Academic Press, 2002), 52; E. Joy Bowles, *The Chemistry of Aromatherapeutic Oils* (Crows Nest, Australia: Allen & Unwin Academic, 2004), 148; Hirokazu Tsubone and Meiji Kawata, "Stimulation to the Trigeminal Afferent Nerve of the Nose by Formaldehyde, Acrolein, and Acetaldehyde Gases," *Inhalation Toxicology* 3, no. 2 (1991): 211–22.

65 *"most aromatic compounds can [also] stimulate trigeminal nerve fibers":* Jackson, *Wine Tasting*, 52.

65 *There at the northern reaches of the world, stationed along the Polar Circle:* See

K. Sieg, E. Starokozhev, E. Fries, S. Sala, and W. Püttmann, "N-Aldehydes (C6–C10) in Snow Samples Collected at the High Alpine Research Station Jungfraujoch during CLACE 5," *Atmospheric Chemistry and Physics,* vol. 9 (2009), 8071–99, www.atmos-chem-phys-discuss.net/9/8071/2009; and "Atmospheric Chemicals Seen in a New Light," *CNN,* March 23, 1999.

65 *"I finally captured it, but not without effort, because the first aldehydes that I was able to find were unstable and unreliably manufactured":* Beaux, "Souvenirs."

65 *Constantin Weriguine, later remembered: a "winter melting note":* Constantin Weriguine, *Souvenirs et Parfums: Mémoires d'un Parfumeur* (Paris: Plon, 1965); Weriguine notes that Ernest Beaux was working with the memory of what the Russians call *chernozem* ("black soil"), a humus-rich soil scent, to capture the idea of melting snow in the spring, 162.

65 *He warned Coco Chanel that a perfume with this much jasmine would be fabulously expensive:* According to Pierre Galante, *Les années Chanel,* 85, Ernest Beaux told her, "There are in this bottle more than twenty ingredients. This perfume will be expensive." She asked, "Ah, what is it that's so expensive in there?" "The jasmine," he told her. "Nothing is more expensive than jasmine." To which she replied, "Ah, good! Use more. I want to make the most expensive perfume in the world."

67 *" was the first fragrance to make use of synthetically replicated molecules taken from products of natural origin called aldehydes":* Susannah Frankel, "The Chanel No. 5 Story," *The Independent,* October 15, 2008, www.independent.co.uk/news/people/profiles/the-chanel-no-5-story-961226.html; Nigel Groom, *The New Perfume Handbook* (London: Chapman and Hall, 1997), 61, also calls it "The first of the aldehyde perfumes." Kate Shapland, "Chanel No. 5: Enduring Love," *The Telegraph,* May 7, 2009, www.telegraph.co.uk/fashion/labels/chanel/5285472/Chanel-No-5-enduring-love.html, credits it with being "the world of scent's first abstract olfactory creation." None of these statements is entirely correct.

67 *Even Robert Bienaimé's groundbreaking scent Quelques Fleurs—which used one of the so-called C–12 aldehydes:* See Kraft, Ledard, and Goutell, "From *Rallet No. 1* to *Chanel No. 5.*"

67 *Pierre Armingeat and Georges Darzens's Reve d'Or (1905) and Floramye (1905) claim the honors:* Bernard Chant, "The Challenge of Creativity," *Newsletter of the British Society of Perfumers,* 1983, www.bsp.org.uk/newsarc/creat.html; see also the excellent discussion by perfume historian and blogger Elena Vosnaki, "Myth Debunking 1: What Are Aldehydes, How Do Aldehydes Smell and Chanel No. 5," *Perfume Shrine,* December 2, 2008, http://perfumeshrine.blogspot.com/2008/12/myth-debunking-1-what-are-aldehydes-how.html. Some sources date Floramye to as early as 1895 or 1903, but the evidence is not conclusive. The sources claiming that Reve d'Or dates to 1925 have likely confused the original launch of the perfume with its relaunch in 1925. See Christie Mayer Lefkowith, *The Art of Perfume* (New York: Thames and Hudson, 1994).

67 *"it is the aldehyde note that, since the creation of Chanel No. 5, has more than any-thing else influenced new perfume compositions":* Beaux, "Souvenirs."

68 *"When did I invent it? In 1920 precisely. After my return from the war":* Ibid.

68 *As Edmonde Charles-Roux, tells it: "the development of No. 5 . . . proceeded in a rather heavy atmosphere . . .":* Charles-Roux, *Chanel,* 202.

69 *named not after the number of the fragrance vial but after the number of "a sta-tion in Coty's laboratory at either Suresnes or at the Rallet factory in the south of France":* Toledano and Coty, *François Coty,* 86.

69 *François Coty's massive perfume company had swallowed up yet another of his smaller competitors:* Kraft, Ledard, and Goutell, "From *Rallet No. 1* to *Chanel No. 5,*" 39; see also Toledano and Coty, *François Coty,* 56.

70 *They were based on a previous formula:* See Kraft, Ledard, and Goutell, "From Rallet No. 1 to Chanel No. 5"; on the basis of GCMS analysis of samples and archival research, the authors demonstrate the relationship among Le Bouquet de Catherine / Rallet No. 1, Chanel No. 5, Mademoiselle Chanel No. 1, and other fragrances, including Quelques Fleurs.

71 *adding to the blend, for example, his own rose-scent invention, "Rose E.B.," and the mixed notes of a jasmine field:* Private correspondence, Philip Kraft, 2009; see also the excellent entry on Chanel No. 5 at http://en.wikipedia.org/wiki/ Chanel_No._5, and the (purported) early Chanel No. 5 cologne formulae available online at http://asylum.zensoaps.com/index.php?showtopic=6800.

CHAPTER SEVEN

76 *wondered aloud, "What was that fragrance?" "The effect," she later said, "was amazing":* Galante, *Les années Chanel,* 85; the version is somewhat different in Madsen, *Chanel,* 134.

77 *we have perfumed ourselves with a remarkably small and consistent number of fragrances, perhaps only a hundred:* See Milinski and Wedekind, "Evidence for MHC-Correlated Perfume Preferences," 147; the authors estimate 100,000 scents in the world and claim that even the most average untrained human nose can recognize upward of ten thousand.

77 *"we are as strongly attracted to roses and violets as any bee":* Watson, *Jacobson's Organ,* 158.

77 *"In the lily of the valley they sell on the 1st of May, I can smell the hands of the kid who picked it":* Baillén, *Chanel Solitaire,* 86; Galante, *Mademoiselle Chanel,* 67.

78 *"share the same peculiar chemical architecture, carrying ten atoms of carbon and sixteen atoms of hydrogen in every molecule":* Watson, *Jacobson's Organ,* 165.

78 *As Lyall Watson writes in her book* Jacobson's Organ, *however, "it does these magical fragrances no favour to reduce them to esthers and aldehydes":* Watson, *Jacobson's Organ,* 165.

79 *Flowers are, after all, the essential machinery of a plant's reproductive organs, and perfumes are often made from their sexual secretions:* Watson, *Jacobson's Organ,* 157. On the difference between storax and styrax, below, see *The New Per-fume Handbook.*

79 *"many classical ingredients of natural origins [in perfume-making are] reminiscent of human body odors":* Milinski and Wedekind, "Evidence for MHC-Correlated Perfume Preferences," 148. This works, of course, at the level of minute sub-scents. The scent of a jasmine flower, for example, is made up of hundreds of different molecules, and the smell of a rose is made up of as many as a thousand. Of those thousand molecules, only a handful give the plant the aroma we recognize as a *rose* smell. All those other hundreds of molecules give a particular rose blossom the qualities that make it unique, and they create a set of sub-scents that operate, more often than not, somewhere below the threshold of our conscious recognition of them. As Milinski and Wedekind put it, while "the scents of . . . rose and jasmine apparently differ. . . . a natural flower oil may contain over 400 different odorants . . . [and] many classical ingredients of natural origins [are] reminiscent of human body odors. . . . It may be because of their subscents that specific species have a long tradition of being used for perfumes," 148; see also discussions in Chandler Burr, *The Emperor of Scent: A Story of Perfume, Obsession, and the Last Mystery of the Senses* (New York: Random House, 2003), 130; and Rachel Herz, *The Scent of Desire: Discovering Our Enigmatic Sense of Smell* (New York: William Morrow, 2007), 18.

79 *poet John Donne wrote about the "sweet sweat of roses":* John Donne, "The Comparison" (elegy 8, line 1), in *John Donne, The Complete English Poems*, ed. A. J. Smith (New York: Penguin, 1971).

79 *indoles are the smell of something sweet and fleshy and just a little bit dirty:* See Drobnick, *The Smell Culture Reader*, 214; jasmine, orange blossom, honeysuckle, tuberose, and ylang-ylang are flowers that, chemically speaking, have particularly high proportions of indoles. Other organic compounds with these same materials and sub-notes include sweat, feces, and rotting bodies.

79 *"several ingredients of incenses resembl[e] scents of the human body":* Lyall Watson writes, "the most interesting feature of incense . . . is that it comes from five principal sources: myrrh, frankincense, laudanum [i.e., labdanum], galbanus and styrax [or storax] . . . [and all] contain resin alcohols, called phytosterols, which biochemically are remarkably similar to human hormones," especially those found in our saliva, sweat, and urine, *Jacobson's Organ*, 152; see also "To Attract a Woman by Wearing Scent, a Man Must First Attract Himself," *The Economist*, December 8, 2008, 136.

79 *When the perfumer Paul Jellinek was writing what is still the standard textbook on the science of fragrance chemistry:* Paul Jellinek and Robert R. Calkin, *Perfumery: Practice and Principles* (Oxford: Wiley Interscience, 1993); cited in Watson, *Jacobson's Organ*, 153.

81 *When Coty was trying to convince a certain Henri de Villemessant, the man in charge of Paris's chic department store Les Grands Magasins:* Toledano and Coty, *François Coty*, 64.

81 *Having established No. 5's appeal, she returned to the idea of giving these samples of the scent to her most loyal clients as holiday gifts:* Details of the perfume's launch,

here and below, from various sources, including Galante, *Mademoiselle Chanel*, 76; Madsen, *Chanel*, 135.

CHAPTER EIGHT

83 *She and Molyneux also shared a certain sense of chaste minimalism:* On Molyneux as a designer, see *Decades of Fashion* (Potsdam, Germany: H. F. Ulmann, 2008).

84 *As Luca Turin writes: "[Edward Molyneux's] Numéro Cinq is surpassingly beautiful and strange":* Luca Turin, "Cinq Bis," *NZZ Folio: Die Zeitschrift der Neuen Zürcher Zeitung*, February 2008, www.nzzfolio.ch/www/d80bd71b-b264–4db4-afd0–277884b93470/showarticle/ee2a4e74–3cd7–4b81–86da–93db1de6f257.aspx; see also *Perfume Intelligence*, www.perfumeintelligence.co.uk/library/perfume/m/houses/Moly.htm. Lefkowith suggests the later date and proposes that Molyneux number three fragrance was named after the address of Maxim's in Paris; see *The Art of Perfume*, 200.

According to archival records at Guerlain, Shalimar was actually invented—and briefly launched—in 1921, the same year as Chanel No. 5 and, perhaps, as Molyneux's Numéro Cinq. When socialites in New York City became enamoured of the fragrance worn by Guerlain's wife, Shalimar was relaunched in 1925, with phenomenal success.

85 *as Misia Sert put it, "success beyond anything we could have imagined . . . the hen laying golden eggs":* Madsen, *Chanel*, 135.

87 *Chanel No. 5, Beaux remembered, "was already a remarkable success":* Beaux went on to say in his "Souvenirs" that " . . .it was the time of the Conférence de Cannes and the factory at La Bocca was the kind of thing that attracted distinguished visitors, who came curious to see my laboratory and the large installations in the soap factory. I had visits from Briand, Loucheur, Lloyd George, and lots of others. The great caricaturist Sem, he also came one day and after having smelled a number of laboratory trials and finished perfumes—he regarded me for an instant—and dubbed me Minister of the Nose."

89 *legendary land of Cockaigne (in French the pays de Cocagne), the mythical land of luxury and ease:* See Herman Pleij, *Dreaming of Cockaigne*, trans. Diane Webb (New York: Columbia University Press, 2001).

90 *"Suffering makes people better, not pleasure . . .":* Baillén, *Chanel Solitaire*, 146.

90 *As neuroscientist Rachel Herz writes in her book* The Scent of Desire, *"the areas . . .":* Herz, *Scent of Desire*, 3.

93 *The Wertheimers had made their fortunes at Bourjois selling perfumes and cosmetics manufactured for the theater and vaudeville stage:* Details here and following drawn from various sources, including the various biographies of Coco Chanel and from Bruno Abescat and Yves Stavridès, "Derrière l'Empire Chanel . . . la Fabuleuse Histoire des Wertheimer," *L'Express*, April 7, 2005, 16–30; July 11, 2005, 84–88; July 18, 2005, 82–86; July 25, 2005, 76–80; August 1, 2005, 74–78; August 8, 2005, 80–84, part 1, 29.

93 *Within just a few years, magazines would begin encouraging women to "analyz[e] one's own personality to discover 'its' style":* Sarah Berry, *Screen Style: Fashion and Femininity in 1930s Hollywood* (Minneapolis: University of Minnesota Press, 2000), 6.

94 *who took pleasure in swallowing up the smaller companies with whom he partnered was already well known:* See Toledano and Coty, *François Coty,* 87; the classic example is the exchange between Coty and Paul Poiret. Coty came to Poiret announcing he was there to buy his business. When Poiret told him it wasn't for sale, Coty said, "You will take fifteen years before you reach any great importance. If you come with me, you will profit from my management, and in two years you will be worth as much as I am." Poiret replied, "But in two years my business would be yours, while in the contrary case, in fifteen years it would still be my own property." As it turned out, fifteen years later Poiret was bankrupt.

94 *She wanted to keep "her association with the Wertheimers . . . at arm's length":* Madsen, *Chanel,* 129.

94 *"her fear of losing control over her fashion house made her sign away the perfume for ten percent of the corporation":* Ibid.

94 *Coco Chanel told them, "Form a company if you like, but I am not interested in getting involved in your business":* Galante, *Mademoiselle Chanel,* 146.

94 *contract read: "Mademoiselle Chanel, dress designer . . . all perfumery products, makeups, soaps, etc.":* Galante, *Mademoiselle Chanel,* 147.

95 *Chanel "only first-class products" that she deemed sufficiently luxurious:* Galante, *Mademoiselle Chanel,* 148.

97 *by 1922 he had broken ties with the company and moved to Charabot, a company specializing in perfume materials:* Biographical details on Ernest Beaux are generally scanty. See Gilberte Beaux, *Une femme libre* (Paris: Fayard, 2006). He is also mentioned in passing during the First World War in Rasskavov, *Notes of a Prisoner,* 1935.

CHAPTER NINE

99 *American women had, in the words of one historian, "the greatest value of surplus [money] ever given to women to spend in all of history":* Berry, *Screen Style,* 2.

100 *"Luxury perfume," the brochure reads, "this term . . .":* Catalog, 1924, Chanel archives.

102 *Coco Chanel shopped there herself on occasion:* See François Chaille, *The Book of Ties* (Paris: Flammarion, 1994), 119.

102 *Her real model was one of Boy Capel's whisky decanters:* Chanel archives.

102 *No. 5 bottle as "solemn, ultra-simple, quasi-pharmaceutical":* Madsen, *Chanel,* 133.

103 *Already "the art of the bottle tend[ing] . . . to simplicity of lines and decoration":* Fontan, *Générations Bourjois,* 78.

103 *The 1907 Lalique bottle for François Coty's La Rose Jacqueminot (1903):* See the image, for example, in Morris, *Fragrance,* 200. Some sources date the release of Coty's blockbuster to 1904, e.g., Michael Edwards, *Perfume Legends,* 290.

104 *At least as early as 1920, Bourjois's bottle for its Ashes of Roses (1909):* See, for example, the image in Fontan, *Générations Bourjois*, 78.

104 *The innovations that directly led to the bottle we know today only happened in 1924:* Chanel archives.

105 *Place Vendôme, the original flask didn't yet have that familiar faceted large stopper:* Chanel archives notes that there is no evidence of any direct connection; Coco Chanel admired octagonal shapes in general and often used them in her designs.

105 *experts have uncovered at least one rare example of Rallet No. 1:* See essay and photography by Philip Goutell, "Le No. 1," *Perfume Projects*, www.perfume projects.com/museum/bottles/Rallet_No1.shtml.

106 *and, when not in the standard* parfum *concentration, it included the strength in* eau de toilette *or* eau de cologne—*two other early:* Chanel archives; according to archivists, the *parfum, eau de toilette,* and *eau de cologne* concentrations were introduced in 1924–25, the *eau de parfum* in the 1950s, and a powder in 1986. Generally, perfumes come in four different "strengths," and sometimes—as in the case of Chanel No. 5—those different strengths are actually different formulas. All perfumes are dissolved in a neutral base, usually an odorless alcohol or a mixture of alcohol and water, and the different terms signal to a consumer what percentage of the final product is aromatic material. The most concentrated version of the scent is the *parfum* version, often known as the *extrait* or extract, which can be anywhere from 15 to 40 percent pure scent, and therefore 60 to 85 percent neutral. This is the kind of perfume that almost always comes only in the small dropper bottles, and its aroma is very concentrated. *Eau de parfum,* however, is often available as a spray, and it typically has 10 to 20 percent aromatics. Obviously, those ballpark numbers mean the percentages across the industry aren't standard. *Eau de toilette* is generally 5 to 15 percent scented material, while *eau de cologne* is reserved for scent concentrations that are usually less than 5 percent aromatic and, for historical reasons, are typically light and fruity.

Chanel No. 5 today is available only in *parfum, eau de parfum,* and *eau de toilette*—or, in the shorthand lingo of the perfume enthusiast, as *extrait, EdP,* and *EdT.* In the late 1970s, when Jacques Polge started at Chanel as the perfumer, there was a rather different lineup: a *parfum,* a classic *eau de toilette,* and an *eau de cologne.* The *eau de cologne* was discontinued in the 1990s, and during his tenure the *eau de parfum* was added.

Chanel No. 5 is also one of those cases where, at each concentration, the formula is slightly different. The reason behind this is a simple one. When Ernest Beaux and his successors thought of artistic creation, it was the already bestselling *parfum* version, and, when the *eau de toilette* was developed, no one wanted to create a scent that would compete with the success of the original. As a result, the current *eau de toilette* version of Chanel No. 5, which dates from the 1950s, increased the sandalwood accord, resulting in a scent that is slightly more sweet and woody. When Polge introduced the *eau de parfum* in the 1980s, it followed the same philosophy. This time, he added a higher vanilla infusion. The *parfum*, meanwhile, is the 1920 original.

Recently, Chanel also introduced Eau Première, which is essentially a lighter, updated version of the original.

106 *The sans-serif font was drawn from contemporary* avant-garde: See Alice Raws-thorn, "Message in a Bottle," *New York Times*, February 22, 2009, www .nytimes.com/indexes/2009/02/22/style/t/index.html#pagewanted=0&page Name=22rawsthorn&. She writes that the bottle's "geometric shape evoked the 'purist villas' that pioneering Modernist architects like Le Corbusier were building for fashionable clients in and around Paris. The sans-serif lettering was similar to the radical typefaces being developed by avant-garde designers like Jan Tschichold and Laszlo Moholy-Nagy in Germany."

107 *American heiress Irène Bretz:* See Mark Hughes, "Logos That Became Leg-ends, Icons from the World of Advertising," *The Independent*, January 4, 2008, www.independent.co.uk/news/media/logos-that-became-legends-icons-from-the-world-of-advertising–768077.html; also Château Crémat website, www.chateau-cremat.com/histoire.php, accessed November 2, 2009.

107 *At the royal château in Blois, the symbol was carved in white in the private apartments:* For details, see Leonie Freida, *Catherine de Medici, Renaissance Queen of France* (New York: HarperCollins, 2005); and (on Queen Claude of France) Desmond Seward, *Prince of the Renaissance, the Life of François I* (London: Constable, 1973).

109 *F. Scott Fitzgerald could write of the character of Nicole, in his masterpiece* Tender Is the Night *(1934), that "She bathed . . .":* F. Scott Fitzgerald, *Tender Is the Night* (New York: Scribner's, 1934), 294; chapter 8.

CHAPTER TEN

112 *Sales of French perfume in America increased more than 700 percent:* Caldwell, "1920–29: French Mystique in the American Perfume Market."

112 *identical bottles . . . an odd way to capitalize on the growing international fame of Coco Chanel's signature scent:* On other perfume houses using standard bottle shapes, see, for example, Michèle Atlas and Alain Monniat, *Guerlain: les fla-cons à parfum depuis 1828* (Toulouse: Éditions Milan, 1997), 42.

113 *it was simply called the "Style Moderne" . . . an "exquisite presentation of a few choice luxury commodities":* Tim Benton and Ghislaine Wood, *Art Deco: 1910–1931* (New York: Bulfinch Press, 2003), 161.

114 *"the promotion of cinema was a means of vaunting the modernity of French indus-trial and cultural production":* Ibid.

114 *fanciful stalls hosted by firms like Houbigant, Parfums de Rosine, Lenthéric, D'Orsay, Roger et Gallet, Molyneux, and Coty:* See Denise Silvester-Carr, "A Celebration of Style," *History Today*, vol. 53, April 2003. Nigel Groom notes that Eugène Rimmel had displayed a perfume fountain at the Great Exhibi-tion of 1851 in London, which was very popular, and that Rimmel, author of *The Book of Perfumes* (1865), sold *Great Exhibition Bouquet* perfume; this was

probably the inspiration for the perfume fountain in Paris in 1925; Groom, *Perfume Handbook,* 285. See also Mitchell Owens, "They Held the Scent of Glamour," *New York Times,* July 20, 1997, www.nytimes.com/1997/07/20/arts/they-held-the-scent-of-glamour.html; Fontàn, *Générations Bourjois;* and *Exposition Internationale des Arts Décoratifs et Industriels Modernes* (1925 catalog), 10 vols. (New York, Garland Publishing, 1977).

As David B. Boyce writes: "The 'Exposition Internationale des Arts Décoratifs et Industriels Modernes' made such a cultural impact at the time that the American Association of Museums organized its own show of 400 works selected from the 'Exposition.' The MFA, Boston, was the first of nine venues to host this touring exhibition from January 15 to February 7, 1926." The exhibits in the United States were "[d]edicated to modern decorative arts and intended to boost the French economy; this ambitious exhibition displayed works from around the globe and attracted over 16 million viewers. More than 20 countries contributed to categories comprising architecture, interior furnishings, costume, and public arts and education"; see Boyce, "Art Deco Exhibit at MFA Is a Dazzling Display," *South Coast Today,* September 15, 2004, B4, http://archive.southcoasttoday.com/daily/09–04/09–15–04/b01li181.htm.

115 *"Perfumery," those sixteen million visitors read, "is an essentially modern art . . .":* *Exposition Internationale des Arts Décoratifs et Industriels Modernes,* 1925, vol. 9, 73.

116 *Tellingly, the perfume wasn't advertised in France until as late as the 1940s:* Chanel archives.

116 *a moment in history when "objects were defined as 'expressive' of the identity of the consumer":* Simon Dell, "The Consumer and the Making of the 'Exposition Internationale des Arts Décoratifs et Industriels Modernes,' 1907–1925," *Journal of Design History* (1999), 311.

116 *"The 1925 exhibition of decorative arts . . . saw her and her friends at the center of the excitement":* Madsen, *Chanel,* 162.

117 *Before long, an advertisement in the French periodical* L'Illustration *flaunted another new perfume, Cadolle's Le No. 9:* L'Illustration, May 4, 1929, Chanel archives.

117 *names like Rallet No. 3 and Rallet No. 33:* On these scents and for images of early Rallet fragrance bottles and advertisements, see Philip Goutell, "A. Rallet and Company," *Perfume Projects,* www.perfumeprojects.com/museum/marketers/Rallet.shtml.

118 *Like Chanel No. 22 (1922)—also one of the original reformulations of Rallet:* Some perfumers suspect that it was Chanel No. 22 (presumably sample number 22 in the original series) that had the accidental overdose of aldehydes. However, the story of the overdose has never been confirmed for either of the perfumes, and Ernest Beaux' earlier experiments with the materials in Le Bouquet de Catherine / Rallet No. 1 suggest that he was familiar with the effect of aldehydes in large doses by 1920.

118 *Jay Thorpe advertised the "light and sparkling" Chanel No. 5 as "the most famous"*
of the Chanel perfumes: New York Times, 1928, Chanel archives.

CHAPTER ELEVEN

120 *thirty billion dollars—the equivalent of $4,080,000,000,000—simply vanished:*
calculated using nominal GDP per capita.

120 *Now came the collapse of the American economy—and of the dollar:* On the period
between the wars in France and the United States and on the effect of the
economic crisis on the luxury markets, see particularly Carol Mann, *Paris
Between the Wars* (New York: Vendome Press, 1996); Alfred Sauvy, "The
Economic Crisis of the 1930s in France," *Journal of Contemporary History* 4,
no. 4 (October 1969): 21–35; and Robert S. McElvaine, *The Great Depression:
America, 1929–1941* (New York: Times Books, 1981); on the role of credit
and luxury, see McElvaine, 41.

120 *from 1929 to 1941, more than a quarter of America's workforce were unemployed:*
Tom Reichert, *The Erotic History of Advertising* (Amherst, NY: Prometheus
Books, 2003), 99.

121 *dropped precipitously: from $3.4 billion in 1929 to $1.3 billion four years later:*
Ibid.

122 *Madeleine Vionnet and the house of Lenthéric had launched lines of fragrances:* On
these various lettered and numbered perfumes, see Lefkowith, *Paul Poiret
and His Rosine Perfumes,* 210; Madsen, *Chanel,* 140; and *Perfume Intelligence,*
www.perfumeintelligence.co.uk/library/perfume/a/a1/a1p1.htm.

122 *Designer Lucien Lelong, rather unoriginally, countered with A, B, C, J, and N
(1924) fragrances:* Lelong company history, www.lucienlelong.com/history
.shtml.

123 *"were pioneers in the art of enhancing and contextualizing commodities by using
exotic backdrops":* See Ellen Furlough, "Selling the American Way in Interwar
France: 'Prix Uniques' and the Salons des Arts Menagers," *Journal of Social
History* 26, no. 3 (Spring 1993): 491–519.

123 *one that emphasized "elaborate displays [and] the cultivation of the shopping experience":* Furlough, "Selling the American Way," 493.

123 *"Perfume," visitors to the pavilion learned, "is a luxury naturally adapted . . . to
feminine fantasy":* *Exposition Internationale des Arts Décoratifs et Industriels
Modernes,* 77; see also Owens, "They Held the Scent of Glamour."

125 *clever new "cocktail" themes that year:* Lefkowith, *Paul Poiret and His Rosine
Perfumes,* 211.

125 *"women were seen by Hollywood as the primary consumers of cinema":* Berry,
Screen Style, xiv, 53.

126 *Art deco was a phenomenon in America:* Berry, *Screen Style,* 6.

126 *the equivalent of over $75 million today:* Calculated using nominal GDP per
capita.

126 *According to an article in* Collier's *magazine in 1932, "The Grand Duke . . .":*
Quoted in Galante, *Mademoiselle Chanel,* 155.

127 *"see what the pictures have to offer me and what I have to offer the pictures":* Madsen, *Chanel*, 195. She ultimately designed the costumes for three Hollywood films, *Palmy Days* (1931), *Tonight or Never* (1931), and *The Greeks Had a Word for It* (1932).

127 *Coco Chanel and Paul Iribe had known each other for decades:* Paul Bachollet, Daniel Bordet, and Anne-Claude Lelieur, *Paul Iribe* (Paris: Editions Denoël, 1984), 74. Iribe had been born Iribarnegaray.

127 *Paul Iribe's first wife, the famed vaudeville actress Jeanne Dirys:* Bachollet et al., *Paul Iribe*, 106.

128 *"My nascent celebrity," she later told a friend, "had eclipsed . . .":* Bachollet et al., *Paul Iribe*, 194–98.

128 *His views were only marginally less narrow than those of another former lover, the Duke of Westminster:* On the controversies surrounding the Duke of Westminster's politics, see Richard Griffiths, *Patriotism Perverted: Captain Ramsay, the Right Club and British Anti-Semitism 1939–40* (London: Constable, 1998).

128 Time *magazine reported on March 16, 1931, "In Manhattan . . .":* "People, March 16, 1931," *Time*, March 16, 1931.

CHAPTER TWELVE

131 *Notably, it was during these years that some of the first numbered perfumes finally began disappearing from the Chanel advertising:* By 1929, the French sales catalog advertised only Chanel No. 5 and Chanel No. 22 among the numbered perfumes, and the United States catalogs in 1931 and 1934 included only Chanel No. 2, Chanel No. 5, Chanel No. 11, Chanel No. 14, Chanel No. 20, Chanel No. 21, Chanel No. 22, Chanel No. 27, and Chanel No. 55—presumably a reflection of the relative popularity of those fragrances; Chanel archives.

131 *the scent "worn by more smart women than any other perfume":* New York Times, December 15, 1935, 41.

132 *By 1928, the partners had assigned an in-house lawyer to handle their prickly celebrity designer:* Madsen, *Chanel*, 137.

133 *Part of the problem was a simple matter of dividends:* Details of this growing conflict, here and below, drawn from various sources, including Galante's *Mademoiselle Chanel*, 143–53, *et passim*; and Bruno Abescat and Yves Stavridès's extensive three-part history, "Derrière l'Empire Chanel . . . la Fabuleuse Histoire des Wertheimer," published in *L'Express* in the spring and summer of 2005.

133 *What prompted her outrage was ostensibly the extension of the Chanel cleansing-cream line, scheduled for 1934:* Pierre Galante tells the story of this conflict in his biography of Coco Chanel, but he has at least one detail wrong: Les Parfums Chanel did not introduce a cleansing cream for the first time in 1934; the first Chanel Crème de Toilette was advertised in the French sales catalog in 1927 and in the United States sales catalog in 1931. Regardless, the

cleansing cream became a point of contention between Coco Chanel and her partners by 1934. See Galante, *Mademoiselle Chanel*, 151; Chanel archives.

134 *"You don't have the right to make a cream," she told the partners; "I demand . . .":* Galante, *Mademoiselle Chanel*, 151.

134 *literally more than a ton of paperwork gathered in files in his offices:* Madsen, *Chanel*, 201.

134 *before the beginning of the Second World War alone, there would be three or four different lawsuits:* Galante, *Mademoiselle Chanel*, 149.

134 *railing against the "Judeo-Masonic Mafia":* Charles-Roux, *Chanel*, 290.

134 *By 1931, the Nazis were already the second largest party in Germany:* On the early rise of fascism in the 1930s, see, for example, Richard Bessel, *Political Violence and the Rise of Nazism: The Storm Troopers in Eastern Germany, 1925–1934* (New Haven, CT: Yale University Press, 1984); Bruce Campbell, *The S.A. Generals and the Rise of Fascism* (Lexington: University of Kentucky Press, 1998).

134 *"In the first number, Iribe inscribed his journal in the line of far-right publications during the period":* Bachollet et al., *Paul Iribe*, 205; the journal had been published earlier and was revived during this period, and commentators have noted that in issue five, published on January 7, 1934, the cover image depicts Coco Chanel as Marianne—the figure of France—on trial. The caption reads "L'Accusée," or "the accused." Coco Chanel's image was used to represent Marianne in Iribe's journal on several occasions.

134 *she "developed a delusion that intensified her anti-Semitism":* Abescat and Stavridès, "Derrière l'Empire Chanel," 29.

135 *remembered Coco Chanel as an "appalling troublemaker" and told how she lumped the Jewish men with whom she did business:* Ibid.

135 *to vote Iribe—and by extension Coco Chanel—off the board of directors at the end of the meeting:* For an account of this and the following, see, for example, Galante, *Mademoiselle Chanel*, 151 ff.; Madsen, *Chanel*, 205 ff.; Abescat and Stavridès, "Derrière l'Empire Chanel."

137 *"Madame Gabrielle Chanel [as] above all an artist in living":* Photograph by Melle Kollar, 1937, Chanel archives, number 10818.

137 *designers of the moment were Elsa Schiaparelli, Lucien Lelong, and Cristóbal Balenciaga:* See Katherine Fleming, "Coco Chanel: From Rags to Riches," *Marie Claire*, October 7, 2008, http://au.lifestyle.yahoo.com/marie-claire/features/life-stories/article/-/5877952/coco-chanel-from-rags-to-riches/.

137 *This, she said to those who criticized her, was no time for fashion:* Charles-Roux, *Chanel*, 306.

138 *Coffee was replaced with chicory, and chocolate all but disappeared:* On daily life in occupied France, see D. Veillon, *Vivre et survivre en France, 1939–1947* (Paris: Payot, 1995).

CHAPTER THIRTEEN

139 *"The ground-floor boutique,"* one historian writes, *"was filled with German sol-diers":* Madsen, *Chanel,* 238.

140 *"During the war we could sell only about twenty bottles of perfume a day":* Haed-rich, *Coco Chanel,* 146.

140 *sons-in-law, Raoul Meyer and Max Heilbronn:* "Galeries Lafayette S.A., Company History," *Funding Universe,* www.fundinguniverse.com/company-histories/Galeries-Lafayette-SA-Company-History.html.

140 *Although old French families, their backgrounds were Jewish:* Details on the Wertheimer family, here and below, drawn from Abescat and Stavridès, "Derrière l'Empire Chanel," 83–85, *et passim;* on Estée Lauder, see *Estée: A Success Story* (New York: Ballantine Books, 1986).

141 *Thomas had been the president of the perfume house of Guerlain before the war:* On H. Gregory Thomas, Jacques Wertheimer, and the problem of bringing jasmine into the United States, see Abescat and Stavridès, "Derrière l'Empire Chanel"; and the obituary published in the *New York Times,* October 10, 1990, www.nytimes.com/1990/10/10/obituaries/h-gregory-thomas-chanel-executive-82.html?pagewanted=1.

142 *something composed— "like a dress":* Galante, *Les années Chanel,* 79–80.

143 *"in Grasse, where all flowers were called by their proper [Latin] names, jasmine was simply known [in the 1920s] as 'the flower'":* Toledano and Coty, *François Coty,* 57.

143 *the jasmine plants grow to only half their normal height, and they have lower proportions of those so-called indoles:* Christopher Sheldrake, Chanel, interview, 2009.

143 *It also has about it a distinct note that smells like tea:* Jacques Polge, Chanel, interview, 2009.

144 *a concrete or the highly purified scent of an absolute:* Joseph Mul and Jean-François Vieille, Grasse, interview, 2009.

144 *"Louis Chiris had set up his first workshop based on solvent extraction,"* having *wisely already secured "a patent . . .":* Toledano and Coty, *François Coty,* 58.

145 *each small, thirty-milliliter bottle of Chanel No. 5 parfum is the essence of more than a thousand jasmine flowers and the bouquet of a dozen roses:* Jacques Polge, Chanel, interview, 2009.

145 *"With a great deal of foresight, the Wertheimer brothers sent people to France to round up stocks while it was still possible to do so:* Galante, *Mademoiselle Chanel,* 183.

146 *"eighty kinds of aldehydes, [and was] unique in the world":* Abescat and Stav-ridès, "Derrière l'Empire Chanel," 86.

146 *Those seven hundred pounds were enough to produce perhaps 350,000 small bottles of the celebrated parfum:* This is a broad approximation, which assumes a stable dosage of jasmine, based on the calculation of a thousand jasmine flowers in a

thirty-milliliter bottle of Chanel No. 5 perfume, which translated to roughly 500,000 flowers or five hundred bottles in a pound of concrete.

146 *"No. 5 [was] probably the only perfume whose quality remained the same through-out the war":* Galante, *Mademoiselle Chanel,* 183.

147 *The large-scale campaign that began in 1934:* Archival research reveals three times as many advertisements for Chanel No. 5 in the *New York Times* in 1940, for example, as in 1941 or in 1942. The advertising was scaled back even more dramatically in 1943 and 1944, and it resumed actively in 1945, suggesting a general approach of not attempting to advertise actively in tra-ditional outlets during the Second World War. However, there was consider-able exposure through the United States Army commissary, perhaps making additional advertisements seem unnecessary. Among the Bourjois advertise-ments during the war, by far the most frequent were pitches for Ernest Beaux' newest perfume, Evening in Paris, which was heavily promoted.

147 *companies like Yardley, Elizabeth Arden, Helena Rubenstein—and Coty—championed their products intensively during the war:* See, for example, the advertising collection at Duke University Library, http://library.duke.edu/ digitalcollections/adaccess/browse/. These same publications do not include any advertisements for Chanel No. 5.

147 *fine fragrances were being manufactured in the United States, which still repre-sented the world's largest luxury market:* See Stanley Marcus, *Quest for the Best* (Denton: University of North Texas Press, 2001), 117.

147 *the partners were preparing to launch a "vast publicity campaign to showcase No. 5":* Abescat and Stavridès, "Derrière l'Empire Chanel," 86.

147 *Yet, from 1940 to 1945, perfume sales in the United States increased tenfold":* Galante, *Mademoiselle Chanel,* 183.

148 *By the early 1930s, he was leading the way in introducing a wider model to France with popular new* prix-unique *chains like Monoprix and the now-forgotten Lanoma:* See Max Heilbronn, *Galeries Lafayette, Buchenwald, Galeries Lafay-ette* (Paris: Éditions Economica, 1989).

149 *"I couldn't bring back an awful lot," she said. But there was one thing she treasured: "Chanel, you know, the perfume":* Margaret Reynolds, undated interview, Indi-ana University Southeast, Floyd County Oral History Project, A Community Project Operated under the Indiana University Southeast Applied Research and Education Center, http://homepages.ius.edu/Special/OralHistory/ MREYNOLDS.htm.

150 *Estée Lauder in the beginning even helped the brothers:* Abescat and Stavridès, "Derrière l'Empire Chanel," 86. The American company Chanel, Inc. and a British company Chanel Ltd. were first established in 1924, when the part-nership was created; Chanel archives.

150 *The Jewish partners of Les Parfums Chanel had sold their shares of the business to a daredevil pilot and industrialist named Félix Amiot:* Details from various sources, the most comprehensive being Abescat and Stavridès, "Derrière l'Empire Chanel."

CHAPTER FOURTEEN

151 *The occupying German forces, along with their French administrative collabora-tors:* For information on Vichy France, see, for example, Robert O. Paxton, *Vichy France: Old Guard and New Order, 1940–1944* (New York: Columbia University Press, 2001).

152 *"You have bought the Bourjois and Chanel perfumeries":* Abescat and Stavridès, "Derrière l'Empire Chanel," 87.

152 *"worth more than four million francs—over seventy million dollars in today's num-bers":* based on nominal GDP per capita.

152 *"it is still the property of Jews":* Abescat and Stavridès, "Derrière l'Empire Chanel," 85; the article includes a photographic reproduction of the letter, signed by Chanel.

152 *He had worked until 1931 as the commercial director at Les Parfums Chanel:* Chanel archives.

152 *"it is still a Jewish business" . . . Coco Chanel and the administrator "appreciated each other":* Abescat and Stavridès, "Derrière l'Empire Chanel," *L'Express,* 88.

152 *"I have," she wrote, "an indisputable right of priority":* Abescat and Stavridès, "Derrière l'Empire Chanel," *L'Express,* 85.

153 *She still thought of Pierre Wertheimer, in particular, as "that bandit who screwed me":* Madsen, *Chanel,* 137.

153 *"any presence of Pierre and Paul [Wertheimer] in the capital of the company had of-ficially disappeared":* Abescat and Stavridès, "Derrière l'Empire Chanel," 87.

153 *In order to backdate the stock transfers that would "ma[k]e indisputable the purchase of the business," they probably had to bribe German officials:* Ibid.

153 *"bought almost 50 percent of an airplane propeller company":* Dana Thomas, "The Power Behind the Cologne," *New York Times,* February 24, 2002, www.nytimes.com/2002/02/24/magazine/the-power-behind-the-cologne.html?pagewanted=3.

154 *"the perfume company of Bourjois . . . passed to Aryan hands in a manner that is legal and correct":* Abescat and Stavridès, "Derrière l'Empire Chanel," 88.

154 *In February of 1942, the case was reopened, and Félix Amiot once again subjected to a long interrogation:* Abescat and Stavridès, "Derrière l'Empire Chanel," 86.

155 *loaded them on the final convoy of trains sent creeping from the industrial western suburbs of Pantin:* See "Histoire de Pantin," www.ville-pantin.fr/fileadmin/MEDIA/Histoire_de_Pantin/histoire.pdf.

155 *In the last days of the war, Théophile Bader's son-in-law, Max Heilbronn, was on one of them:* See Max Heilbronn, *Galeries Lafayette, Buchenwald, Galeries Lafayette* (Paris: Éditions Economica, 1989).

155 *Out of the silence, the ringing bells of the cathedral of Notre Dame echoed over the Seine:* Recollections of John Mac Vane, "On the Air in World War II," interview, 1979; Martin Blumenson, "Liberation," interview, 1978, www.eyewitnesstohistory.com/parisliberation.htm.

155 *the French "swept the [soldiers] into their arms, dancing, singing, often making love to them":* Levenstein, *We'll Always Have Paris.*

156 *Only one-in-four Parisian residents had enough food during those years:* Sharon Fogg, *The Politics of Everyday Life in Vichy France* (Cambridge: Cambridge University Press, 2009), 4.

156 *Some have called the occupation not the crazy years but* les années érotiques—*the erotic years—instead:* Patrick Buisson, *1940–1945, Années Érotiques: Vichy ou les Infortunes de la Vertu* (Paris: Albin Michel, 2008).

156 *the American troops liberated Paris, "there was one souvenir of the city they all wanted":* Kennett, *Coco,* 127.

157 *"Not only was it the only French perfume the American G.I. had ever heard of, it was the only one he could pronounce":* Philippa Toomey, "Shop Around," *The Times,* November 26, 1977, 26; Issue 60171, col. D.

157 *the American president, Harry S. Truman, went looking for it:* Letter from Harry S. Truman to Bess Wallace Truman, July 22, 1945, National Archives, ARC Identifier 200660, Collection HST-FBP: Harry S. Truman Papers Pertaining to Family, Business and Personal.

157 *Before the celebrations had even ended,* les épurations—*the purges—began:* See Eugen Weber, "France's Downfall," *Atlantic Magazine,* October 2001, www.theatlantic.com/doc/200110/weber; Glenys Roberts, "Sleeping with the Enemy: New Book Claims Frenchwomen Started a Baby Boom with Nazi Men During Vichy Regime," *Daily Mail,* July 17, 2008, www.dailymail.co.uk/femail/article-1035804/Sleeping-enemy-New-book-claims-Frenchwomen-started-baby-boom-Nazi-men-Vichy-regime.html#ixzz0V9xfteQ9; and Jon Elster, *Retribution and Reparation in the Transition to Democracy* (Cambridge: Cambridge University Press, 2006), who writes, "It was proposed that women who slept with the Germans would be conducted into prostitution, shorn, and registered, after having been examined for venereal diseases," 97.

157 *Christiane, the daughter of Coco Chanel's old friend and now archrival, François Coty, was among those brutalized:* Toledano and Coty, *François Coty,* 255.

158 *Christiane Coty had been humiliated on the grounds that she had simply socialized with German officers":* Toledano and Coty, *François Coty,* 204–206, 254–55.

158 *Coco Chanel's wartime companion:* Details on her liaison and wartime activities, here and below, from various sources; the most complete accounts are Madsen, *Chanel,* 237–70; Charles-Roux, *Chanel,* 311–49.

158 *all she could think to do in the days that followed was ask a German-American soldier if perhaps he would help her:* Madsen, *Chanel,* 264–65.

159 *When friends had warned her that the liaison with von Dincklage was dangerous:* Haedrich, *Coco Chanel,* 147. Some have suggested, although without any corroboration, that von Dincklage was a double agent, also working for the British during the war; see discussion in Madsen, *Chanel,* 246.

159 *At her age, she wryly announced, when she had the chance of a lover she was hardly going to inspect a man's passport:* Madsen, *Chanel,* 262.

159 *She had done more during those years than simply carry on a romance with a German officer:* See Kate Muir, "Chanel and the Nazis: What *Coco Avant Chanel* and Other Films Don't Tell You," *The Times*, April 4, 2009, http://entertainment.timesonline.co.uk/tol/arts_and_entertainment/film/article6027932.ece. The use of the term "Nazi" is historically complicated, and I refrain from using it here only because the question of von Dincklage's association with the Nazi Party proper has never been satisfactorily settled. In many cases officers of other branches of the German fascist government were formally barred from party membership. However, insofar as von Dincklage acted as a German diplomat and later as an officer working with the fascist administration in Nazi-occupied France, Coco Chanel must have understood the political complexity of her liaison.

159 *Walter Friedrich Schellenberg—the powerful German officer best known to history for his memoirs of Nazi Germany, written after his conviction for war crimes:* Walter Schellenberg, *The Labyrinth: Memoirs of Walter Schellenberg, Hitler's Chief of Counterintelligence* (London: DaCapo Press, 2000).

159 *Declassified documents show that Coco returned to Berlin again in December of 1943:* For a narrative summary of the materials in the National Archives, Washington D.C., and for the best brief account of the Schellenberg and Lombardi affairs, see Christophe Agnus, "Chanel: un parfum d'espionnage," *L'Express,* March 16, 1995, www.lexpress.fr/informations/chanel-un-parfum-d-espionnage_603397.html. Details here and following draw from this article and, as noted, from unpublished materials in the Churchill Archives, Churchill College, University of Cambridge.

In her article on "Chanel and the Nazis," Kate Muir writes, "Schellenberg was interrogated by the British after the war concerning the visit in 1943 from 'Frau Chanel a French subject and proprietress of the noted perfume factory.' According to the transcript: 'This woman was referred to as a person Churchill knew sufficiently to undertake political negotiations with him, as an enemy of Russia and as desirous of helping France and Germany whose destinies she believed to be closely linked together.' Operation Modelhut [as the Schellenberg affair was known] fell apart, and the mutual friend of Churchill and Chanel denounced her as a German agent."

On Chanel's connections with other German officers in occupied France, see also Uki Goñi, *The Real Odessa: Smuggling Nazis to Perón's Argentina* (London: Granta Books, 2002).

160 *Remembering those meetings, Mumm later declared that she had "a drop of the blood of Joan of Arc in her veins":* Quoted in Agnus, "Chanel: un parfum d'espionnage."

160 *according to top secret memos sent between the United States government and the office of Winston Churchill—had deliberately exaggerated her old friend's use to German intelligence:* Churchill Archive Centre, University of Cambridge, CHAR 20/198A, items 61–91; item 87, a top secret letter dated December 28, 1944, reads: "When Madame Lombardi was in Paris in December, 1941,

her friend Madame Chanel deliberately exaggerated her importance in order to give the Germans the impression that she (Madame Lombardi) might be useful to them."

160 *She wrote to Churchill that summer protesting Coco's treachery:* Churchill Archive Centre, University of Cambridge, CHAR 20/198A, item 75, letter from V. Lombardi, Madrid, August 8, 1944, to Winston Churchill.

160 *Coco had the idea that Vera would help, and it seems that, when Vera refused, von Dincklage may have been the one who thought to have her arrested:* Agnus, "Chanel: un parfum d'espionnage."

161 *"Madame Chanel," the report reads, "apparently instigated the special facilities afforded by the German Gestapo to Madame Lombardi":* Churchill Archive Centre, University of Cambridge, CHAR 20/198A, item 86, letter from S. S. Hill-Dillon, Allied Force Headquarters, U.S. Army, December 3, 1944, to J. J. Martin, Prime Minister's Principal Secretary, 10 Downing Street (Top Secret).

161 *Files in the British Foreign Office were mistakenly declassified for a brief window:* Madsen, *Chanel*, 263. Madsen suggests that Coco Chanel knew details of Nazi collaboration by the Duke and Duchess of Windsor; see also Toledano and Coty, *François Coty*, 122. While this may or may not have been the case, unpublished archival materials suggest that the British and the American governments were satisfied that Coco Chanel had not actively collaborated.

161 *Churchill followed the investigation into Coco's wartime imbroglio carefully . . . despite the "suspicious circumstances":* Churchill Archive Centre, University of Cambridge, CHAR 20/198A, item 86.

161 *"By one of those majestically simple strokes which made Napoléon so successful as a general . . .":* Madsen, *Chanel*, 263.

CHAPTER FIFTEEN

165 *Her object: "to create total confusion among her haute-couture clients, her friends, and the distributors of the authentic Chanel No. 5":* Abescat and Stavridès, "Derrière l'Empire Chanel," 83.

166 *Paris would be "gay and animated," filled with art, music, and entertainment:* Charles Bremner, "Andre Zucca's Portraits of Gay Paris at War Paint an Uneasy Portrait of City Collaboration," *The Times*, April 18, 2008, http://entertainment.timesonline.co.uk/tol/arts_and_entertainment/visual_arts/article3767951.ece.

166 *the Bourjois factory on Queen's Way in Croydon was destroyed in a terrible air raid in the summer of 1940:* The bombing of the factory is occasionally in the news because of claims by former employees that a World War Two–era airplane remains buried in the ruins of the building; see most recently Kirsty Whalley, "Is Perfume House Hiding Secret Aircraft?," *Croydon Guardian*, August 2, 2008, www.croydonguardian.co.uk/news/heritage/3565445.Is_perfume_warehouse[IQ]_hiding_secret_aircraft_/.

166 *"after the defeat of France," writes one historian, "Germany received a supply*

of luxury goods such as she had not seen for years": Marshall Dill, *Germany: A Modern History* (Ann Arbor: University of Michigan Press, 1970).

167 *It was $15,000—today worth a cool million dollars:* Based on nominal GDP per capita.

167 *in the United States she received only 10 percent of a 10 percent dividend:* Galante, *Mademoiselle Chanel,* 198.

167 *"It is monstrous," she insisted. "They produced it in Hoboken!":* Abescat and Stavridès, "Derrière l'Empire Chanel," 83; see also Kennett, *Coco,* 83.

167 *"From Miami to Anchorage, from Naples to Berlin . . . next to milk chocolate":* Abescat and Stavridès, "Derrière l'Empire Chanel," 83; also quoted in the official Chanel history of No. 5, François Ternon, *Histoire du No. 5 Chanel: Un numéro intemporel* (Nantes, France: Éditions Normant, 2009), 45.

167 *In her private war with the Wertheimers, though, she now declared, "We need to get our weapons . . . and I have some!":* Abescat and Stavridès, "Derrière l'Empire Chanel," 83.

167 *she threatened to produce a scent simply called Mademoiselle Chanel No. 5:* Madsen, *Chanel,* 268.

168 *Just outside Zürich, for example, in the village of Dübendorf, a small perfumery called Chemische Fabrik Flora:* Philip Kraft, personal correspondence, 2010.

168 *He paid about five dollars each—more than sixty dollars a bottle in modern figures—for flasks:* The notebooks, along with a collection of vintage perfumes, were sold in an auction in Britain during 2010 to an undisclosed buyer, and details here are based on photographic records from the sale; calculations based on consumer price index.

169 *This mossy, green scent with jasmine and roses went on to become . . . "the celebrated No. 19" fragrance:* Fiemeyer, *Coco Chanel,* 133. See also Angela Taylor, "Coco Left a Legacy—It's Chanel No. 19," *New York Times,* September 11, 1972, 46: "A few years before her death in 1971, Mlle. Chanel got a little bored with smelling like everyone else, according to H. Gregory Thomas, her good friend and chairman of Chanel, Inc. here. She wanted a perfume all her own. . . . It was numbered 19." Named after Coco Chanel's birth date, on August 19, it was based on the red-label formula and updated sometime after 1965 by Chanel's perfumer Henri Robert, who added to it a recently discovered synthetic jasmine compound, Hedione. See Galante, *Mademoiselle Chanel,* 275.

169 *"A perfume ought to punch you right on the nose":* Claude Delay, *Chanel Solitaire* (Paris: Gallimard, 1983), 88.

169 *She boasted that it was the scent of Chanel No. 5—"but even better":* Galante, *Mademoiselle Chanel,* 193.

170 *"When he came in," the lawyer remembered, "I showed him the samples . . .":* Ibid.

171 *"The suit asks that the French parent concern [Les Parfums Chanel] be ordered to cease manufacture . . .":* New York Times, June 3, 1946, 24.

172 *eight million dollars—$240 million today":* Calculated using nominal GDP per capita.

172 *Several sources speculate that it must have been Ernest Beaux:* For the best discussion, see Kraft, Ledard, and Goutell, "From *Rallet No. 1* to *Chanel No. 5*"; perfumer and fragrance historian Elena Vosnaki notes that it is a "violet-orris" with a structure that "is a common thread in Beaux creations": private correspondence, 2009.

173 *Gilberte Beaux, Ernest's daughter-in-law is equally confident that he wasn't the nose behind those fragrances, and her observation is also a good one*: Gilberte Beaux, interview, 2010.

Mademoiselle Chanel No. 1 resembles Rallet No. 1, but no one could have confused it with Chanel No. 5 if they sniffed either appreciatively. While they have the floral heart in common, there is one crucially important difference. Unlike both Chanel No. 5 and Rallet No. 1, Mademoiselle Chanel No. 1 doesn't have any aldehydes. Those scent materials transformed the world of perfumery in the 1920s, but they were no longer cutting edge in the late 1940s. The success of Chanel No. 5 meant that perfumers had readily incorporated these materials into their fragrances for several decades.

Instead of the aldehyde bouquet, the perfumer made a new innovation. Aldehydes might have become a familiar part of the scent idiom of the 1940s, but a-n-methyl ionone (alpha, nu; marketed by Givaudan as Raldeine A)—a synthetic compound with the unique scent of woody florals and orris butter—was still uncharted territory. It allowed perfumers, who could never have afforded to use large proportions of natural orris, a prohibitively expensive compound made naturally from the rhizome roots of iris flowers, to experiment with the full range of its aromas. Mademoiselle Chanel No. 1 used a-n-methyl ionone for nearly 25 percent of its entire formula. "As a result," researchers have discovered, "Mademoiselle Chanel No. 1 becomes somewhat of a violet-orris modification of the Chanel No. 5 theme"; Kraft, et al., 46.

175 *"If one took seriously the few disclosures that Mademoiselle Chanel allowed herself to make about those black years of the occupation":* Haedrich, *Coco Chanel*, 144.

175 *Pierre Wertheimer's worry was how "a legal fight might illuminate Chanel's wartime activities and wreck her image—and his business":* Madsen, *Chanel*, 272; Phyllis Berman and Zina Sawaya, "The Billionaires Behind Chanel," *Forbes*, April 3, 1989, 104.

176 *Walter Schellenberg, one of the principal operatives in the failed diplomatic mission to Berlin:* Fiemeyer, *Coco Chanel*, 136; the funds were paid in 1958.

176 *"Pierre [Wertheimer]," he told Coco Chanel's lawyer, "is standing here next to me":* Abescat and Stavridès, "Derrière l'Empire Chanel," 82.

176 *Parfums Chanel would give Coco Chanel $350,000—a sum today worth nearly nine million dollars:* figures here and below based on nominal GDP per capita.

CHAPTER SIXTEEN

181 *a light "boy-meets-girls" comic opera called* Chanel No. 5: Composed by Friedrich Schröder, with lyrics by B. E. Lüthge and Günther Schwenn; *Chanel No. 5* (Berlin: Corso, 1946). The operetta was obviously quite popular and

well known, since a number of individual songs were printed separately, including "That Is the Smile with Tears" ("*Das Ist das Lächeln der Tränen*"), "In My Thoughts I Already Say 'Du' to You," and "Tango Érotique." Curiously, the story is not particularly focused on Chanel No. 5, despite the title. Instead, Chanel No. 5—as the most famous scent of a generation—stands in for a larger category of luxury French perfumes. The cover page depicts a large bottle of Chanel No. 5 with a woman beside it.

181 *"We know the ladies . . . the blond and blue-black [haired] ones, the large and the slender ones":* Chanel No. 5, Berlin: Corso, 1946.

183 *"based on a businessman's passion for a woman who felt exploited by him":* Berman and Sawaya, "The Billionaires Behind Chanel," 104.

183 *"Pierre returned to Paris full of pride and excitement":* Ibid. There are divergent accounts of this story, however. See, for example, Galante, *Les années Chanel*, 188.

183 *"Pierre," she said, "let's launch a new perfume" . . . "It's too risky":* Ternon, *Histoire du No. 5 Chanel*, 45; Madsen, *Chanel*, 282.

184 *he was now the only partner left at Les Parfums Chanel:* Madsen, *Chanel*, 270.

184 *offended at being taxed under French law as a "spinster," she would even insist that Pierre Wertheimer pay her taxes:* Galante, *Mademoiselle Chanel*, 151.

184 *"Pierre Wertheimer, you see, had been one of those* entreteneurs *(like Balsan) of a type that no longer existed, whence Gabrielle's attraction for him":* Charles-Roux, *Chanel*, 322; see also Edmonde Charles-Roux, *L'Irrégulière, ou Mon Itinéraire Chanel* (Paris: Grasset, 1994); and Edmonde Charles-Roux, *Chanel and Her World* (New York: Vendome, 2005).

184 *"a man who had had many mistresses in his day, [and he] was used to paying women's personal expenses . . .":* Charles-Roux, *Chanel*, 322.

185 *She lived in a simply decorated room at the Ritz Hotel and took to writing . . . a book of aphorisms that she imagined one day publishing:* Ann Brower tells of seeing the notebook during an interview with Coco Chanel in 1954; she recalls it as being approximately 6" x 4" and blue. When Brower had resigned a modeling position with the designer, she was asked in for an interview, and Coco Chanel asked her what she wanted to be. Brower replied that she wanted to be a writer, and Chanel told her, "I am a writer, too" and showed her the book.

186 *The reality, however, is that Warhol didn't create the Chanel No. 5 silk screens until the mid-1980s:* My thanks to Matt Wrbican and Tresa Varner, at the Andy Warhol Museum, Pittsburgh, PA, for their assistance in dating this work.

187 *"removed from their conventional context of advertising and sales" and selected "for excellence":* The Package, The Museum of Modern Art, 1959, catalog, 27:1 (Fall 1959), 24.

187 *"This is a most sophisticated use of bold black lettering on a white ground":* The Package, 19.

188 *In the fifteen years from 1940 to 1955, the gross national product in the United States . . . soared 400 percent:* Richard Shear, "The Package Design: A Lead-

ing or Trailing Indicator, 1950–1960," October 14, 2009, http://richardshear
.wordpress.com/2009/10/14/package-design-a-leading-or-trailing-indicator–
1950–1960/.

188 *For the first time "The package became an independent communicator of its own
brand personality":* Vance Packard, *The Hidden Persuaders* (New York: David
McKay, 1957), 19–20.

188 *Americans threw themselves into the pleasures of material comforts and cozy domesticity:* Donica Belisle, "Suburbanization and Mass Culture in North America," *History Cooperative Journal* 57 (Spring 2006), www.historycooperative
.org/journals/llt/57/belisle.html.

188 *Writes one historian, "In 1955, $9,000,000,000 was poured into United States
advertising . . . A cosmetics tycoon, probably mythical, was quoted as saying, 'We
don't sell lipstick, we buy customers' ":* Packard, *The Hidden Persuaders,* 21.

189 *"any product not only must be good but must appeal to our feelings":* Packard, *The
Hidden Persuaders,* 32.

189 *One 1950s advertiser claimed, "Infatuation with one's own body . . . and sex [were]
now used differently to sell products":* Packard, *The Hidden Persuaders,* 84.

189 *"A perfume is different on different women because every woman has a skin chemistry
all her own":* To a limited extent, perfumes do smell differently on the skin of
individual people. Scientists have suspected that the rate at which a scent dif-
fuses on our skin and the way it is perceived by others is influenced by everything from skin hydration and body temperature to the effect of our diet and
the depth of our wrinkles. The differences, however, are largely overstated.
The primary factors in how a scent unfolds on our bodies turn out to be simply
room temperature and a perfume's concentration. This means that the effect
of our skin's unique chemistry is actually minimal and limited to the first few
moments of the experience—the appreciation of those fleeting top notes. So
two friends comparing the scent of a perfume on their skin at a department-
store beauty counter might notice a distinction at the moment of application.
The friend with the oilier skin will find that the scent does last longer. Fifteen
minutes later, however, the differences between how it smells on one arm or
another literally start to evaporate. Unless you are applying Chanel No. 5 a
couple of times an hour, no one will be getting "your" unique impression. Since
fine fragrances at the perfume strength are designed to last five or six hours
(and will often last much longer if applied to skin that is well moisturized),
such frequent application would be expensively overpowering. See R. Schwarzenback and L. Berteschi, "Models to Assess Perfume Diffusion from Skin,"
International Journal of Cosmetic Science 23 (2001): 85–98; 85, 92.

189 *Chanel No. 5 was the first fragrance ever advertised on television:* Chanel archives.

190 *"Nothing but a few drops of Chanel No. 5":* in Haedrich, *Coco Chanel,* 177.

190 *Marilyn Monroe said about that interview, "People are funny":* Marilyn Monroe
then went on to explain to the interviewer: "Someone once asked me, 'What
do you wear in bed? Pajama tops? Bottoms? Or a nightgown?' So I said,

'Chanel No. 5.' Because it's the truth. You know, I don't want to say 'nude,' but . . . it's the truth"; see Kremmel, ed., *Marilyn Monroe and the Camera*, 15, quoting a 1960 interview with *Marie Claire* editor George Belmont.

190 *For some reason, the fashion for Chanel No. 5 was fading:* Madsen, *Chanel*, 282.

190 *Even more important, "In France, in Europe, in the United States, the sales outlets exploded"*: Abescat and Stavridès, "Derrière l'Empire Chanel," 78.

190 *With the expansion, "the price [of a bottle] went lower, lower, lower"*: Ibid.

CHAPTER SEVENTEEN

193 *idea behind pop art was to use mass-cultural imagery playfully:* See Princeton Museum of Art, *Pop Art: Contemporary Perspectives* (New Haven, CT: Yale University Press, 2007), 10, 100. Also Jean-Michel Vecchiet, dir., *Andy Warhol, L'Oeuvre Incarnée: Vies et Morts de Andy Warhol*, France Télévisions, 2005 (film).

193 *"Being good in business is the most fascinating kind of art":* Andy Warhol, *The Philosophy of Andy Warhol: From A to B and Back Again* (New York: Mariner Books, 1977), 92.

193 *In her book* Deluxe: How Luxury Lost Its Luster*:* Dana Thomas, *Deluxe: How Luxury Lost Its Luster* (New York, Penguin, 2007).

194 *While Jacques was, by all accounts, brilliant at raising racehorses:* For the best discussion, see Abescat and Stavridès, "Derrière l'Empire Chanel."

195 *Coco Chanel simply called him "the kid":* Jocelyn de Moubray, "Jacques Wertheimer" (obituary), *The Independent*, February 10, 1996, www.independent.co.uk/news/people/obituaryjacques-wertheimer–1318229.html.

195 *Jasmine production was in decline:* For details in this paragraph, see "Business Abroad: King of Perfume," *Time*, September 14, 1953.

196 *"Chanel dominated the Paris fashion world . . .":* "Chanel, the Couturier, Dead in Paris," *New York Times*, January 11, 1971.

196 *"It was," the column read . . . :* Ibid.

196 *share in the all-important American market had slipped to under 5 percent:* "Chanel S.A. Company History," *Funding Universe*, www.fundinguniverse.com/company-histories/Chanel-SA-Company-History.html.

197 *"Chanel was dead. . . . Nothing was happening":* Thomas, *Deluxe*, 150.

197 *"From the age of eighteen, when he first joined Chanel, [Jacques Helleu] focused his efforts on turning the signature black-and-white packaging"—and especially the trademark bottle—"into a universally recognized brand":* Laurence Benaïm, *Jacques Helleu and Chanel* (New York: Harry N. Abrams, Inc., 2006), 8.

198 *Marilyn Monroe, as the perfume critic Tania Sanchez puts it, wore Chanel No. 5 because it was sexy:* Turin and Sanchez, *Perfumes*, 260.

198 *there on the cover of* Look *magazine, he read the caption "Most Beautiful Woman in the World":* Chanel archives.

198 *"Chanel," Laurence Benaïm has perceptively noted, "chooses its models as carefully as any harvest of May roses or jasmine from Grasse":* Benaïm, *Jacques Helleu and Chanel*, 8.

199 *Best remembered today are Chanel No. 5 shorts such as* La Piscine *(1979),* L'invitation au rêve *(1982),* Monument *(1986), and* La Star *(1990):* For a de-tailed account of the advertising films, see Ternon, *Histoire du Chanel No. 5 Chanel*, 133 ff. Information here and below supplied by Chanel archives.

200 *Only a "handful of major brands—Hermès and Chanel in particular—strive to maintain and seem to achieve true luxury," Thomas claims. "The quality . . .":* Thomas, *Deluxe*, 323.

200 *Many credit this revitalization of Chanel during the 1970s to the new, energetic leadership of Pierre's grandson, Alain Wertheimer:* See, for example, Madsen, *Chanel*, 334; Thomas, *Deluxe*, 150.

202 *fragrances "based on the complicated trajectory of the founder's difficult and flam-boyant life . . . scents she cherished, outdoors and at home": Allure*, February 2007, 178.

203 *According to Polge, it is the scent of Chanel No. 5:* Jacques Polge, Chanel, inter-view, 2009.

CHAPTER EIGHTEEN

205 *"Rules put famous perfumes 'at risk'" and "Allergen rules may alter scents of great perfumes":* Chris Watt, "Rules Put Famous Perfumes 'At Risk,'" *The Herald* (Glasgow), September 25, 2009, 3; Basil Katz, "Allergen Rules May Alter Scents of Great Perfumes," Reuters wire service, September 24, 2009, www.reuters.com/article/idUSTRE58N3LQ20090924?pageNumber=1&virtualB randChannel=11604; and Geneviève Roberts, "The Sweet Smell of Success."

205 *the end of Chanel No. 5 was near and that "twentieth-century perfumery [is] history":* See, for example, the online discussion by perfumer Octavian Coifan, "1000 Fragrances," http://1000fragrances.blogspot.com/2009/04/endangered-fragrances.html.

205 *Word spread that the notorious forty-third IFRA amendment would limit jasmine to 0.7 percent:* See IFRA, "Standards,"www.ifraorg.org/Home/Code,+Standards+Compliance/IFRA+Standards/page.aspx.

206 *"When the new IFRA standards were issued we immediately checked the percent-ages of* jasmine grandiflora *and* [jasmine] sambac": quoted in Katz, "Allergen Rules May Alter Scents of Great Perfumes."

208 *the scent of warm, clean skin:* For a discussion, see, for example, Burr, *Emperor of Scent*, 216.

208 *the world's first "nitro-musk":* For an excellent discussion, see Turin and San-chez, *Perfumes*, 35; also Burr, *Emperor of Scent*, 216. As Turin explains to Burr in *The Emperor of Scent*, today perfumers work with a new generation of synthetic musks, and there have been several stages in the evolution of these materials.

The first substitutes for the original nitro-musks were a family of synthet-ics known as polycyclic musks, which didn't have the nitrogen-and-oxygen combination that made the nitro-musks unstable. In fact, that was precisely the new dilemma they posed: they weren't biodegradable, making them less than ideal environmentally; Burr, *Emperor*, 217.

The next—and current stage in the development of synthetic musks— are a group known as macrocyclics and, more recently, alicyclics, which are safe, sustainable, and increasingly affordable. The macrocyclics, in particular, have the distinctive smell of natural musk and sometimes an additional fruit aroma. See Philip Kraft, "Aroma Chemicals IV: Musks," in *Chemistry and Technology of Flavours and Fragrances*, ed. David J. Rowe (London: Blackwell, 2004); and Till Luckenbach and David Epel, Marcus Eh, "New Alicyclic Musks: The Fourth Generation of Musk Odorants," *Chemistry and Biodiversity*, 1, no. 12 (2004): 1975–84.

209 *Today musk ketone is still permitted only with strict limitations*: See annex III of the European Cosmetic Directive.

209 *As Christopher Sheldrake explains, while those nitro-musks were wonderful, powerful, and inexpensive:* Christopher Sheldrake, Chanel, interview, 2009.

209 *And, as perfumer Virginia Bonofiglio quips, "You can't make cheap that smells like Chanel No. 5":* Virginia Bonofiglio, Fashion Institute of Technology, interview, 2009.

210 *Polge tells a story about how his predecessor, Henri Robert, used to watch Ernest Beaux correct an entire batch of Chanel No. 5 perfume in the production facility:* Jacques Polge, Chanel, interview, 2009.

210 *Responding to this threat, in the early 1980s Chanel brokered a long-term agreement with the Mul family:* Chanel, interview, 2009; also reported in Roberts, "The Sweet Smell of Success."

211 *Soon, Chanel hopes simply to have resolved the problem of jasmine sensitivity entirely:* Christopher Sheldrake, Chanel, interview, 2009.

BIBLIOGRAPHY

Abescat, Bruno, and Yves Stavridès. "Derrière l'Empire Chanel . . . la Fabuleuse Histoire des Wertheimer." *L'Express*, April 7, 2005, 16–30; July 11, 2005, 84–88; July 18, 2005, 82–86; July 25, 2005, 76–80; August 1, 2005, 74–78; August 8, 2005, 80–84.

Agnus, Christophe. "Chanel: un parfum d'espionnage." *L'Express*, March 16, 1995, www.lexpress.fr/informations/chanel-un-parfum-d-espionnage_603397.html.

Anonymous. *Decades of Fashion*. Potsdam: H. F. Ulmann, 2008.

———. *Exposition Internationale des Arts Décoratifs et Industriels Modernes*. 10 vols. New York: Garland Publishing, 1977.

———. *Green Girls*. Paris: Bouillant, 1899.

———. *Russian Diary of an Englishman, Petrograd, 1915–1917*. London: William Heinemann, 1919.

Atlas, Michèle, and Alain Monniat. *Guerlain: les flacons à parfum depuis 1828*. Toulouse: Éditions Milan, 1997.

Bachollet, Paul, Daniel Bordet, and Anne-Claude Lelieur. *Paul Iribe*. Paris: Éditions Denoël, 1984.

Baillén, Claude. *Chanel Solitaire*. Trans. Barbara Bray. New York: Quadrangle, 1973.

Baker, Jean-Claude. *Josephine Baker: The Hungry Heart*. New York: Cooper Square, 2001.

Beaux, Gilberte. *Une femme libre*. Paris: Fayard, 2006.

Benaïm, Laurence. *Jacques Helleu and Chanel*. New York: Harry N. Abrams, Inc., 2006.

Benton, Tim, and Ghislaine Wood. *Art Deco: 1910–1931*. New York: Bulfinch Press, 2003.

Berry, Sarah. *Screen Style: Fashion and Femininity in 1930s Hollywood*. Minneapolis: University of Minnesota Press, 2000.

Bessel, Richard. *Political Violence and the Rise of Nazism: The Storm Troopers in Eastern Germany, 1925–1934*. New Haven: Yale University Press, 1984.

Blavatsky, Helena Petrovna. *The Secret Doctrine*. Wheaton, IL: Theosophical Publishing House, 1993.

Bohn, Michael K. *Heroes and Ballyhoo: How the Golden Age of the 1920s Transformed American Sports*. Dulles, VA: Potomac Books, 2009.

Budin, Stephanie. *The Myth of Sacred Prostitution*. Cambridge: Cambridge University Press, 2008.

Buisson, Patrick. *1940–1945, Années Érotiques: Vichy ou les Infortunes de la Vertu*. Paris: Albin Michel, 2008.

Burr, Chandler. *The Emperor of Scent: A Story of Perfume, Obsession, and the Last Mystery of the Senses*. New York: Random House, 2003.

———. *The Perfect Scent: A Year Inside the Perfume Industry in Paris and New York*. New York: Henry Holt, 2007.

Campbell, Bruce. *The S.A. Generals and the Rise of Fascism*. Lexington: University of Kentucky Press, 1998.

Castle, Vernon, and Irene Castle. *Modern Dancing*. New York: Harper, 1914.

Charles-Roux, Edmonde. *Chanel*. Translated by Nancy Amphoux. London: Harvill Press, 1995.

———. *Chanel and Her World*. New York: Vendome, 2005.

———. *L'Irrégulière, ou mon itinéraire Chanel*. Paris: Grasset, 1974.

Churchill Archive Centre, University of Cambridge. Archives, CHAR 20/198A, items 61–91.

du Closal, Jacques. *Les Grands Magasins: Cent Ans Après*. Paris: Clotard et Associés, 1989.

Cowley, Malcolm. *Exile's Return: A Literary Odyssey of the 1920s*. New York: Penguin, 1994.

Crémieux, Hector Jonathan, and Ernest Blum. *La Jolie Parfumeuse, An Opera-Comique in Three Acts*. New York: Metropolitan Print, 1875.

Davis, Mary E. *Classic Chic: Music, Fashion, Modernism*. Berkeley: University of California Press, 2006.

Davis, Tracy C. *Actresses as Working Women: Their Social Identity in Victorian Culture*. London: Routledge, 1991.

Delay, Claude. *Chanel Solitaire*. Paris: Gallimard, 1983.

Dill, Marshall. *Germany: A Modern History*, Ann Arbor: University of Michigan Press, 1970.

Drobnick, Jim, ed. *The Smell Culture Reader.* Oxford, UK: Berg Publishers, 2006.

Dufresne, Claude. *Trois Grâces de la Belle Époque.* Paris: Bartillat, 2003.

Dumas, Alexandre. *La Dame aux Camélias* (1847). New York: Oxford University Press, 2000.

Edwards, Michael. *Perfume Legends.* Levallois: H.M. Editions, 1996.

Elster, Jon. *Retribution and Reparation in the Transition to Democracy.* Cambridge: Cambridge University Press, 2006.

Faber, Toby. *Fabergé's Eggs: The Extraordinary Story of the Masterpieces That Outlived an Empire.* New York: Random House, 2008.

Fiemeyer, Isabelle. *Coco Chanel: Un Parfun* [sic] *de Mystère.* Payot: Paris, 1999.

Fitzgerald, F. Scott. *Tender Is the Night.* New York: Scribner's, 1934.

————. *The Jazz Age.* New York: New Directions, 1996.

Fitzpatrick, Sheila. *The Russian Revolution.* Oxford: Oxford University Press, 2008.

Fogg, Sharon. *The Politics of Everyday Life in Vichy France.* Cambridge: Cambridge University Press, 2009.

Fontan, Geneviève. *Générations Bourjois.* Toulouse, France: Arfon, 2005.

Freida, Leonie. *Catherine de Medici, Renaissance Queen of France.* New York: HarperCollins, 2005.

Furlough, Ellen. "Selling the American Way in Interwar France: 'Prix Uniques' and the Salons des Arts Menagers." *Journal of Social History*, 26, no. 3 (Spring 1993): 491–519.

Galante, Pierre. *Les années Chanel.* Paris: *Paris-Match* / Mercure de France, 1972.

————. *Mademoiselle Chanel.* Translated by Eileen Geist and Jessie Wood. Chicago: Henry Regnery Company, 1973.

Gold, Arthur. *Misia: The Life of Misia Sert.* New York: Vintage, 1992.

Golden, Eve. *Vernon and Irene's Ragtime Revolution.* Lexington: University Press of Kentucky, 2007.

Goñi, Uki. *The Real Odessa: Smuggling Nazis to Perón's Argentina.* London: Granta Books, 2002.

Grasse, Marie-Christine, Elisabeth de Feydeau, and Freddy Ghozland. *L'un des sens. Le Parfum au XXème siècle.* Toulouse: Éditions Milan, 2001.

Griffiths, Richard. *Patriotism Perverted: Captain Ramsay, the Right Club and British Anti-Semitism 1939–40.* London: Constable, 1998.

Groom, Nigel. *The New Perfume Handbook.* London: Chapman and Hall, 1997.

Haslip, Joan. *Madame du Barry: The Wages of Beauty.* London: Tauris Parke, 2005.

Heilbronn, Max. *Galeries Lafayette, Buchenwald, Galeries Lafayette.* Paris: Éditions Economica, 1989.

Herz, Rachel. *The Scent of Desire: Discovering Our Enigmatic Sense of Smell.* New York: William Morrow, 2007.

Jellinek, Paul, and Robert R. Calkin. *Perfumery: Practice and Principles.* Oxford: Wiley Interscience, 1993.

Kennett, Frances. *Coco, the Life and Loves of Gabrielle Chanel*. London: Victor Gollancz, 1989.

Kidd, Colin. *The Forging of Races: Race and Scripture in the Protestant Atlantic World*. Cambridge: Cambridge University Press, 2006.

Kraft, Philip, Christine Ledard, and Philip Goutell. "From *Rallet No. 1* to *Chanel No. 5* versus *Mademoiselle Chanel No. 1*." *Perfume and Flavorist*, October 2007, 36–41.

Kremmel, Paul, ed. *Marilyn Monroe and the Camera*. London: Schirmer Art Books, 1989.

Laty, Dominique. *Misia Sert et Coco Chanel*. Paris: Jacob, 2009.

Lauder, Estée. *Estée: A Success Story*. New York: Ballantine Books, 1986.

Laurie, Alison. *The Language of Clothes*. New York: Random House, 1981.

Leaska, Mitchell A., ed. *The Virginia Woolf Reader*. San Diego: Harcourt, 1984.

Lefkowith, Christine Mayer. *Paul Poiret and His Rosine Perfumes*. New York: Editions Stylissimo, 2007.

———. *The Art of Perfume*. New York: Thames and Hudson, 1994.

Levenstein, Harvey. *We'll Always Have Paris: American Tourists in France Since 1930*. Chicago: University of Chicago Press, 2004.

Longstreath, Richard. *The American Department Store Transformed, 1920–1960*. New Haven: Yale University Press, 2010.

Luckenbach, Till, David Epel, and Marcus Eh. "New Alicyclic Musks: The Fourth Generation of Musk Odorants." *Chemistry and Biodiversity* 1, no. 12 (2004): 1975–84.

Madsen, Axel. *Chanel: A Woman of Her Own*. New York: Henry Holt, 1990.

Mann, Carol. *Paris Between the Wars*. New York: Vendome Press, 1996.

Manniche, Lisa. *Sacred Luxuries: Fragrance, Aromatherapy, and Cosmetics in Ancient Egypt*. Ithaca, NY: Cornell University Press, 1999.

Marcus, Stanley. *Quest for the Best*. Denton: University of North Texas Press, 2001.

Margueritte, Victor. *La Garçonne*. New York: A. Knopf, 1923.

Marquet, Alfred. *From Fauvism to Impressionism*. New York: Rizzoli, 2002.

McElvaine, Robert S. *The Great Depression: America, 1929–1941*. New York: Times Books, 1981.

Mendes, Peter. *Clandestine Fiction in English 1800–1930, A Bibliographical Study*. Aldershot, UK: Scolar Press, 1993.

Mienert, Marion. *Maria Pavlovna: A Romanov Grand Duchess in Russia and in Exile*. Mainz, Germany: Lennart-Bernadotte-Stiftung, 2004.

Milinski, Manfred, and Claus Wedekind. "Evidence for MHC-Correlated Perfume Preferences in Humans," *Behavioral Ecology* 12, no. 2 (2001): 140–49.

Momas, Alphonse. *Green Girls*. Paris: Renaudie, 1899.

Moore, Lucy. *Anything Goes: A Biography of the 1920s*. New York: Overlook Press, 2010.

Morand, Paul. *L'Allure de Chanel*. Paris: Hermann, 1996.

Morris, Edwin. *Fragrance: The Story of Perfume from Cleopatra to Chanel.* New York: Charles Scribner's, 1984.

Museum of Modern Art. *The Package,* 27:1, Fall 1959.

Obazine, Étienne. *La Vie de Saint Étienne Fondateur et Premier Abbé du Monastère d'Obazine.* Ed. Monsignor Denéchau. Tulle: Jean Mazeyrie, 1881.

Otis Skinner, Cornelia. *Elegant Wits and Grand Horizontals.* New York: Houghton Mifflin, 1962.

Packard, Vance. *The Hidden Persuaders.* New York: David McKay, 1957.

Pavlovna, Marie. *A Princess in Exile.* New York: Viking Press, 1932.

Paxton, Robert O. *Vichy France: Old Guard and New Order, 1940–1944.* New York: Columbia University Press, 2001.

Pereira, Jonathan. *The Elements of Materia Medica and Therapeutics.* Philadelphia: Blanchard and Lea, 1854.

Pleij, Herman. *Dreaming of Cockaigne.* Trans. Diane Webb. New York: Columbia University Press, 2001.

Poiret, Paul. *The King of Fashion: The Autobiography of Paul Poiret.* London: V & A Publishing, 2009.

Princeton Museum of Art. *Pop Art: Contemporary Perspectives.* New Haven, CT: Yale University Press, 2007.

Proust, Marcel. *À la recherche du temps perdu.* Paris: Gallimard, 2002.

Radcliffe, Herbert. "Is There a Fourth Dimension?" *World Theosophy* (February–June 1931): 293–296.

Radzinsky, Evard. *The Rasputin File.* New York: Anchor, 2001.

Rain, Patricia. *Vanilla: The Cultural History of the World's Favorite Flavor and Fragrance.* New York: Penguin, 2004.

Ralls, Karen. *Knights Templar Encyclopedia: The Essential Guide to the People, Places, Events, and Symbols of the Order of the Temple.* Franklin Lakes, NJ: New Page Books, 2007.

Rasskavov, Pavel P. *Notes of a Prisoner.* Arkhangel: Sevkraigiz, 1935.

Reichert, Tom. *The Erotic History of Advertising.* Amherst, NY: Prometheus Books, 2003.

Rowe, David J., and Philip Kraft. *Chemistry and Technology of Flavours and Fragrances.* Oxford: Blackwell, 2004.

Sabetay, Hermine. "Creative Asymmetry." *The Theosophist Magazine* (August 1962): 301–8.

Salhab, Walid Amine. *The Knights Templar of the Middle East.* San Francisco: Red Wheel, 2006.

Samuel, Larry. *Rich: The Rise and Fall of American Wealth Culture.* New York: ACOM, 2009.

Samuels, S. "Souvenirs d'un Parfumeur." *Industrie de la Parfumerie* 1, no. 7 (October 1947): 228–31.

Sandrini, Francesca, et al. *Maria Luigia e le Violette di Parma.* Parma, Italy: Pubblicazioni del Museo Glauco Lombardi, 2008.

Sauvy, Alfred. "The Economic Crisis of the 1930s in France." *Journal of Contemporary History* 4, no. 4 (October 1969): 21–35.

Schellenberg, Walter. *The Labyrinth: Memoirs of Walter Schellenberg, Hitler's Chief of Counterintelligence*. London: DaCapo Press, 2000.

Schröder, Friedrich, B. E. Lüthge, and Günther Schwenn. *Chanel No. 5*. Berlin: Corso, 1946.

Schwarzenback, R., and L. Berteschi. "Models to Assess Perfume Diffusion from Skin." *International Journal of Cosmetic Science* 23 (2001): 85–98.

Seaton, Beverly. *The Language of Flowers: A History*. Charlottesville: University of Virginia, 1995.

Sell, Charles. *The Chemistry of Fragrances: From Perfumer to Consumer*. London: Royal Society of Chemistry Publishing, 2005.

Sert, Misia. *Misia and the Muses: The Memoirs of Misia Sert*. New York: John Day Company, 1953.

———. *Misia par Misia*. Paris: Gallimard, 1952.

Seward, Desmond. *Prince of the Renaissance, The Life of François I*. London: Constable, 1973.

Shipman, Pat. *Femme Fatale: Love, Lies, and the Unknown Life of Mata Hari*. New York: Harper Perennial, 2008.

Shteir, Rachel. *Striptease: The Untold History of the Girlie Show*. Oxford: Oxford University Press, 2005.

Stamelman, Richard. *Perfume: Joy, Obsession, Scandal, Sin*. New York: Rizzoli, 2006.

Tamagne, Florence. *A History of Homosexuality in Europe: Berlin, London, Paris, 1919–1939*. New York: Algora Publishing, 2006.

Ternon, François. *Histoire du No. 5 Chanel: Un numéro intemporel*. Nantes: Éditions Normant, 2009.

Thomas, Dana. *Deluxe: How Luxury Lost Its Luster*. New York: Penguin, 2007.

Toledano, Roulhac B., and Elizabeth Z. Coty. *François Coty: Fragrance, Power, Money*. Gretna, LA: Pelican Publishing, 2009.

Turin, Luca. *The Secret of Scent: Adventures in Perfume and the Science of Smell*. New York: Harper Perennial, 2006.

Turin, Luca, and Tania Sanchez. *Perfumes: The Guide*. New York: Viking, 2008.

Vecchiet, Jean-Michel, dir. *Andy Warhol, L'Oeuvre Incarnée: Vies et Morts de Andy Warhol*. Paris: France Télévisions, 2005 (film).

Veillon, D. *Vivre et survivre en France, 1939–1947*. Paris: Payot, 1995.

Verdi, Giuseppe. *La Traviata* (1853). New York: G. Schirmer, 1986.

Warhol, Andy. *The Philosophy of Andy Warhol: From A to B and Back Again*. New York: Mariner Books, 1977.

Watson, Lyall. *Jacobson's Organ and the Remarkable Nature of Smell*. New York: Plume, 2001.

Weriguine, Constantin. *Souvenirs et Parfums: Mémoires d'un parfumeur*. Paris: Plon, 1965.

Whalley, Kirsty. "Is Perfume House Hiding Secret Aircraft?" *Croydon Guardian*, August 2, 2008.

Whitaker, Jan. *Service and Style: How the American Department Store Fashioned the Middle Class.* New York: St. Martin's, 2006.

Wilson, Edmund. *The American Earthquake: A Chronicle of the Roaring Twenties, the Great Depression, and the Dawn of the New Deal.* New York: DaCapo Press, 1996.

Wiser, William. *Crazy Years: The Twenties in Paris.* London: Thames and Hudson, 1990.

Youssoupoff, Felix. *Lost Splendor: The Amazing Memoirs of the Man Who Killed Rasputin.* New York: Helen Marx Books, 2007.

INDEX

Abdy, Lady, 39
absolutes, 143–45, 146
accords:
  as building blocks of perfumes, 39
  in chypre perfumes, 43
  containing lavender, 41
  in oriental perfumes, 40
advertising:
  of Chanel No. 5, *see* Chanel No. 5,
    marketing and advertising of
  in cosmetics industry, 188–89
  expansion in 1950s of, 198
alcohols, 78
aldehydes, 78
  arctic concentrations of, 65
  in Chanel No. 5, xvi, 60, 62, 63,
    65–67, 71, 76, 115, 118
  chemistry and impact of, 62–65
  as fleeting, 64, 76
  introduction of, 45, 144
  in L'Aimant (perfume), 118
  as novelty, 62
  as organic, 63–64

responses stimulated by, 64–65
  stabilizing of, 63
Alexandra Feodorovna, czarina of
  Russia, 49, 50, 51, 52, 55, 71
Alexei Nikolaevich, czarevitch of
  Russia, 49, 51
Alméras, Henri, 124
ambergris, 19
Ambre (perfume), 109
Amélie, 201
Amiot, Félix, 150, 151–54, 166, 168,
  216
Anthony, Mark, 40
anti-Semitism, 134–35
Aphrodite, perfume dedicated to, 19,
  42, 77, 79
A. Rallet & Co, 52, 54–55, 92
Armingeant, Pierre, 67
art deco
  Chanel's influence on, 116, 126
  launched at 1925 exhibition,
    113–16, 126
  popularity in U.S. of, 116, 126

À Sainte Marie, 14
Ashes of Roses (perfume), 104
Aubazine Abbey:
    architecture and aesthetics of, 5–6,
        90, 102, 187
    Coco as orphan at, 4, 5–11
    flowers and gardens at, 7, 10
    scent as part of life at, 6–8, 37, 61
    symbolism and numbers at, 8–10, 61

Babani, Maurice, signature scent
    launched by, 27
Bader, Théophile, 92, 95, 99, 123, 134,
    140, 148, 184
Baker, Josephine, xv, 14
Balenciaga, Cristóbal, 117, 137
Ballet Russes, 127
Balsan, Étienne, 17–18, 19, 23–24, 28,
    34, 184, 185, 201
Bauer, Albert, 208
Beautiful (perfume), xiii
Beaux, Ernest, 53, 54–57, 142
    as celebrated perfumer, 55–56,
        61–62, 87
    Chanel No. 5 production rate of, 81,
        82, 92
    as drawn to arctic scents, 56, 65
    innovative use of aldehydes by,
        61–62, 65, 66–67, 115, 206
    at Les Parfums Chanel, 97, 100,
        117, 172, 210
    as perfumer for Chanel No. 5,
        59–62, 65–72, 96–97, 101, 143,
        172–73, 202, 206, 210, 215
    pride in Chanel No. 5 of, 172–73
    at Rallet, 54–55, 69, 96–97, 105
    during World War II, 173
Beaux, Gilberte, 173
beavers, musk from, 208
Bécu, Jeanne (Madame du Barry), 19
Beene, Geoffrey, 41
Belle de Jour (film), 198, 199
Benaïm, Laurence, 198
Berlin, Germany:
    allied occupation of, 181–82
    Coco's wartime trip to, 159–60,
        161, 181
Bernard of Clairvaux, Saint, 6–7

Bernhardt, Sarah, 10
Besson, Luc, 200–201
Bianco, Renato, 31
Bienaimé, Robert, 45, 67, 70–71
Blaise, E. E., 62
Bois des Îles (perfume), 167, 202
Bonaparte, Josephine, Empress of
    France, 10, 20
Bonaparte, Marie Louise, Empress of
    France, 44
Bonaparte, Napoléon, Emperor of
    France, 2, 10, 44
Bonofiglio, Virginia, 209
Bonwit Teller, 112
bottom notes, 78
Bouquet, Carole, 199
Bourjois, 29, 42, 93, 97, 104, 112, 141,
    172, 189
    at 1925 Paris Expo, 114, 115
    see also Les Parfums Chanel
Bow, Clara, xv
Bretz, Irène, 107
Brosse, 103
Brower, Ann Montgomery, 216–17
Brut Cologne, 41
Buchenwald, 140, 155, 158
Buñuel, Luis, 198
Burr, Chandler, xvii, 197

Cadolle, 117
Campbell's Soup, 186
Capel, Arthur "Boy," 49, 61, 108, 185
    bottles belonging to, 102
    Coco as mistress to, 24, 27–28,
        33–35, 201
    death of, 35, 48, 53, 90, 91, 137
Castle, Irene, 27
Castle, Verne, 27
castoreum, 80
Catherine the Great, Empress of
    Russia, 55
Chambrun, Josée de, 170
Chambrun, René de, 134, 136, 170, 183
Chanel, Albert, 4, 137
Chanel, Gabrielle "Coco":
    anti-Semitism of, 135–36, 185
    attempts to undermine Chanel No.
        5, 164–66, 165, 167–77

Aubazine aesthetics as influence on, 5–6, 8–10, 61

as Balsan's mistress, 17–18, 19, 23–24, 28, 34, 201

Berlin trip of, 159–60, 161, 181

boutiques of, 24, 25, 27, 82, 105, 137–38, 202

business doubts of, 85, 116, 129–30, 133–34

as business woman, 84–85, 92, 94, 95–96, 104, 116, 126, 134

cabaret career of, 14, 16–17, 29, 34, 88–89, 93, 127, 201

and Capel's death, 35, 48, 53, 90, 91

as Capel's mistress, 24, 27–28, 33–35, 201

Chanel No. 5 rights released by, 91–97

charges of collaboration against, 158–62

Coty's competition with, 70, 106, 117–18

couturier business of, 23–25, 27, 51–52, 94–95, 96, 122–23, 136, 152, 183–85, 195

death of, 196

de Medici manuscript purchased by, 32, 53

early childhood of, 4–11

Eau Chanel trademarked by, 32

Émilienne d'Alençon admired by, 18, 20–21, 37

fame and celebrity of, 22, 28–29, 48, 66, 75, 87, 90, 93, 97, 116, 119, 125, 128, 129, 132–33, 186

as fashion arbiter and icon, 45–46, 86, 116, 126, 137, 182

fictional childhood created by, 7

fictional portrayals of, 201

first sportswear introduced by, 27

as Hollywood designer, 125, 126–27, 128–29, 132, 190, 199

La Pausa estate of, 119

as Les Parfums Chanel partner, *see* Les Parfums Chanel

living at Ritz Hotel, Paris, 35, 138, 140, 157, 184, 186

living in Switzerland, 161, 162, 167, 173, 176

logo design of, 106–7

as milliner, 23–25, 127, 185

Molyneux competition with, 83–85, 86

musks disliked by, 20

number five as talisman for, 9–10, 11, 60–61, 82, 84

as orphan at Aubazine, 4–11

as part of *demi-monde*, 16–18, 33–34, 88–90, 184

as Pavlovich's lover, 53

perfume philosophy of, 46, 61, 129

perfume studied by, 38–39, 40–45, 104, 143

Pierre Wertheimer's business relationship with, 153, 183–85

in post-liberation Paris, 157–62

press and media portrayals of, 27–28, 86–90

probable abortion undergone by, 17

public image of, 28, 89–90, 91, 162, 174–76

reaction to Wertheimers' management, 151–54, 185

relationship with scent of, 6–8, 11, 20–21, 33, 37–38, 72, 77, 136

retirement of, 137, 182

return to Paris of, 182

Sem illustrations of, 88–90

sensuality of, 14, 16–18, 21–22, 37

as shopgirl and seamstress, 14

shop on rue Cambon of, 24, 137–38, 156–57, 163–64

signature scent of, *see* Chanel No. 5

style and aesthetics of, 5–6, 41, 83, 102, 124, 137, 202

U.S. trip of, 128–30

von Dincklage's relationship with, 158–62, 167, 182

wartime reputation of, 162, 174–76, 182

as wary of press, 28

wealth and financial success of, 29, 38, 96, 177, 185

work with Beaux of, 59–62, 65–72

Chanel, Inc.:
  see also Les Parfums Chanel
  "address-inspired" scents from, 202
  establishment of, 150
  Les Parfums Chanel in relationship
    to, 167
  21st century relaunches from, 202–3
Chanel, Jeanne, 4
Chanel logo, 106–7
Chanel No. 1 (perfume), 109
Chanel No. 2 (perfume), 109
Chanel No. 5 (perfume):
  abandoned by Coco as signature
    scent, 169
  as artificial abstraction, 45, 46, 103,
    142
  Beaux embrace of modernity in,
    61–62
  bottle and packaging of, xvi-xvii,
    101–6, 108, 121–22, 148, 187–88,
    199
  challenges of 1960s facing, 193–95
  Coco's early planning for, 30–33,
    38–39, 40–45
  Coco's identification with, 84–85,
    88–90, 89–90, 91, 92, 94–95, 96,
    129–30, 136, 164, 176, 186, 215
  Coco's plans to undermine, 164–66,
    165, 167–77
  commercial success and sales of,
    xiv, xvii, 84–86, 87–88, 91, 92,
    95–96, 97, 115, 116, 132–33, 139,
    146–47, 158, 163–64, 176, 183,
    195, 213, 215–16
  in contemporary art, xvi-xvii,
    186–87
  cost of, 3, 65, 71, 112, 118, 124,
    149–50, 190, 195, 209
  Dmitri Pavlovich's influence on, 52
  early 20th-century tensions
    encapsulated by, 162–63
  enthusiastic response to test of,
    75–76, 81–82
  exclusivity as element of, 81–82,
    85–86, 97, 111, 149, 200
  exhibited at MOMA, xvi-xvii, 187
  fame and iconic status of, xiii, xvii,
    42, 67, 68, 88, 99, 104, 106, 108,

    109–10, 113, 118, 125, 129, 131,
    138, 148, 149, 162, 175, 181, 186,
    187–88, 199, 213, 215, 215–17
  imitations and alternatives of, 67,
    69, 117–18, 169, 170, 173–75, 203,
    212, 214
  introduction and launch of, xiv, 27,
    67, 75–76, 81–90, 105
  late 1950s drop in popularity of,
    190–91
  legends and stories surrounding,
    xiii, xv-xvi, xv-xvii, xvi, xvi-xvii,
    32–33, 53, 57, 67, 68–72, 86–87,
    96, 96–97, 100, 102, 105–6,
    112–13, 115, 215
  as le monstre among perfumes, xvii,
    63, 186, 197, 202
  linked to Chanel fashions, 122–23,
    132
  luxury associated with, 3, 95, 111,
    121, 122, 133, 147, 148, 149, 170,
    188, 194, 195, 214
  name chosen for, 60–61
  as originally envisioned by Coco,
    37–38, 45–46, 47, 53, 59–60,
    65–66, 70, 72, 100, 101–3, 194,
    198
  overexposure of, 133, 148–49,
    190–91, 193–94, 200, 211
  parfum concentration of, 212
  perfumer sought for, 48, 53
  production and distribution of,
    81–82, 85–86, 92–97, 140–44,
    166–67, 171, 190–91, 194
  public following for, xvii-xviii, 85,
    92, 115, 214–17
  revitalized popularity of, 199–200,
    203
  rooted in Coco's life experiences,
    3–4, 11, 37–38, 88–90, 95, 102,
    184, 197, 201, 214, 215
  scent and quality consistency over
    time of, 146–47, 171, 207–12
  Sem illustrations of, 86–90, 92, 104
  sold through military commissaries,
    148–49, 167, 190–91, 194
  spirit of Roaring Twenties captured
    by, 3, 67, 118

spokesmodels for, 197–201
stopper design for, 104–5
as symbol and souvenir of France, 139, 149, 157, 159, 162–64, 216–17
Truman's search for, 157, 162, 181
voted most seductive scent, xiii-xiv, 76
Warhol silk screens of, xvi, 186, 199
Chanel No. 5, marketing and advertising of, 97, 108–9, 111–16, 121, 121–23, 133–34, 147–50, 211, 213
demi-monde as related to, 201
during 1950s, 190–91
during 1960s, 194–96, 198
during 1970s and 80s, 199–200
during 1990s and 2000s, 200–201
earliest, xvi-xvii, 75–76, 81–82, 86, 99–101
Hollywood element to, 125, 126
Les Parfums Chanel European strategy for, 113, 115–16
Little Red Riding Hood campaign for, 200–201
as luxury vs. mass market item, 148–49, 190–91, 193–94, 200
middle class as target of, 121–22
as one of several fragrances, 109, 112–13, 116, 131
in pocket sizes, 121–22, 148
spokesmodel campaigns in, 197–201
on television, 189–90
as understated and modest, 100–101, 112
in U.S. market, 99–100
word of mouth, 81–82, 86
World War II era, 147–50
Chanel No. 5 (opera), 181–82
Chanel No. 5 formula:
aldehydes used in, xvi, 60, 62, 63, 65–67, 71, 76, 80, 115, 205–6, 208
changes made to, 207–11
development of, 59–62, 65–72
floral-aldehyde balance of, 66, 71, 149, 205–6
IFRA regulation risks to, 205–7, 211

impact of aldehydes on, 65, 66, 67, 80
as inherently and structurally sensual, 80
jasmine in, 60, 61, 65–66, 71, 76, 79, 124, 141–46, 205–6, 208, 210–11
musks used in, 207–9
nitro-musks used in, 208–9
origins of, 32–33, 68–72, 96–97, 213
quality and quantity of materials in, 43, 78–79, 142, 145
as revolutionary, xvi, 22, 60, 62, 66, 67, 68, 71, 78–79
rose in, 60, 61, 66, 71, 76, 79, 124, 141–46
World War II acquisition of raw materials for, 141–46
Chanel No. 7 (perfume), 109, 112
Chanel No. 9 (perfume), 112
Chanel No. 11 (perfume), 109, 112
Chanel No. 14 (perfume), 109
Chanel No. 18 (perfume), 202
Chanel No. 19 (perfume), 202
Chanel No. 20 (perfume), 109
Chanel No. 21 (perfume), 109
Chanel No. 22 (perfume), 109, 112, 118, 168, 174, 202, 212
Chanel No. 27 (perfume), 109
Chanel No. 46 (perfume), 212
offered as post-War No. 5, 174–75
Chaplin, Charlie, xv
Charabot, 97
Charles-Roux, Edmonde, 6, 68–69, 184
Charlie (perfume), 43
Charvet, 102
Château Crémat, 107
Chemische Fabrik Flora, 168
Chiris:
Coty's loyalty to, 117
distillery process developed by, 144–45
Rallet as part of, 54, 96, 105
taken over by Coty, 69–70
Chiris, Louis, 144
Choix (Iribe), 127
Churchill, Winston, 160, 161

Chypre (Chanel perfume), 109
Chypre de Coty (perfume), 42–43
Chypre de Limassol (perfume), 42
Chypre de Paris (perfume), 42
chypre perfumes, 40, 42–43
    accords in, 43
    as oldest perfume family, 42
cinnamaldehyde, 64
Cistercian orders, 5, 6, 8–9
civet cats, musk from, 80, 208
Claude, Queen of France, 107
cleanliness, as Coco's preferred scent,
    8, 21, 37, 46
Cleopatra, 40
Coco (perfume), 202
Coco Avant Chanel (film), 201
Coco Mademoiselle (perfume), 202
Cocteau, Jean, 127
Collier's, 126, 156
concretes, production of floral, 143–45
Cool Water (perfume), 41
cosmetics industry, advertising in,
    188–89
Côte d'Azur, 143
Coty, Christiane, 157–58
Coty, Elizabeth, 33
Coty, François, 25, 29–30, 32, 44, 54,
    94, 157, 158
    Chypre introduced by, 42–43
    Coco's competition with, 70, 106,
    117–18
    as inspiration for Coco, 30, 81, 92
    and origins of Chanel No. 5, 68–69
    strategy for challenging Chanel No.
    5, 117–18
Coty, Henri, 157–58
Coty, Inc., 29–30, 114, 147, 174
    Chiris takeover by, 69–70
    as perfume powerhouse, 103–4
    perfumes from, *see specific perfumes*
Coty, Yvonne, 30, 32, 69
coumarin, 41, 115
couturiers and designers:
    perfumes launched by, 25–27, 59,
    92, 122–23
    see also specific couturiers and designers
Crawford, Joan, 126
Cristal Baccarat, 101

cuir de Russie, 42
Cuir de Russie (perfume), 167, 202

d'Alençon, Émilienne, 18
    scent used by, 18, 20–21, 37
Darzens, Georges, 62, 67
Davidoff, perfume house of, 41
Deluxe: How Luxury Lost Its Luster
    (Thomas), 193–94, 200
de Medici, Catherine, 31, 107–8
de Medici, Marie:
    manuscript of, 31, 32, 33, 53
    and roots of French perfume
    industry, 31–32
demi-monde:
    Coco as part of, 16–18, 33–34,
    88–90, 184
    divide between respectability and,
    18, 33–34
    as note in Chanel marketing, 201
Deneuve, Catherine, 198–99, 200, 208
department stores:
    marketing driven by, 123
    see also specific stores
de Villemessant, Henri, 81
Diaghilev, Sergei, 127
Dior, perfume house of, 42, 43
Dirys, Jeanne, 127
Dmitri Pavlovich of Russia, Grand
    Duke, 49–53, 126
    childhood scents recalled by, 52, 55,
    71, 72, 215
    in exile, 50–51, 52
    in Rasputin murder plot, 49–50
d'Obazine, Étienne, Saint, 5, 7, 10, 17
Donne, John, 79
D'Orsay, perfume house of, 114
Dumas, Alexandre, 10

Eau Première (perfume), as update of
    Chanel No. 5, 203
economy, U.S., during Roaring Twen-
    ties, xiv-xv
Einstein, Albert, xiv
Elizabeth Arden, 147
Elizabeth Feodorovna of Russia,
    Grand Duchess, 49, 51
Emeraude (perfume), 84

enfleurage, 144
esters, 78
Eternity (perfume), xiii

Fabergé, 54
Fahrenheit (perfume), 42
fashion:
  Coco as arbiter of, 45–46, 86, 116,
    126, 137, 182
  Coco's millinery beginning in,
    23–25, 127, 185
  during Great Depression, 120
  personal style as factor in, 93
  of Roaring Twenties, 22, 45–46
  see also couturiers
Fitzgerald, F. Scott, 48, 109, 156
floral-aldehydic, Chanel No. 5 as
    first, 67
floral perfumes, 40
  considered less respectable, 18, 20,
    44
  considered respectable, 20, 34, 44
  quality materials needed for, 43
  re-imagined by Coco, 43–45
  soliflore style, 43–44
floral scents:
  balance of aldehydes with, 66, 71
  in Chanel No. 5, *see* Chanel No. 5
    formula
  as head notes, 78
Floramye (perfume), aldehydes first
    used in, 67
flowers:
  at Aubazine Abbey, 7, 10
  symbolism of, 10
Fontaine, Anne, 201
Forbes, 175
Forces of the French Interior, 155
fougére perfumes, 40, 41
Fougére Royale (perfume), 41
fragrance:
  compounds, 78
  see also perfumes; scent
France:
  Depression-era economy of, 120
  luxury industry in, 113–16, 120
  Nazi occupation of, 139–40,
    151–55, 166, 185

frankincense, 79
  in oriental perfumes, 40
French Resistance, 140, 155, 157
fruits verts, 21–22, 137
  see also garçonnes style

Galeries Lafayette, 92, 123, 148
Garbo, Greta, 125
garçonnes style, 22, 27, 45–46, 137
  see also fruits verts
gardenia, as respectable scent, 44
geraniol, 44
Germany, rise of Nazi Party in, 134
Gibbons, Cedric, 126
Givaudan, Léon, 173
Goebbels, Joseph, 166
Goldwyn, Sam, 125, 126
Goude, Jean-Paul, 200
Goursat, Georges "Sem," 27
grande horizontales, 18, 201
  see also demi-monde
Grasse, France:
  floral materials from, 43, 54, 65,
    141–46, 195
  as fragrance capital, 31–32, 142–46
  jasmine smuggled out of, 141–46,
    206
Great Britain, Chanel production
    facilities in, 166
Great Depression, 118, 119, 154
  Hollywood influence during,
    125–26
  luxury marketing during, 119–21,
    124
Grey Flannel (perfume), 41
Groom, Nigel, 31
Guerlain, perfume house of, 141
Guerlain, Aimé, 40
Guerlain, Jacques, 40, 42, 114, 115,
    174

Haedrich, Marcel, 175
head notes, 78
heart notes, 78
Heilbronn, Max, 135, 140, 155
heliotropine, 40
Helleu, Jacques, 102, 106
  Chanel marketing vision of, 197–99

Helleu, Jean, 102, 105–6, 197
Hemingway, Ernest, 120, 156
Henry II, King of France, 31
Hermès, perfume house of, 200
Hollywood:
    Chanel as designer for, 125, 126–27,
        128–29, 132, 190, 199
    first talkies from, 119
    luxury goods pushed by, 125–26
honeysuckle, 79
Houbigant, perfume house of, 41, 55,
        114
    multiflores introduced by, 44–45

Imperial Porcelain Factory, 54
indole, 79
International Fragrance Association
        (IFRA), 205–7, 211
ionones, 44
Iribe, Maybelle, 127
Iribe, Paul:
    anti-Semitism of, 134
    Coco's affair with, 127–28
    as Coco's representative at Les Par-
        fums Chanel meetings, 134–35
    death of, 136, 137
    political views and activities of, 127,
        128, 134
Iris Gris (perfume), 174
iris root, in Chanel No. 5, 71

Jacobson's Organ (Watson), 78
jasmine:
    absolutes of, 145, 146
    Chanel agreement with Mul's for,
        210–11
    in Chanel No. 5, 60, 61, 65–66, 71,
        76, 79, 205–6, 208, 210–11
    cross-breeding of, 211
    as erotic scent, 18, 20, 44, 76
    from Grasse, 43, 141–46, 166, 195,
        205, 206, 210–11
    IFRA regulations regarding, 205–7,
        211
    production decline of, 195, 210–11
    as scent at Russian court, 52
Jasmophore, 71
Jay Thorpe, 118

Jellinek, Paul, 79
Jeunet, Jean-Pierre, 201
Jicky (perfume), 40
Joy (perfume), 43
    cost of, 124
    scent consistency over time of, 209
    scent salon for, 124
Joyce, James, 120

ketones, 78, 209
Kidman, Nicole, 201
Kitmar, textile house of, 51–52
Klein, Calvin, 40
Knights Templar, 8
Knowing (perfume), 43
"Ko Ko Ri Ko" (song), 88–89

labdanum, 19, 79
La Dame aux Camélias (Dumas), 10
La Garçonne (Margueritte), 21
L'Aimant (perfume), as reinterpreta-
        tion of Chanel No. 5, 69, 118, 173
L'Air du Temps (perfume), 43
La Jolie Parfumeuse, 14–15, 18
Lalique, René:
    1925 Paris Expo fountain designed
        by, 114
    perfume bottles designed by, 103
L'Ami du Peuple, 158
Lancôme, 42
Lanoma, 148
La Piscine, 199
La Rose Jacqueminot (perfume), 44,
        81, 103
La Rotonde, 14
La Star, 199
La Traviata (Verdi), 10
Lauder, Estée, 43, 141, 150
lavender, accords containing, 41
leather perfumes, 40, 41–42
Le Bouquet de Catherine (perfume),
        see Rallet No. 1
Le Bouquet de Napoléon (perfume), 55
Le Dix (perfume), 117
Le Fabuleux Destin d'Amélie Poulain
        (*Amélie*), 201
Le Figaro, 158
legacy perfumes, xiii, 209

Lelong, Lucien, 122, 137
Le Minaret (perfume), 26
Le No. 9 (perfume), 117
Lenthéric, house of, 114, 122
les années folles, 48, 154
    see also Roaring Twenties
lesbianism, as bohemian fashion, 21
Les Grands Magasins, 81, 92
Les Parfums Chanel:
    Beaux at, 97, 100, 117, 210
    bottle design ordered by, 104, 105
    Coco voted off board of, 135–36
    Coty's plans to challenge, 117–18
    establishment of, 91–97, 132
    expansion of Chanel No. 5 product
        line by, 121–22, 133–34, 148–49
    expansion during World War II of,
        147–50
    Jewish partners wartime exile from,
        140, 141–46, 150, 151–54, 185
    legal battles at, 133–34, 136–37,
        138, 151–54, 162, 169, 170,
        171–72, 176–77, 195
    marketing of Chanel No. 5 by, *see*
        Chanel No. 5, marketing and
        advertising of
    missing from 1925 Paris Exposition,
        113–16
    multiple Chanel perfumes of,
        108–9, 112
    partnership tensions at, 122,
        129, 132–36, 141, 166–67, 168,
        169–70, 176–77
    renegotiation of Coco's contract
        with, 176–77, 183–85, 195
    and Wertheimers' return to France,
        167
    Wertheimers' sale to Amiot of
        shares in, 151–54, 185
Lewy, Claude, 176
L'Exposition Internationale des
    Arts Décoratifs et Industriels
    Modernes (1925), 113–16, 120,
    126
    economic impact on designers of,
        120
    marketing trends launched at,
        123–24

    perfume pavilion at, 114–15,
        123–24
Lights of New York, The, 119
lilac, as respectable scent, 44
lilies, as respectable scent, 44
L'Illustration, 117
Lindbergh, Charles, xv, 119
L'invitation au rêve, 199
Little Red Riding Hood campaign,
    200–201
Liù (perfume), 174
Lombardi, Vera, 160
London Daily Mail, xiii–xiv
Louis XV, King of France, 19
Lurhmann, Baz, 201

Mademoiselle Chanel fragrance line,
    creation of, 165, 167–77, 202
Mademoiselle Chanel No. 1 (perfume),
    165, 168
    perfumer behind, 172–74
    Rallet No. 1 as basis for, 172–74
    reformulated as Chanel No. 19,
        202
    as "super" Chanel No. 5, 169, 170,
        172, 173
Mademoiselle Chanel No. 2 (perfume),
    165, 168
Mademoiselle Chanel No. 31 (per-
    fume), 165, 168, 169
Madoux, Georges, 152
Malhame, Bichara, 42
Mao Tse-Tung, 186
Marcus, Stanley, 171
Margueritte, Victor, 21
Maria Pavlovna of Russia, Grand
    Duchess, 49, 51–52
Marilyn, 200
marketing
    of Chanel No. 5, *see* Chanel No. 5,
        marketing and advertising of
    changes in perfume industry,
        123–25
    of Coty's perfumes, 81
    driven by department stores, 123
    of luxury during Great Depression,
        119–21, 124
    mid-century shifts in, 188–91

marketing (*cont.*)
  of perfumes during World War II, 147–50
  of Poiret's signature scents, 26–27
Matisse, Henri, 13
memory, scent linked to, 52, 90–91, 102, 210
Meyer, Raoul, 135, 140
Miss Dior (perfume), 43
Mitsouko (perfume), 182
Modern Dancing (Castle and Castle), 27
Molyneux, Edward, 83–85, 86, 114
Monoprix, 148
Mon Parfum (perfume), 93
Monroe, Marilyn, xiv, xvi, 186, 190, 198, 200
Monument, 199
Morand, Paul, 57
Moulin Rouge, 201
Moulins sur Allier, France, 13–17
Mudyug Island, 56
multiflores, 55, 70–71
  Chanel No. 5 as standout, 65–66
  introduction of, 44–45
Mumm, Theodore, 159–60
Museum of Modern Art (MOMA), xvi–xvii, 187
musk ketone, 209
musks:
  as bottom notes, 78
  as erotic scent, 18, 20, 79–80
  in oriental perfumes, 40
  origin of, 80
  synthetic, 208–9
  used in Chanel No. 5, 71, 76
myrrh, 79

Napoléon, Emperor of France, 2, 10, 44
Neiman Marcus, 171
New York, N.Y.:
  perfume market in, 111–12
  during Roaring Twenties, xiv
New York Times, xvii, 112, 132, 171
  Chanel's obituary in, 196
Nicholas II, Czar of Russia, 49, 50, 51
Nips, 187

Nuit Persane (perfume), 26, 123
number five, as Coco's talisman, 9–10, 11, 60–61, 82, 84
numbers, as symbolic, 8–10, 60–61
Numéro Cinq (perfume), 84–85

oakmoss, in fougére accord, 41
Obsession (perfume), 40
Offenbach, Jacques, 15
Old Spice Cologne, 40
Opium (perfume), 40
orange blossom, 79
oriental perfumes, 40–41
Our Dancing Daughters, 126

Pantin, France, Chanel production facilities in, 166
Parfum Delettrez, 114
Parfums d'Orsay, 42, 114
Parfums de Rosine, 26, 30, 114
Paris, France:
  as bohemian, 13
  Chanel No. 5 as symbol of, 216–17
  collaborators sought and charged in, 157–62
  as fashion capital, 113
  liberation of, 155–61
  perfume sales to soldiers in, 24, 29, 139–40
  perfume as souvenir of, 29, 34, 111, 139–40, 149, 216–17
  during Roaring Twenties, xiv
  during World War II, 137–40, 151–57
Parma violet, as respectable scent, 44
Parquet, Paul, 41
patchouli:
  as erotic scent, 18, 76
  in oriental perfumes, 40
Patou, Jean, 43
  scent salon created by, 124–25
Paul Alexandrovich of Russia, Grand Duke, 49, 51
perfume industry:
  at 1925 Paris exhibition, 114–15
  during Great Depression, 120, 121
  duty free business model of, 167

innovations and changes in, 39,
40, 41, 44–45, 54–55, 93, 115,
144–45, 208–9
late–20th century glamour of, 201–3
Marie de Medici and roots of, 31–32
marketing changes in, 123–25
secrecy within, 97
perfume(s):
accords as building blocks of, 39
aldehydes in, *see* aldehydes
American market for, 29, 30, 100,
111–12, 120, 124, 197
in ancient world, 19
categories of, 39–45
on couture scene, 25–27, 59
as feat of engineering and inspiration, 47
"golden age" of, xvi, 33, 45, 144, 214
historically linked to prostitution, 19
legacy, xiii, 209
"lifted" by aldehydes, 64
marketing of, 81, 123–25, 147–50
natural vs. synthetic materials in, 41
personal style as factor in, 93
processing of florals for use in,
143–45
scent salons for merchandising,
123–25
social distinctions defined by, 18,
43, 44, 46
as souvenir of Paris, 29, 34, 111,
139–40, 149, 157, 159, 162–64,
216–17
structure of, 78
studied by Coco, 38–39, 40–45,
104, 143
world's oldest, 19
on World War II black market, 138,
146
see also fragrance; scent; *specific
perfumes*
perfumer, task and skills of, 39, 210
phenylethyl alcohol, 44
Piaf, Édith, 155
Picasso, Pablo, 45
plant resins, as head notes, 78
Poiret, Paul, 127

signature scent launched by, 25–27,
30, 122, 123
Polanski, Roman, 198
Polge, Jacques, 64, 202, 203, 210
prostitution, perfumes linked to, 19
Proust, Marcel, 18

Quelques Fleurs (perfume), 45, 55, 67,
70–71
quinolines, 42

Rallet No. 1 (perfume), 52, 55–56
as basis for Chanel No. 5, 70–72,
96–97, 105–6, 118, 173, 174
bottle design for, 105–6
Mademoiselle Chanel No. 1 based
on, 172–74
re-release of, 117
Rallet No. 3 (perfume), 117
Rallet No. 33 (perfume), 117
Rallet O-De-Kolon No. 1 Vesovoi, *see*
Rallet No. 1
Rasputin, Grigori, 49–50, 55
red label Chanel, *see* Mademoiselle
Chanel perfumes
Remembrance of Things Past (Proust),
18
Renoir, Pierre-Auguste, 31
Repulsion, 198
respectability, divide between *demi-
monde* and, 18, 33–34
Reve d'Or (perfume), aldehydes first
used in, 67
Ricci, Nina, 43
Ritz Hotel, Paris, 35, 138, 140, 155,
157, 184, 186
Roaring Twenties, xiv–xvi
Chanel No. 5 captures spirit of, 3,
67, 118
fashion and style of, 22, 45–46
see also les années folles
Robert, Henri, 210
Robert, Joseph, 97
Roger et Gallet, 114
rose
in Chanel No. 5, 60, 61, 66, 71, 76,
79, 124

rose (*cont.*)
    from Grasse, 43, 44, 143
    as respectable scent, 43, 44
    as scent at Russian court, 52
    smuggled during WWII, 206
Rose (Chanel perfume), 109
Roubert, Vincent, 117–18, 173–74
Rubenstein, Helena, 147
Russian Revolution of 1917, 51
Ruth, Babe, xv

Saint Laurent, Yves, 40
Saks Fifth Avenue, 116, 171
sandalwood:
    in Chanel No. 5, 62
    in oriental perfumes, 40
    as sexual scent, 76–77
Scandal (perfume), 182
scents:
    chemical architecture of, 78
    language of, 39–40, 78
    memories linked to, 52, 90–91, 102,
        210
    reminiscent of human odors, 21, 60,
        77–78, 79–80
    sexuality revealed through, 18–22
    see also fragrance; perfumes
scent salons, 123–25
Schellenberg, Walter Friedrich, 159,
    176
Schiaparelli, Elsa, 137
Scott, Ridley, 199
Sergei Alexandrovich of Russia, Grand
    Duke, 49, 51
Sert, Misia, 30–31, 32, 35, 57, 102–3,
    127
Seventeen, 199
Shalimar (perfume), 84, 114, 115
    as oriental reference perfume, 40
    scent consistency over time of, 209
Sheldrake, Christopher, 206–7, 209
soldiers, U.S., French perfume as
    souvenir for, 29, 34, 157, 159,
        162–64, 168
soliflores, 43–44
Stamelman, Richard, 45
State Porcelain Factory, 54
Stein, Gertrude, 120

storax, 79
Stravinsky, Igor, 107, 127
Style Moderne, *see* art deco
styrax, 79
Sulka, house of, 102
Summers, Steven, 168
suntans, made fashionable by Coco, 48
Switzerland:
    Coco living in, 161, 162, 167
    perfume production in, 168, 170,
        173
symbolism, of numbers at Aubazine,
    8–10, 61
synthetics:
    first used in Fougére Royale, 41
    in floral perfumes, 45
    in leather perfumes, 42
    mid-century generation of, 195
    musk, 208–9
    in oriental perfumes, 40
    perfume industry changed by, 39,
        40, 41, 44–45, 54–55, 144–45,
        208–9
    wariness about use of, 63
    see also aldehydes

Talbot, J. Suzanne, 122
Tautou, Audrey, 201
Tender Is the Night (Fitzgerald), 109
31 rue Cambon (perfume), 202
Thomas, Dana, 193–94, 200
Thomas, H. Gregory, floral materials
    acquired by, 141–46, 206
Time, 128–29
Toulouse-Lautrec, Henri, 31
Truman, Bess, 157, 162, 181
Truman, Harry S, 157, 162, 181
tuberose, as erotic scent, 18, 44, 76, 79
Turin, Luca, 84
28 La Pausa (perfume), 202

United States:
    Coco's visit to, 128–30, 171
    Depression-era luxury market in,
        119–20
    marketing of Chanel No. 5 in,
        99–100, 111–13, 138, 141,
        147–50, 199

perfume market in, 29, 30, 100, 111–12, 120, 124, 197
perfume production in, 141, 145–46, 147, 166–67, 171
during Roaring Twenties, xiv-xv

Valéry, Paul, 46
van Ameringen, Arnold, 141
vanilla, in oriental perfumes, 40, 115
vanillin, 40, 115
Verdi, Giuseppe, 10
Victoria, Queen of England, 49
violet fragrances, as respectable scent, 44
Violetta di Parma (perfume), 44
Vionnet, Madeleine, 122
von Boineburg, Hans, 158
von Dincklage, Hans Günther, Coco's relationship with, 158–62, 167, 182

Warhol, Andy, xvi, xvii, 186, 193, 199
Warren, Estella, 200–201
Watson, Lyall, 78
Weriguine, Constantin, 65
Wertheimer, Alain, 197, 200
Wertheimer, Jacques, 141, 194–95, 197
Wertheimer, Paul, 104, 123, 135
Coco's initial agreement with, 92–97
death of, 184
move to New York of, 140
shares sold to Amiot by, 151–54
see also Les Parfums Chanel
Wertheimer, Pierre, 104, 123, 135, 175
Coco's business relationship with, 153, 183–85
Coco's expenses paid by, 184
Coco's initial agreement with, 92–97
Coco's renegotiated agreement with, 176–77, 183–85, 195
death of, 194

move to New York of, 140
shares sold to Amiot by, 151–54
see also Les Parfums Chanel
Westminster, Hugh Grosvenor, Duke of, 128
white camellia:
as Coco's personal symbol, 10
popularity of, 10
White Russians, in exile, 48–49, 51–53, 56, 88
women, number five as symbolic of, 9–10
Woolf, Virginia, 24
World War I, 27, 28–29, 50–51, 54, 55, 70, 113
Beaux service during, 56
perfume as souvenir after, 29, 34
World War II:
black market during, 138, 146
Chanel No. 5 as soldiers 'souvenir during, 139–40, 157, 164
Chanel No. 5 production during, 140–46, 166–67, 171
Chanel No. 5 sales during, 138–40, 146–47, 158, 176
collaborators sought and charged after, 157–62
floral material supplies during, 196
shop at rue Cambon during, 137–38
shortages during, 138, 141–46, 156
Wyndham, Diana Lister, 34, 35, 43

XXIII (perfume), 114

Yardley, perfume house of, 147
ylang-ylang:
in Chanel No. 5, 62
as erotic scent, 44
Yusopov, Felix, 49–50

Zelle, Margaretha Geertruida (Mata Hari), 13, 14, 16
Zizanie (perfume), 187

About the author

2 Meet Tilar J. Mazzeo

About the book

5 Following the Scent of Chanel No. 5

Read on

10 Science and Why Scent Is Sexy

14 Further Reading

Insights,
Interviews
& More . . .

Meet Tilar J. Mazzeo

I GREW UP in one of those famously charming small villages on the coast of Maine, where parts of my family have been eking out their existence for the better part of two hundred years, and my Sicilian-American father grew some grapes in my parents' vastly ambitious gardens there. Contrary to what you might expect, though, my brothers and I weren't raised on fine wine; that fruit mostly got turned into more cases of grape jelly than any family knew what to do with. In the late summers of my childhood, whole days were given over to stacking wood for winter fires and canning garden vegetables, so it might not seem obvious that I would have ended up writing about the distinctly cosmopolitan world of French luxury, from its celebrated champagnes to its most famous perfume.

But in my early twenties I moved to the West Coast, and, as chance would have it, ended up becoming a wine aficionado within months of reaching the legal drinking age. In those days, Washington state was already making great wines, and, with the help of a friendly clerk in the wine department at the local Thriftway in Seattle's Ballard neighborhood, I drank my way through my doctoral program in some reasonable approximation of *la dolce vita*. By the late 1990s, when I finished my doctorate in English literature at the University of Washington, in Seattle, I knew a lot about a few things—early nineteenth-century British poetry, the ins and outs of having a city garden (during the summers, not coincidentally, my dissertation languished and my tomatoes flourished), the essentials of traveling France on a lean student budget, and the wines of the Pacific Northwest. I would soon end up learning a good deal more about those wines when, the next fall, I got my first appointment as an English professor at Oregon State University, in the heart of Oregon's wine country. There, on rural weekends in the Willamette Valley, I honed my cooking skills, practiced my rusty French with neighbors, took up croquet, and, of course, sampled more than my fair share of the local pinot noir.

From there, I moved on to a second professorship at a branch campus of the University of Wisconsin system, and it was a bad match. Midwesterners were friendly and welcoming, and I lived during those years in a rundown but wonderful old house just a block or two from Lake Michigan, which for ▶

> " With the help of a friendly clerk in the wine department at the local Thriftway in Seattle's Ballard neighborhood, I drank my way through my doctoral program in some reasonable approximation of *la dolce vita*. "

Meet Tilar J. Mazzeo *(continued)*

someone who grew up by the ocean was surprisingly comforting. But this wasn't wine country. Along with some girlfriends, I threw myself during those years into the enjoyment of fine French champagne as a winter solace, and it was then that I first began thinking about how someday I would write *The Widow Clicquot*, the story of the world's first modern businesswoman—and the history of one of the world's great wines.

By then I had married, and we left the Midwest when my husband took a professorship in Sonoma County and I began teaching at Colby College in Maine. We lived bicoastally for several years, alternating between a sunny New England cottage with red fir floors and a low-slung Californian ranch with a huge garden overgrown with honeysuckle; the vineyards started in the fields down at the end of the lane. Of course, I quickly developed an enthusiastic appreciation for the celebrated local wines. Before long, I was writing guidebooks to my favorite back-lane discoveries in Napa and Sonoma counties and training my nose to enjoy thoroughly that most exquisite of the senses—scent.

The Secret of Chanel No. 5 began with just such simple pleasures: the scent of jasmine in a well-loved backyard garden and the passing thought that perhaps perfume and fine wine are not, in what makes them gorgeous, so different. I am fascinated, too, by the complex human stories behind the business of beautiful things. ∾

> ❝ I am fascinated, too, by the complex human stories behind the business of beautiful things. ❞

Following the Scent of Chanel No. 5

MY MOTHER NEVER WORE Chanel No. 5. In fact, when I started writing this book, I knew only as much about the storied history of the world's most famous perfume as any practiced devotée of all things luxurious.

I knew, of course, that Chanel No. 5 came in that gorgeous iconic square flask and had been invented by the incomparable Coco Chanel sometime in the early decades of the last century. I knew that Marilyn Monroe had quipped that the only thing she wore to bed was a splash of it. I could have told you that it had been the world's best-selling fragrance for nearly a century and that the phenomenon of its amazing success still had marketing executives around the globe scratching their heads.

Of course I also knew what it smelled like, in a general sort of way. I had a bottle at home, and at one point I had worn it regularly as a kind of experiment that had more to do with my interest in scent than in perfume particularly. After all, as a wine writer and an enthusiastic admirer of the good things that can happen when you capture aromatics in some quality alcohol, I was more than a little curious about the whole idea of a "vintage" fragrance.

But this book had its origins in an emotion stronger than mere curiosity. The story of how Chanel No. 5 captured my imagination—and of the ultimately charmed few years I spent in pursuit ▶

> 66 I knew Marilyn Monroe had quipped that the only thing she wore to bed was a splash of it. 99

5

Following the Scent of Chanel No. 5
(continued)

of its many secrets—began rather differently, in a small seaside village south of Boston, at the end of a very bad couple of days in the spring of 2008.

I had flown back to New England from the Californian wine country for just seventy-two hours on some of that grim business of adult life. Late that autumn, my then-husband had announced over dinner—and with heartbreaking appetite—that our love affair was over, and now all that remained was a long afternoon of waiting in court for the judge to sign the last bits of paper. The next morning I drove to Boston, where friends had promised expensive wine as the only sensible remedy.

I had already tried expensive wine as a remedy for much of what had come before. During the last months of our marriage, I lived at home in California, finishing my guidebook to the wines of Sonoma County. I lay in bed that winter alternately reading mystery novels and weeping until noon. And then, with a book to write, I went to work—wine tasting.

For four hours a day, I sniffed wine in the company of the experts. But alone in bed at night, I could still smell the scent of my husband in the sheets. With the windows open to the spring air, the fragrance of lavender and honeysuckle crept in from a garden I knew I would soon never see again. I already knew

I was saying a long goodbye with my nose.

Now, here in my friends' New England kitchen, they offered every pleasant diversion. Including perfume. One of these friends had a new fascination with fragrances and a little collection, and sampling it was a simple and unexpected pleasure. Luca Turin and Tania Sanchez had just published their book *Perfumes: The A-Z Guide* that spring, and before long we were reading the descriptions aloud. The vivid one describing Chanel No. 5—"more beautiful than an object has any right to be"—was arresting.

"Alone among fragrances known to me," Luca Turin had written, only Chanel No. 5 "gives the irresistible impression of a smooth, continuously curved, gold-colored volume that stretches deliciously, like a sleepy panther" (260). It was, we read, almost too beautiful to look at, a Brancusi of the olfactory senses. I knew just what he meant. There are wines like that. Once, at a restaurant in Napa, someone at the next table passed me a glass containing just the barest whisper of a Château Pétrus from the 1950s. It was like nothing I ever imagined could exist, and unspeakably lovely.

That night, as I drifted off to sleep, I thought to myself, "I wonder what actually makes a perfume beautiful?" About Chanel No. 5 specifically, I wondered what we all wonder when ▶

we think of one of the world's most iconic luxury brands: was it just brilliant marketing? Later that summer, as I kept turning over in my mind the idea of a book on the secrets of Chanel No. 5, something else interested me, too: the fact that this celebrated fragrance had its origins for Coco Chanel in a love affair gone wrong. Chanel No. 5, I remember thinking, is not a story about mothers. It's a story about men and women and all the complicated things that happen between them.

That autumn, when I started research for the book I had now decided I would write, it was the same human complexity that kept emerging, again and again, in the story behind Coco Chanel's signature perfume. It was at the heart of how the scent began for the designer in the months after a failed liaison, and it was at the heart of the tangled and sometimes bruising business relationships she had with the men who helped make it famous. It was the biggest part of the reason why, in old photographs from the 1940s, there are smiling faces of American soldiers lined up outside the Chanel boutique in Paris waiting to buy bottles for their girls back home. It's why it is still a scent that instantly conjures up the very idea of sexy.

This book is about that dramatic history and the Chanel No. 5 story. But it began with some late-night wondering, and, behind the scenes, I still always

66 It's a story about men and women and all the complicated things that happen between them. 99

wanted to know the answer to that question: What actually makes a perfume beautiful? And so I didn't spend the entire year or two that I dedicated to the secret of Chanel No. 5 with my nose in dusty archives—not remotely. Along the way, I studied perfume in New York City. I tramped through the rose plantations of the south of France in the springtime. I met with odor artists in Berlin and chemists in New Jersey. I fell in love at least once, disastrously. I smelled the rare scents of fragrances that haven't been produced for decades in a small museum outside of Paris and—the ultimate experience—talked with more than a dozen of the world's most renowned perfumers and heard their answers to that question. ❧

Science and Why Scent Is Sexy

THE SECRET OF CHANEL NO. 5 is the "biography" of the world's most famous perfume, and it's the story of a tumultuous business history and of one of the twentieth century's most complicated—and undeniably stylish—entrepreneurs. One somewhat tangential element of the subject that fascinated me in the course of my research for the book was where the science of the fragrance industry came together behind the scenes with questions of marketing and sex appeal. I suspect it fascinates other people, too, because there are two questions I always get asked when I talk about perfume. The first: Why does perfume seem to change its scent on the skin of different people? And second: What's the story with pheromones—do some scents make us genuinely irresistible? Here are the brief answers to both questions and some suggestions for further reading if you're still curious about where marketing meets science in the world of fragrance.

Skin Chemistry and Perfume

In 1959, the campaign for Chanel No. 5 featured the tagline "Chanel *becomes* the woman you are." "A perfume is different on women because every woman has a skin chemistry of her own," the advertisement continued. "Chanel *becomes* you because it becomes *you*." Thus the popular legend that a perfume smells differently on each woman was invented.

People still insist it's true today. It's a perception many of us would swear to. Sometimes I have thought I noticed it myself. According to scientists, though, we are mostly imagining it. Sure, they say, skin hydration, body temperature, and even the effect of our diet and the depth of our wrinkles make a small difference in how quickly a perfume fades on each of us. But they are small differences and happen in the first few minutes, when the skin reacts with the volatile—and fleeting—so-called "top notes" of a fragrance. So two friends comparing the scent of a perfume on their skin at a department store beauty counter might notice slightly different scents at the moment of application. The friend with the oilier and cooler skin, for example, will find that the perfume lasts a bit longer.

Give it fifteen minutes, however, and the differences between how a perfume smells on one arm or another literally start to evaporate. Unless you are applying Chanel No. 5 a couple of times an hour, what the science says is that no one will be getting "your" unique impression.

Fragrance and Pheromones

How about those advertisements we've all seen in the back pages of a magazine touting a perfume guaranteed to drive the men or women wild? These advertisements are based on the idea of a human pheromone—a smell ▶

compound that is hardwired into
our sexual neurobiology. Fortunately
or unfortunately, depending on your
perspective and on how much of a
certain formula you just ordered,
the scientific consensus is also
overwhelmingly against the idea
that we are moved to passion by the
mere whiff of a pheromone.

It's not that, as humans, we don't
release pheromones or that we don't
respond to them. There is a good deal
of evidence to suggest that, in fact, we
do. The trouble is, scientists also tell
us, that how our bodies process the
message of these pheromones isn't about
scent. Animals that react to pheromones
by smell have an organ in their noses
that specifically processes pheromones.
If humans ever had such an organ, it
was disconnected a couple hundred
thousand years ago. So, instead, it
appears that we respond to our
pheromones only through skin contact.
The only love potion worth buying, in
other words, is one you can rub on the
object of your most passionate desires.
And chances are, if you've already
managed to get that close, you
could have saved your money.

But there is some good news for the
perfume industry and for the lovelorn
perfume aficionado. Just because
pheromones don't make a fragrance
irresistibly alluring doesn't mean that
a signature perfume won't make you
more attractive. What the science of
scent also shows is that any perfume

you choose for yourself probably *will* accentuate your appeal. Anyone who has ever been in love knows that the smell of someone you are crazy about is powerful. It's why the fact that their mother wore Chanel No. 5 matters to so many people.

Why? Well, it turns out that the unique scent of our skin reveals something called MHC—a kind of individual advertisement to the strengths and weaknesses of our immune system. When it comes down to evolutionary biology, getting clues to the immune system of a potential partner is an important bit of information. About the fragrance of your skin, here's the interesting thing: perfume doesn't cover it up. In fact, it's just the opposite. It seems, most fortunately, that we humans have the uncanny ability to choose for ourselves perfumes that intensify our natural scent.

That means that the question of the best perfume to wear if you want to be irresistible has a very simple answer: ignore the marketing and advertisements, ignore all the celebrity endorsements. Wear a fragrance that you like the smell of, and it will highlight what's already attractive about you. It's that simple.

Further Reading

"To Attract a Woman by Wearing Scent, a Man Must First Attract Himself," *The Economist*, December 8, 2008, 136.

Chandler Burr, *The Emperor of Scent: A True Story of Perfume and Obsession*, New York: Random House, 2004.

R. Douglas Fields, "Sex and the Secret Nerve," *Scientific American*, February/March 2007, 21–27.

Rachel Herz, *The Scent of Desire: Discovering Our Enigmatic Sense of Smell*, New York: William Morrow, 2007.

Lyall Watson, *Jacobson's Organ and the Remarkable Nature of Smell*, New York: Plume, 2001.

Technical Further Reading for the Science Buff

Manfred Milinski and Claus Wedekind, "Evidence for MHC-Correlated Perfume Preferences in Humans," *Behavioral Ecology*, 12:2 (2001): 140–149.

R. Schwarzenback and L. Berteschi, "Models to Assess Perfume Diffusion from Skin," *International Journal of Cosmetic Science* 2001, 23, 85–98.

Don't miss the next book by your favorite author. Sign up now for AuthorTracker by visiting www.AuthorTracker.com.